Welfare Reform in East Asia

In many Western countries, social welfare payments are increasingly being made conditional on recipients doing voluntary work or attending job training courses, a system known as 'welfare-to-work' or 'workfare'. Although social welfare in Asia is very different from that in the West, with much smaller social welfare budgets, a strong self-reliance and a much higher dependency on family networks to provide support, the workfare approach is also being adopted in many Asian countries. This is the first book to provide a comprehensive overview of how welfare reform around work is implemented in leading East Asian countries.

Based on the experiences of seven East Asian economies – including China, Japan, South Korea, Taiwan, Singapore, Hong Kong and Macau – this book critically analyses current trends, the social, economic and political factors that lead to the implementation of workfare, and compares the similarities and differences of workfare in the different polities and assesses their effectiveness.

Chak Kwan Chan is Reader in Social Policy at Nottingham Trent University, UK.

Kinglun Ngok is Professor and Director of the Institute for Social Policy, China Centre for Public Administration Research, School of Government at Sun Yat-sen University, China. They recently co-authored *Social Policy in China: Development and Well-Being*.

Comparative Development and Policy in Asia Series
Edited by Ka Ho Mok
Faculty of Social Sciences, The University of Hong Kong, China

Rachel Murphy
Oxford University, UK

Yongjin Zhang
Centre for East Asian Studies, University of Bristol, UK

1 **Cultural Exclusion in China**
   State education, social mobility and cultural difference
   Lin Yi

2 **Labour Migration and Social Development in Contemporary China**
   Edited by Rachel Murphy

3 **Changing Governance and Public Policy in East Asia**
   Edited by Ka Ha Mok and Ray Forrest

4 **Ageing in East Asia**
   Challenges and policies for the twenty-first century
   Edited by Tsung-hsi Fu and Rhidian Hughes

5 **Towards Responsible Government in East Asia**
   Trajectories, intentions and meanings
   Edited by Linda Chelan Li

6 **Government and Policy-Making Reform in China**
   The implications of governing capacity
   Bill K.P. Chou

7 **Governance for Harmony in Asia and Beyond**
   Edited by Julia Tao, Anthony Cheung, Martin Painter and Chenyang Li

8 **Welfare Reform in East Asia**
   Towards workfare?
   Edited by Chak Kwan Chan and Kinglun Ngok

Welfare Reform in East Asia
Towards workfare?

**Edited by
Chak Kwan Chan and Kinglun Ngok**

LONDON AND NEW YORK

This edition published 2011
by Routledge
2 Park Square, Milton Park, Abingdon, Oxon OX14 4RN

Simultaneously published in the USA and Canada
by Routledge
711 Third Avenue, New York, NY 10017

Routledge is an imprint of the Taylor & Francis Group, an informa business

First issued in paperback 2013

© 2011 Chak Kwan Chan and Kinglun Ngok for selection and editorial material. Individual chapters, the contributors.

The right of the editor to be identified as the author of the editorial material, and of the authors for their individual chapters, has been asserted in accordance with sections 77 and 78 of the Copyright, Designs and Patents Act 1988.

All rights reserved. No part of this book may be reprinted or reproduced or utilised in any form or by any electronic, mechanical, or other means, now known or hereafter invented, including photocopying and recording, or in any information storage or retrieval system, without permission in writing from the publishers.

Trademark notice: Product or corporate names may be trademarks or registered trademarks, and are used only for identification and explanation without intent to infringe.

British Library Cataloguing in Publication Data
A catalogue record for this book is available from the British Library

Library of Congress Cataloging-in-Publication Data
Welfare reform in East Asia : towards workfare? / edited by Chak Kwan Chan & King Lun Ngok. – 1st ed.
  p. cm. – (Comparative development and policy in Asia series)
Includes bibliographical references and index.
 1. East Asia–Social policy. 2. Public welfare–East Asia. 3. East Asia–Politics and government. I. Chan, Chak Kwan. II. Ngok, King Lun.
 HN720.5.A8W454 2011
 362.5'84095–dc22
     2010054105

ISBN13: 978-0-415-59026-6 (hbk)
ISBN13: 978-0-415-72837-9 (pbk)
ISBN13: 978-0-203-81014-9 (ebk)

Typeset in Times
by Taylor & Francis Books

Contents

List of illustrations vii
List of abbreviations viii
List of contributors xi
Preface xiv

PART I
Introduction 1

1 Understanding workfare in Western and East Asian welfare states 3
  CHAK KWAN CHAN

PART II
Workfare in seven East Asian economies 15

2 Workfare in mainland China: a reaction to welfare dependency? 17
  KINGLUN NGOK, WING KIT CHAN AND ZHAIWEN PENG

3 Workfare in Hong Kong 41
  JOE C.B. LEUNG

4 From workfare to cash for all: the politics of welfare reform in Macau 60
  ALEX H. CHOI AND EVA P.W. HUNG

5 Workfare in Taiwan: from social assistance to unemployment absorber 78
  CHIN-FEN CHANG

6 Workfare in Japan 100
  SHOGO TAKEGAWA

vi *Contents*

7 Workfare in South Korea: delivering unemployment
   benefits in the developmental welfare state   115
   HUCK-JU KWON AND JOOHA LEE

8 Workfare in Singapore   131
   IRENE Y.H. NG

PART III
Conclusion   149

9 Workfare in East Asia: development and characteristics   151
   CHAK KWAN CHAN

   Index   167

Illustrations

Tables

2.1	Local workfare measures in China	27
2.2	The MLSS in urban China, 2009	35
3.1	Hong Kong labour force participation rates by sex, 1996–2009	44
3.2	Comprehensive social assistance scheme demographics	49
4.1	WCEA and ALSS, 2006–09	70
4.2	Migrant workers, unemployed population and unemployment rate, 2001–09	71
5.1	Conditions at times of workfare and unemployment measures' implementation in Taiwan	92
6.1	Japanese single-parent households	103
6.2	Unemployed Japanese aged 15–34 years	104
6.3	Households receiving livelihood protection	105
6.4	Japanese people with disabilities	106
7.1	The Employment Insurance Programme's structure	119
7.2	Social insurance coverage by employment status	121
7.3	Composition of Employment Insurance Programme participants and non-participants	121
7.4	FGI participants' personal profiles	126

Figures

5.1	Taiwan's social insurance programmes	80
5.2	Taiwan economic statistics, 1978–2009	81
5.3	Scale of Taiwan workfare, 1993–2009	94
7.1	Government spending on social protection	120
7.2	ALMP expenditure as a percentage of GDP	125
8.1	Number of cases and disbursement amounts in Work Support and ComCare Transitions	137
8.2	Disbursement amounts of WIS and Workfare Bonus, 2006–08	138
8.3	Gini coefficient among employed households, 2000–09	142

Abbreviations

ALMP	Active labour market policies
ALSS	Active Life Service Scheme
CCT	ComCare Transitions
CCT	Conditional Cash Transfer
CDC	Community Development Council
CET	Continuing education and training
CLA	Council of Labour Affairs of Taiwan
CPF	Central Provident Fund
CSD	Census and Statistics Department
CSSA	Comprehensive Social Assistance Scheme
DGBAS	Directorate-General of Budget, Accounting and Statistics of Taiwan
DPJ	Democratic Party of Japan
DPP	Democratic Progressive Party of Taiwan
EATC	Employment Assistance and Training Course
EEP	Ending Exclusion Project
EIP	Employment Insurance Programme
EITC	Earned Income Tax Credit
EPM	Employment Promotion Measure of Unemployed Workers due to Plant Closure or Shutdown
EPP	Employment Promotion Programme
ERB	Employees Retraining Board
ERES	Measure of 921 Earthquake Restoration Employment Services, Vocational Training and Temporary Work Allowance
ESS	Employability Skills System
FGI	Focus group interview
FSC	Family service centre
GDP	Gross domestic product
HKSAR	Hong Kong Special Administrative Region
IEA	Intensive Employment Assistance Fund
IEAP	Intensive employment assistance project
ILO	International Labour Organization
IMF	International Monetary Fund

List of abbreviations

KMT	Kuomintang of Taiwan (Nationalist Party)
LDP	Liberal Democratic Party
MCA	Ministry of Civil Affairs of Taiwan
MCLWW	Ministerial Committee on Low Wage Workers
MCYS	Minister for Community Development, Youth and Sports
MEP	Measure for the Implementation of the Employment Promotion Allowance
MFTU	Macau Federation of Trade Unions
MHLW	Ministry of Health, Labour and Welfare
MIC	Ministry of Internal Affairs and Communications
MLSG	Minimum Living Standard Guarantee
MLSS	Minimum living standard scheme
MOL	Ministry of Labour
MOM	Ministry of Manpower
MSAR	Macau Special Administrative Region
NEET	Not in education, employment or training
NGO	Non-governmental organization
NP	Nationalist Party of Taiwan
NPP	National Pension Programme
NTD	New Taiwan dollar
OECD	Organisation for Economic Co-operation and Development
PA	Public Assistance
PAA	Public Assistance Act
PEE	Plan for Expanding Employment through Public Service
PRC	People's Republic of China
SARS	Severe acute respiratory syndrome
RMB	Renminbi
ROC	Republic of China
RSC	Re-employment service centre
SCCSA	Standing Committee for the Coordination of Social Affairs
SDF	Skills Development Fund
SDL	Skills Development Levy
SJA	Special Job Attachment programme
SOE	State-owned enterprise
SPUR	Skills Upgrading and Resilience programme
SRC	Re-employment Service Centre
SReP	Self-Reliance Programme
TANF	Temporary Assistance for Needy Families
TSS	Transport Support Scheme
UAM	Unemployment Assistance Measure
UN	United Nations
UNDP	United Nations Development Programme
UR	Unemployment Relief
US	United States
WAP	Work Assistance Programme

WCEA	Workfare – Community-Based Employment Assistance Programme
WDA	Workforce Development Agency
WIS	Workfare Income Supplement
WS	Work Support
WSE	Work Support Employment
WSQ	Workfare Skills Qualification
YES	Youth Employment Start
YMETS	Youth Work Experience and Training Scheme
YPTP	Youth Pre-employment Training Programme

Contributors

Chak Kwan Chan is Reader in Social Policy at Nottingham Trent University. His research interests include social security, poverty and comparative social policy. Chak Kwan's most recent book is *Social Policy in China: Development and Well-being* (with Kinglun Ngok and David Phillips; Policy Press, 2008), and his research work has been published in *Journal of Social Policy*, *Social Policy and Administration* and *Critical Social Policy*.

Wing Kit Chan is Assistant Professor at the Institute for Social Policy, China Center for Public Administration Research, School of Government at Sun Yat-sen University, China, and deputy managing editor for the *Journal of Public Administration* (Chinese). His main research areas include educational inequality, graduate unemployment and social assistance. His latest paper '*Employability not necessarily leads to competitiveness: An employment gap left by ascribed factors*' will be published in *Chinese Education and Society* in 2011.

Chin-fen Chang is a Research Fellow at the Institute of Sociology in Academia Sinica, Taiwan. Her research interests include the sociology of labour, gender and the labour market, and social stratification. One of Chin-fen's recent publications is 'Who cares for unions? Public attitudes toward union power in Taiwan, 1990–2005' (with Heng-hao Chang; *China Perspectives* 2010/3: 64–78).

Alex H. Choi is Assistant Professor of Government and Public Administration at the University of Macau. His research interests include migrant workers, regulation of work, casino and development, and democratization. He has written extensively on the economy and politics of Macau. His papers have appeared in *Studies in Political Economy*, *Critical Asian Studies* and other edited book volumes.

Eva P.W. Hung is Assistant Professor of Sociology at the University of Macau. Her research interests centre on state–society relations and post-socialist transformation in China. She has published papers in *Modern China*, *Communist and Post-Communist Studies* and *Social Indicators Research*.

xii *List of contributors*

Huck-ju Kwon is Professor and Director of the Asia Development Institute, Graduate School of Public Administration, Seoul National University, South Korea. He was previously Research Coordinator at the United Nations Research Institute for Social Development (UNRISD). Huck-ju serves as East Asian editor of *Global Social Policy* (Sage). His most recent publication was *Transforming the Developmental Welfare State in East Asia* (London: Palgrave, 2005).

Jooha Lee is Assistant Professor of Public Administration at Dongguk University, Seoul, South Korea. He was previously Head of the Research and Policy Development Team at the United Nations Project Office on Governance. His recent publications include 'Another dimension of welfare reform' (*International Journal of Social Welfare*, 2009) and 'The diversity of democracy and publicness' (*Korean Journal of Public Administration*, 2010). Lee is co-author of *The Korean State and Social Policy* (Oxford University Press, 2011).

Joe C.B. Leung is Professor at the Department of Social Work and Social Administration, Hong Kong University. His research and publications focus on social welfare reforms in Hong Kong and mainland China. Specific research areas include social assistance, the care of older people, social development, community building and family services. Joe has published papers in *Journal of Social Policy*, *Social Policy and Administration* and *International Journal of Social Welfare*.

Irene Y.H. Ng is an Assistant Professor of Social Work at the National University of Singapore and managing editor of *Asia Pacific Journal of Social Work and Development*. Her research areas include poverty and inequality, intergenerational mobility, youth crime and social welfare policy. She is principal investigator of an evaluation of a national Work Support programme, co-principal investigator of the National Youth Survey 2010 and a collaborator in a research project in Michigan studying delinquents processed through the adult criminal system. Irene's teaching areas include youth work, policy, research and programme planning.

Kinglun Ngok is Professor and Director of the Institute for Social Policy, China Center for Public Administration Research, School of Government at Sun Yat-sen University, China. His research interests include education policy, labour policy, social security and social development in China. His English articles have been published in academic journals such as *Social Policy and Administration*, *Critical Social Policy*, *Chinese Law and Government*, *International Review of Administrative Sciences*, and *Problems of Post-communism*. Kinglun serves as editor of *Chinese Public Policy Review*. His most recent book is *Social Policy in China: Development and Well-being* (with Chak Kwan Chan and David Phillips; Policy Press, 2008).

Zhaiwen Peng is Assistant Professor at the Institute for Social Policy, China Center for Public Administration Research, School of Government at Sun Yat-sen University, China. His main research areas include local governance and social policy, social expenditure and health policy in China.

Shogo Takegawa is a Professor in the Graduate School of Humanities and Sociology, Tokyo University, Japan. His research focuses on comparative social policy. He is author of 'Japan's welfare-state regime: Welfare politics, provider and regulator' (*Development and Society*, 2005), 'International circumstances as factors in building a welfare state: Welfare regimes in Europe, Japan and Korea' (*International Journal of Japanese Sociology*, 2009) and 'Liberal preferences and conservative policies: The puzzling size of Japan's welfare state' (*Social Science Japan Journal*, 2010).

Preface

Workfare is now a dominant welfare approach in Western democratic countries; it stresses personal duties, using stringent and punitive measures such as limiting the time period for receiving public assistance and the withdrawal of benefits to push social security recipients to the labour market. Since 1997, workfare has been introduced by some Asian governments. We are very concerned about the well-being of welfare beneficiaries because Asian governments traditionally do not emphasize the social and political rights of citizens. Also, some Asian polities have few channels for welfare recipients to express their grievances and defend their rights.

Moreover, we are puzzled by East Asian governments' adoption of workfare. This is because workfare was introduced by Western capitalist states to control high social security expenditure and tackle welfare dependency. On the other hand, East Asian governments have always had a minimal social security system, and most Asian people are still strongly attached to the ideologies of self-reliance and family support. The introduction of workfare in East Asia is obviously a mystery. Thus, this book aims to explore why Asian governments have implemented workfare measures, examining their development and discussing whether workfare is a wise approach for East Asian societies.

We would like to express our gratitude to the authors of the seven case studies for their support for this book project. We are grateful to Professor Ka Ho Mok for his swift and excellent comments on our book proposal and manuscript. Our thanks also go to Peter Sowden and his colleagues from Routledge. Their patience and effective work has contributed to the successful publication of this title.

Chak Kwan Chan and Kinglun Ngok
January 2011

Part I
Introduction

1 Understanding workfare in Western and East Asian welfare states

Chak Kwan Chan

Introduction

Many Western welfare states have adopted workfare as their dominant approach to provide welfare services. This has made social security conditional, with welfare beneficiaries having to fulfil assigned duties in order to receive their benefits. Traditional pro-welfare social democratic parties in Europe and the United States (US), as well as pro-market conservative parties, now support this approach to welfare provision (Lodemel & Trickey 2000a). Welfare reforms based on the ideology of workfare have occurred in all the countries in Western Europe (Handler 2003) and, since the mid-1990s, the European Union (EU) has regarded *activation*, which refers to activating the incentive to work among unemployed people, as the 'cornerstone of social policy development' (Lodemel & Trickey 2000b: 14).

The impact of workfare has not been restricted to Western capitalist states. An increasing number of Asian countries have introduced welfare-to-work measures since the late 1990s. Asia's socioeconomic conditions are different from those in Europe, however, so it is important to examine why East Asian welfare states have introduced workfare and what the main features of their workfare measures are. The first part of this introductory chapter therefore critically examines the socioeconomic factors contributing to the implementation of workfare in Western capitalist states. It then points out the nature of East Asian welfare states and this book's key concerns.

What workfare is

Although many European countries have had workfare programmes since the mid-1990s, much disagreement exists about what the word workfare actually means (Lodemel & Trickey 2000b; Grover & Stewart 2002). It was originally associated with the US welfare policy that required welfare beneficiaries to work in both governmental and non-governmental organizations (Mead 1997). The concept later became broader to include the requirement to be actively job-hunting (Grover & Stewart 2002).

Despite its lacking a single definition, scholars have noted that workfare has several common elements. The first of these is ideological and involves the conviction that citizenship involves both rights and duties rather than that its main concern should be citizens' rights. This involves attaching obligations to rights and changing the nature of social citizenship from being a status to a matter of contract (Handler 2004). The social contract between the state and the public now emphasizes the responsibility of welfare beneficiaries to perform required duties in order to access rights. This new view of citizenship has justified governments in demanding that welfare beneficiaries do assigned work as a prerequisite for receiving benefits (Lodemel & Trickey 2000b). This new citizenship ideology therefore accords more power to governments to regulate poor people's behaviour.

Another common element of workfare is that it stresses the need of welfare systems to be active rather than passive in response to welfare beneficiaries' needs and problems. This has become 'a universal trend in developed welfare states' due to its widespread perception as an effective means of addressing social deprivation (Lodemel & Trickey 2000b: 15), and that the provision of training and education that leads to inclusion in the labour market is also the stablest, most certain route to social inclusion (Handler 2004). This view that the extension of states' control over their citizens' employment behaviour is beneficial to their social and psychological well-being leads to the conclusion that governments have to improve the employability of disadvantaged groups proactively by requiring them to do community work, attend job-training programmes and pursue further education.

Yet another common element is the conviction that it is proper for states to use coercive means to improve welfare beneficiaries' employability and to reward those who have done their assigned duties. The US government, for example, passed the Personal Responsibility and Work Opportunity Reconciliation Act in 1999, which strictly enforces work requirements and also restricts the assistance period to a maximum of two consecutive years with a five-year lifetime limit (Handler 2004). This approach also concentrates on limiting the amount of benefits. The United Kingdom (UK) government, for example, is typical in this regard in ensuring that the least well-paid workers receive better incomes than those who are not in paid employment (Grover & Stewart 2002). This means that governments use incentives to make having a job more attractive than receiving a benefit (Lodemel & Trickey 2000a). These key common elements indicate a definition of workfare as *a welfare approach that uses coercion and rewards to push welfare beneficiaries into the labour market or to require them to participate in certain activities to strengthen their work ethics or to enhance their employability.*

Socioeconomic challenges and workfare in the West

The emergence of workfare in the West needs to be examined from the context of the economic and social changes that have challenged the US and Western

European welfare systems. Their advanced capitalist economies have experienced serious declines in their manufacturing sectors while having to compete with developing economies in a global financial market for international investment. Furthermore, their societies have become characterized by ageing populations and the disintegration of traditional families, which have put the democratic welfare states under considerable financial strain.

Economic changes

Fierce global competition has frustrated the development of Western welfare states since the mid-1980s, as Western governments have found that they can no longer just increase corporate and income taxes to finance expensive welfare programmes and, at the same time, achieve the objective of relatively full employment. This is because capital has become more mobile and international corporations can easily transfer their investments and production lines to developing countries that offer them low taxes and cheap labour. An increasing number of countries with advanced economies have begun to try to reduce their tax rates in order to maintain their competitive positions in the global market. For example, when he was the UK's Chancellor of the Exchequer in 2007, Gordon Brown announced a reduction in corporation and personal income tax rates of 2 per cent, putting the UK's corporate tax rate well below both the Organisation for Economic Co-operation and Development (OECD) and EU15 average (Tax-News.com 2007).

Globalization has had a dramatic impact on the advanced economies' labour markets in addition to having put pressure on their tax revenues. Having high labour costs, Western capitalist states experienced a decline in their manufacturing industries as corporations moved many factory operations to Asia and Africa. The number of workers in the manufacturing sectors of ten major developed economies dropped from 69.7 million in 1970 to 63.7 million in 1992 (ILO 2010). The average unemployment rate in fifteen members of the EU was 10 per cent from 1992 to 1997 (Eurofound 2009).

Although the advanced economies have created new jobs, many unemployed workers have had difficulty being hired for them because of poor education and inadequate skills. The European Centre for the Development of Vocational Training (2010) estimated that the share of jobs that require high qualifications in the EU will increase from 29 per cent in 2010 to about 35 per cent in 2020, and that the share of those requiring low qualifications will drop from 20 per cent to 15 per cent. This means that workers with low skill and educational levels are being excluded from the new labour market.

In the early part of the twenty-first century, 20 per cent of the UK's working population had inadequate skills and were effectively illiterate. Nickell (2003: 104) concluded that the solution to poverty in the new economy is to reduce 'the long tail in the skill distribution'. Similarly, the European Centre for the Development of Vocational Training (2010: 4) pointed out that Europe's occupational structure has been becoming one dominated by jobs requiring high levels of knowledge and skills, adding that 'Europe needs to make sure its human resources can respond to the economy's needs. Policy must enable people to raise and broaden their skills'. In order to address the problem of unemployment in their knowledge-based economies, the Western welfare states have obviously had little choice but to take effective measures to improve their unemployed workers' skills.

The Western welfare states have also had to devise more effective ways of encouraging welfare beneficiaries to accept increasingly unattractive jobs. A rapidly increasing number of jobs have become part-time and low-paid, with unsocial working hours and short-term contracts or casual employment arrangements. Based on the employment data from 1985 to 2000, the OECD (2002) concluded that temporary jobs were a significant part of the employment structure in all its countries, with one in three jobs in Spain, for example, being temporary. Workers in temporary jobs also tend to be paid less than those in full-time employment and also have less access to paid holidays, sick leave, unemployment insurance and training. Many temporary workers have expressed dissatisfaction with their work because of inflexible work schedules and monotonous work tasks (OECD 2002).

Grover and Stewart (2002) argued that workfare helps capitalist economies to address some of the dilemmas involved in the neoliberal capital accumulation process because its deterrent effect forces more people to search for jobs in the labour market, which helps to reduce wage levels. The provision of in-work benefits for subsidized jobs suppresses wages further, allowing for the creation of more jobs. Workfare's deterrent effects therefore push more unemployed beneficiaries to accept insecure jobs in unattractive labour markets that help to maintain their economies' wage competitiveness.

Social changes

Western welfare states have also faced the challenges of ageing populations and an increasing number of single-parent families. Advanced medical technology and comprehensive health care services have rapidly increased the life expectancy of the general public in the developed world. The proportion of people aged 65 and older in twenty-five EU countries increased from 26.1 per cent in 1975 to 29.5 per cent in 2000 (Zaidi 2008), and the EU's Economic Policy Committee (2001) expected the size of this demographic to rise dramatically from 61 million in 2000 to 103 million in 2050. These ageing populations have created a heavy financial burden. As the International Labour Organization (ILO) (2009, n.p.) reported,

> social security expenditure throughout Europe is heavily dominated by spending on pensions and health care. There is evidence that this is also the case in non-EU countries. Other programmes, such as unemployment benefit schemes, family programmes, housing and social assistance, are consequently at risk of being crowded out.

The EU's Economic Policy Committee (2001) also expected expenditure on the public pensions of those aged 55 and older as a share of gross domestic product (GDP) to increase from 10.4 per cent in 2000 to 13.3 per cent in 2050. Having to pay pensions to this growing demographic is another pressure for Western welfare states to encourage beneficiaries to accept jobs in order to make more contributions to state pension funds. Jozefowicz and Pearce (2000: 19) noted that the social security systems of post-industrial countries with ageing populations have accentuated their need to make 'the economically inactive population active', and these countries have therefore attempted to reduce the dependence burden, unemployment and therefore the need to recruit foreign workers.

In addition to this increase in the number of elderly people, the Western welfare states have also had to address the needs of an increasing number of families with no one in paid employment, due mainly to family breakdown and disabilities. The number of UK males receiving incapacity benefit, for example, doubled between the early 1980s and the mid-1990s. Some have argued that generous invalidity benefits had pushed these men into inactivity (Nickell 2003).

The number of divorces in the EU increased by 55 per cent between 1980 and 2005, and in the enlarged EU, the breakdown of approximately 13.5 million marriages affected more than 21 million children between 1990 and 2005 (*Bloomberg* 2007). In some Western countries, more than a quarter of all households are headed by single parents, and single-parent families often involve child poverty and unemployment, which directly increase the public's welfare burden. The number of female-headed families in the US receiving Aid to Families with Dependent Children (AFDC), for example, increased from 3,771,000 in 1989 to 4,981,000 in 1993 (US Department of Health and Human Services 2008a). The real growth of the cost of the AFDC programme to the federal government consequently increased over those five years from US$13,733 million to US$16,212 million, or by 18 per cent (US Department of Health and Human Services 2008b). Similarly, prior to the UK's New Labour government, more than 20 per cent of working-age jobless households were 'cut off from jobs and careers' (Department for Education and Employment 1997, cited in Finn 1998: 106).

Jobless households are one of the key factors contributing to child poverty. More than half of the single parents in the UK in 2000 had no paid employment and lived on public assistance, and 53 per cent of the children living under the poverty line lived in jobless households (Nickell 2003). The New Labour government therefore introduced its New Deal programme, which, according to former Chancellor Gordon Brown, was 'an onslaught against the unacceptable culture of worklessness that grew up in some of our communities in the 1980s and early 1990s' (cited in Carpenter and Speeden 2007: 143).

In addition to demographic and family changes, the emergence of workfare is related to the discourse on welfare dependence and social exclusion. Such US neoliberal and neoconservative analysts as Charles Murray, Lawrence Mead and Michael Novak accused the US welfare system of increasing family breakdowns and welfare dependence (Grant 2000). Murray (1990: 8), for example, pointed out that 'long-term welfare dependency is a fact, not a myth, among young women who have children without husbands'. He went on to assert that a social consequence of single parenthood is the emergence of an underclass in which 'large numbers of young, healthy, low-income males choose not to take jobs' (Murray 1990: 17). Based on this analysis, Murray (1994: 227) advocated the elimination of benefits for single mothers, asserting that doing so would 'drastically reduce births to single teenage girls' and 'reverse the trendline in the break-up of poor families'.

In the UK, the major impetus for workfare policies was politicians' concern that the unconditional receipt of social security benefits was making beneficiaries dependent upon them (Cebulla 2005). An increasing number of political leaders have claimed that generous welfare states discourage the seeking of paid employment and encourage a culture of dependence (Handler 2004). Those with this perspective, therefore, are convinced that stringent welfare measures are necessary to address welfare dependency and family breakdown.

From a more positive perspective, those advocating welfare reform have insisted that employment is the most effective means of combating the problems of poverty and social exclusion. Furthermore, governments on both sides of the Atlantic came to the conclusion that paying people cash benefits had failed to help a large proportion of them to become self-sufficient, and that welfare-to-work programmes can enhance self-reliance and promote personal and family responsibility (Lodemel & Trickey 2000b). The UK's New Labour government asserted that paid employment can increase social mobility (Department of Social Security 1998), and that the opportunity to have a job 'opens up the chance to progress, to develop and to participate fully in society. We know that people in work are often healthier, and more fulfilled, than people who are not' (Department for Work and Pensions 2007: 25). Western governments therefore now associate paid employment with social and economic well-being and consider it to be a more acceptable means of achieving independence and freedom than public assistance.

Western capitalist states have therefore used workfare as a mechanism for coping with new economic and social challenges to their welfare systems. By pushing more welfare beneficiaries into the labour market, they expect more families to increase their incomes, thereby reducing the number of children living in poverty and increasing their revenues from taxes and national insurance contributions to help pay for old-age pensions. Workfare is therefore a strategy that Western governments employ to solve the problems of an ageing population and families without wage earners in a competitive global economy with deteriorating work conditions.

East Asian welfare states and this book's structure

East Asian welfare systems have been defined as 'Oikonomic welfare [states]', 'Confucian welfare [states]', 'liberal welfare states', 'liberal welfare capitalism', 'conservative welfare state systems' and 'productivist welfare capitalism' (Walker & Wong 2005: 9). These definitions are based on two dimensions: the nature of the economy and the contents of the culture in East Asia. According to Jones (White & Gooman 1998), East Asian societies have been shaped by Confucian values, which emphasize welfare contributions from the family and community organizations and avoid relying on the government. The key features of a Confucian welfare system are:

> Conservative corporatism without (western-style) worker participation; subsidiary without the Church; solidarity without equality; laissez-faire without libertarianism: an alternative expression for all this might be 'household economy' welfare states – run in the style of a would-be traditional, Confucian, extended family.
> Jones (1993, cited in White & Goodman 1998: 12)

As early as 1982, S.K. Lau (1982), a Hong Kong sociologist, had already pointed out the impact of traditional Chinese ideologies in a colonial setting, concluding utilitarianistic familism as Hong Kong's dominant culture. As he explained:

> the normative and behavioural tendency of an individual to place his familial interests above the interests of society and of other individuals and groups, and to structure his relationships with other individuals and groups in such a manner that the furtherance of his familial interests is the overriding concern. Moreover, among the familial interests, material interests take priority over non-material interests.
> Lau (1982: 72)

McLaughlin (1993: 132) also claimed that social welfare in Hong Kong was a matter of 'charity and benevolence', in which the government told people that they 'should look to the family, voluntary agencies and the market for their welfare needs'. In short, Hong Kong people had a low level of dependence on the British colonial government, emphasizing instead mutual support among family members.

Similarly, Ezra Vogel pointed out that the Japanese government had a low level of welfare expenditure because the public relied heavily on the welfare services offered by the family, private companies and a large voluntary sector (White & Goodman 1998). Also, welfare entitlements in Japan were kept low, while the welfare rights of citizens were minimally developed (White & Goodman 1998). The Japanese government's low tax policy and minimal social security system are therefore fundamentally supported by welfare contributions from the family, voluntary organizations and private firms.

From the perspective of political economy, East Asian societies are examples of 'productivist welfare capitalism' (Holliday 2000: 711) and 'developmental welfare states' (Kwon 2005: 3). According to Holliday (2000: 709), East Asian economies are growth-oriented states in which social policies are subordinate to 'economic/industrial objectives'. The key features of East Asian productivist welfare states are strong families with low taxation and limited welfare provisions (Holliday 2000). Kwon (2005: 4) also pointed out that East Asian governments always regard economic development as their top priority. In this environment, social policy is 'only conceived as instrumental to economic and political objectives' (Kwon 2005: 3; see also Chapter 7).

As explained in the previous sections, the key impetuses for the introduction of workfare in the West have been significantly increasing social security budgets and public concerns about welfare dependence. On the other hand, East Asian societies have characteristically had little state expenditure on social welfare, low benefits and governments acting as regulators rather than providers (Walker & Wong 2005). With a small government, a minimal welfare system, a self-reliance and family dependency culture, it is hard to understand why East Asian economies have introduced workfare since the late 1990s. Therefore, this book aims to solve this mystery by examining the social, economic and political factors that have contributed to the adoption of workfare in seven East Asia economies.

It should be noted that workfare in East Asian economies affects the well-being of poor people in undemocratic political systems. The European and American governments introduced welfare-to-work programmes into systems that already had proper mechanisms for checking the power of welfare bureaucrats and addressing welfare recipients' grievances, thereby ensuring the institutional safeguarding of poor people's democratic welfare rights. Some East Asian societies, however, are still ruled by semi-democratic or authoritarian governments in which senior officials, business communities or a combination of both basically decide policies and their means of implementation. Poor people in such polities have limited political participation and few opportunities to voice concerns or defend their rights (Chan & Bowpitt 2005; Chan et al. 2008). The authoritarian governments in East Asia had 'maintained a regressive welfare system and suppressed dissenting voices' (Kwon 2005: 2). As workfare involves stringent welfare measures that impose penalties on those who fail to abide by official regulations, it is important to study its impact on the well-being of welfare claimants in different East Asian political systems.

Unsurprisingly, Western workfare programmes vary (Trickey 2000; Handler 2004; Cebulla 2005). It is therefore also likely that social and political differences shape the contents of these programmes in East Asia. This book therefore analyses the similarities and differences in workfare programmes in China, Hong Kong, Macau, Taiwan, Japan, Korea and Singapore. It has three sections.

This chapter, which has discussed the concept of workfare and analysed the factors contributing to its adoption by Western capitalist states, has been the first section. The second section has seven chapters, each exploring the workfare practices in an East Asian polity by introducing the context of their introduction and examining their key elements. The final chapter analyses the key features and the similarities and differences in workfare programmes in the seven cases. It concludes by discussing whether workfare is a wise approach for East Asian welfare states.

Bibliography

Bloomberg (2007) 'A Portrait of Europe's Aging Population', 9 October. Online. Available at www.businessweek.com/globalbiz/content/oct2007/gb2007109_091747. htm?campaign_id=rss_daily (accessed 12 September 2010).

Carpenter, M. and Speeden, S. (2007) 'Origins and Effects of New Labour's Workfare State: Modernisation or Variations on Old Themes?' in M. Carpenter and S. Speeden (eds) *Beyond the Workfare State*, pp. 133–58, Bristol: The Policy Press.

Cebulla, A. (2005) 'The Road to Britain's New Deal', in A. Cebulla, K. Ashworth, D. Greenbery and R. Walker (eds) *Welfare-To-Work*, pp. 17–33, Farnham, Surrey: Ashgate Publishing Ltd.

Cebulla, A. and Walker, R. (2005) 'Welfare, Work and Welfare-to-work in the UK', in A. Cebulla, K. Ashworth, D. Greenbery and R. Walker (eds) *Welfare-To-Work*, pp. 1–16, Farnham, Surrey: Ashgate Publishing Ltd.

Chan, C.K. and Bowpitt, G. (2005) *Human Dignity and Welfare Systems*, Bristol: The Policy Press.

Chan, C.K., Ngok, K.L. and Phillips, D. (2008) *Social Policy in China: Development and Well-Being*, Bristol: The Policy Press.

Department for Work and Pensions (2007) *In Work, Better Off: Next Steps to Full Employment*, Norwich: HMSO.

Department of Social Security (1998) *A New Contract for Welfare: The Gateway to Work*, London: Stationery Office.

Economic Policy Committee (2001) *Budgetary Challenges Posed by Ageing Populations: The Impact of Public Spending on Pensions, Health and Long-Term Care for the Elderly and Possible Indicators of the Long-Term Sustainability of Public Finances*, Brussels: Economic Policy Committee and the Directorate General for Economic and Financial Affairs of the European Commission. Online. Available at www.europa.eu/epc/pdf/summary_en.pdf (accessed 14 September 2010).

Eurofound (European Foundation for the Improvement of Living and Working Conditions) (2009) *EurLIFE – Unemployment Rate*, 26 August. Online. Available at www.eurofound.europa.eu/areas/qualityoflife/eurlife/index.php?template=3&radioindic=17&idDomain = 2 (accessed 10 September 2010).

European Centre for the Development of Vocational Training (2010) *Jobs in Europe to Become More Knowledge- and Skills-Intensive*, Thessaloniki: European Centre for the Development of Vocational Training. Online. Available at www.cedefop.europa.eu/EN/Files/9021_en.pdf (accessed 14 September 2010).

Finn, D. (1998) 'Labour's 'New Deal' for the Unemployed and the Stricter Benefit Regime', in E. Brunsdon, H. Dean and R. Woods (eds) *Social Policy Review 10*, pp. 105–22, London: Social Policy Association.

Grant, D. (2000) 'Crossing the Atlantic: US Welfare Reform and the Degradation of Poor Women', in H. Dean, R. Sykes and R. Woods (eds) *Social Policy Review 12*, pp. 349–69, Newcastle: Social Policy Association.

Grover, C. and Stewart, J. (2002) *The Work Connection: The Role of Social Security in Regulating British Economic Life*, Basingstoke: Palgrave.

Handler, J.F. (2003) 'Social Citizenship and Workfare in the US and Western Europe: From Status to Contract', *Journal of European Social Policy* 13, 3: 229–43.

—— (2004) *Social Citizenship and Workfare in the United States and Western Europe: The Paradox of Inclusion*, Cambridge: Cambridge University Press.

Holliday, I. (2000) 'Productivist Welfare Capitalism: Social policy in East Asia', *Political Studies* 48, 4: 706–23.

Jones, C. (1993) 'The Pacific Challenge: Confucian Welfare States', in C. Jones (ed.) *New Perspectives on the Welfare State in Europe*, pp. 198–217, London: Routledge.

ILO (International Labour Organization) (2009) *The 8th European Regional Meeting: Facts on Social Protection in Europe and Central Asia*, ILO: Geneva. Online. Available at www.ilo.org/wcmsp5/groups/public/-dgreports/-dcomm/documents/publication/wcms_101657.pdf (accessed 13 September 2010).

—— (2010) *Labour Market Trends and Globalization's Impact on Them*, Geneva: ILO. Online. Available at www.actrav.itcilo.org/actrav-english/telearn/global/ilo/seura/mains.htm (accessed 20 August 2010).

Jozefowicz, A. and Pearce, D. (2000) 'Europe's Population and Labour Market Beyond 2000: An Assessment of Trends and Projections', in A. Punch and D. Pearce (eds) *Europe's Population and Labour Market Beyond 2000*, pp. 17–42, Strasbourg Cedex: Council of Europe Publishing. Online. Available at www.coe.int/t/e/social_cohesion/population/N%B033_Europe's_population_Vol1.pdf (accessed 14 February 2011).

Kwon, H.J. (2005) *Transforming the Developmental Welfare State in East Asia*, Geneva: United Nations Research Institute for Social Development.

Lau, S.K. (1982) *Society and Politics in Hong Kong*, Hong Kong: Chinese University Press.

Lodemel, I (2000) 'Discussion: Workfare in the Welfare State', in I. Lodemel, and H. Trickey (eds) *An Offer You Can't Refuse: Workfare in International Perspective*, pp. 295–344. Bristol: The Policy Press.

Lodemel, I. and Trickey, H. (2000a) 'Preface', in I. Lodemel and H. Trickey (eds) *An Offer You Can't Refuse: Workfare in International Perspective*, pp. xi–xxi, Bristol: The Policy Press.

—— (2000b) 'A New Contract for Social Assistance', in I. Lodemel and H. Trickey (eds) *An Offer You Can't Refuse: Workfare in International Perspective*, pp. 1–40, Bristol: The Policy Press.

McLaughlin, E. (1993) 'Hong Kong: A Residual Welfare Regime', in A. Cochrane and J. Clarke (eds) *Comparing Welfare States: Britain in International Context*, pp. 105–40, London: Sage Publications, in association with the Open University.

Mead, L. (1997) 'From Welfare to Work: Lessons from America', in A. Deacon (ed.) *From Welfare to Work: Lessons from America*, pp. 1–55, London: Institute of Economic Affairs Health and Welfare Unit.

Murray, C. (1990) *The Emerging British Underclass*, London: The IEA Health and Welfare Unit.

—— (1994) *Losing Ground: American Social Policy 1950–1980*, New York: Basicbooks.

Nickell, S. (2003) *Poverty and Worklessness in Britain*, London: Centre for Economic Performance, London School of Economics and Political Science.

OECD (Organisation for Economic Co-operation and Development) (2002) 'Taking the Measure of Temporary Employment', *Employment Outlook 2002*, Paris: OECD. Online. Available at www.oecd.org/dataoecd/36/8/17652675.pdf (accessed 2 October 2010).

Tax-News.com (2007) *Brown Cuts UK Corporate Tax*, 22 March. Online. Available at www.tax-news.com/asp/story/story_open.asp?storyname=26747 (accessed 10 October 2009).

Trickey, H. (2000) 'Comparing Workfare Programs – Features and Implications', in I. Lodemel and H. Trickey (eds) *An Offer You Can't Refuse: Workfare in International Perspective*, pp. 249–94, Bristol: The Policy Press.

US Department of Health and Human Services (2008a) *Trends in the AFDC Caseload since 1962*, Washington: Department of Health and Human Services. Online. Available at www.aspe.hhs.gov/HSP/AFDC/baseline/2caseload.pdf (accessed 15 June 2009).

——(2008b) *Federal and State Expenditures for AFDC*, Washington: Department of Health and Human Services. Online. Available at http://aspe.hhs.gov/hsp/afdc/baseline/4spending.pdf (accessed 14 February 2011).

Walker, A. and Wong C.K. (2005) 'Introduction: East Asian Welfare Regimes', in A. Walker and C.K. Wong (eds) *East Asian Welfare Regimes in Transition: From Confucianism to Globalisation*, pp. 3–20, Bristol: The Policy Press.

White, G. and Goodman, R. (1998) 'Welfare Orientalism and the Search for an East Asian Welfare Model', in R. Goodman, G. White and H.J. Kwon (eds) *The East Asian Welfare Model: Welfare Orientalism and the State*, pp. 3–24, London: Routledge.

Zaidi, A. (2008) *Features and Challenges of Population Ageing: The European Perspective*, Vienna: European Centre for Social Welfare Policy and Research. Online. Available at www.euro.centre.org/data/1204800003_27721.pdf (accessed 12 September 2010).

Part II
Workfare in seven East Asian economies

2 Workfare in mainland China
A reaction to welfare dependency?

Kinglun Ngok, Wing Kit Chan and Zhaiwen Peng[1]

Introduction

The People's Republic of China (PRC) has been undergoing large-scale socioeconomic transformation since the late 1970s. In addition to its shift from a planned to a market economy, it has also fundamentally transformed its social security system. In order to enable inefficient state-owned enterprises (SOEs) to survive in the competitive market economy, the PRC government has made a great effort since the mid-1980s to transform the traditional work unit (*danwei*)-based social security system into a multiple-tier one based on contributory social insurance programmes. In order to pacify such vulnerable social groups as laid-off workers, unemployed people, retirees and poor farmers, in the late 1990s, the PRC government started to reform its public assistance policy and establish a social assistance system with a minimum living standard scheme (MLSS) at its core (Ngok 2010).

China's current social security system is an umbrella of social protection schemes encompassing mainly programmes relating to social insurance, social assistance and social welfare services. The social insurance programmes cover old age, unemployment, health care, maternity and work-related injury. Social welfare programmes provide funds and services to ensure the livelihood of such people as senior citizens, orphans and people with disabilities who are in extraordinarily straitened circumstances. Social assistance programmes provide support for urban and rural poor people and are the system's final safety net (Information Office of the State Council 2004).

Having a transitional economy, China's social security system is undergoing a process of deconstruction and reconstruction. Its social policies have experienced rapid expansion during the twenty-first century in response to the social problems and social pressures caused by unbalanced economic growth. An increasing number of people, especially those from such vulnerable social groups as unemployed workers, disabled people and other poor people, have benefited from this expansion and the extension of the system's coverage. A new welfare philosophy has also accompanied this expansion, in particular in regard to workfare, which has become popular with those setting social assistance policy.

This chapter aims to outline the background and development of workfare in China based on a policy review and fieldwork. The next section briefly introduces China's unemployment situation and anti-unemployment policies. The subsequent section documents the emergence of workfare with a review of policies at both central and local government levels. The main section describes China's workfare initiatives and their implementation by local governments, with a particular focus on Guangzhou, one of China's most prosperous cities. It argues that China's workfare programme is based on a subsistence level of welfare provision and is not a response to genuine welfare dependence.

Unemployment in China's market transition

Mao's China did not accept the concept of unemployment, which it saw as antithetical to its socialist ideology, and those who worked for SOEs were free from any threat of it. Those who were idle were labelled *daiye*, which means waiting for employment. *Daiye* persons were mostly young school leavers waiting for their first job assignments from the government (Wong & Ngok 1997).

As the country's market-oriented economic reform proceeded in the late 1980s, Chinese academics and officials began to accept the reality that unemployment is both inevitable and natural during a transition to a market system (Feng 1988, 1991). The new Labour Law (1994), which became effective in January 1995, used the word unemployment in the legal lexicon for the first time. It defined unemployed people officially as people with urban household registrations who were either women between the ages of 16 and 45 or men between 16 and 50, able and willing to work, with no employment and registered as unemployed with the local employment service agency (Wong & Ngok 1997).

Unemployment has emerged as a serious social problem in China since the mid-1990s as a result of the deepening of its market-oriented reforms, especially the downsizing, closures, bankruptcies and privatization of loss-making SOEs. Between the mid-1990s and the early 2000s, more than 20 million SOE workers' jobs became redundant, releasing them from the production process and making them what came to be called *xiagang*, or laid-off workers (Wong & Ngok 2006). *Xiagang* is a type of institutional or structural unemployment that has been a direct result of China's transition from a planned to a market economy (Gu 2001). Although off duty, the *xiagang* are still counted as belonging to their *danwei* or work units.

The *xiagang* became a formidable social problem in 1997 when the Chinese government decided to introduce a modern enterprise system by restructuring, regrouping, carrying out renovations and reinforcing its management of most SOEs. The government proceeded to retain only the key enterprises and let the rest go. This strategy initiated the revamping of small and medium-sized SOEs and legitimated massive layoffs of the surplus work force (Wong & Ngok 2006). The number of *xiagang* workers consequently rose dramatically and, by 2003, China had 28.18 million of them (Information Office of the State Council 2004).

China's work force consisted of 779.95 million men and women at the end of 2009, 311.20 million of them urban workers. The official registered urban unemployment rate was 4.3 per cent, involving 9.21 million people (Ministry of Human Resources and Social Security 2010). The global financial crisis apparently had had little effect on the Chinese labour market, as this urban unemployment rate was decidedly low in comparison with those in the West. It should be noted, however, that the Chinese authorities deliberately under-report unemployment there, as the statistics exclude the rural population, which includes even those who have left their villages and actually live in cities and towns, and count only registered urban unemployed people. If the figures were to include all of China's jobless people, the real unemployment rate would be much higher (Chan *et al.* 2008).

China's anti-unemployment policies

In view of the financial implications and political sensitivity of the unemployment problem, finding ways to pacify unemployed state workers has become one of the top priorities of Chinese labour policy in the context of market transition, especially since the mid-1990s. In doing so, the PRC government has developed some key policy responses.

It first established an unemployment insurance system in order to provide benefits for unemployed state workers. Next, it set up a system for providing a living allowance for the *xiagang* workers, and has established re-employment service centres nationwide that provide employment-related service to the *xiagang* and other unemployed workers. It then established the MLSS, which provides public assistance for the urban poor, mainly retirees and unemployed workers. It calls these anti-unemployment policies together the *santiao baozhangxian*, or three guarantee lines for providing a basic safety net for those they serve (Chan *et al.* 2008).

Unemployment insurance

The PRC government began developing China's unemployment insurance system in 1986 when it introduced a national labour contract system. It issued the Provisional Regulation on Unemployment (*daiye*) Insurance for Workers and Staff in State-Owned Enterprises (1986), which had the objective of providing social protection for workers whose labour contracts had expired or been terminated, and to facilitate the implementation of the labour contract system. This required enterprises to contribute 1 per cent of workers' basic wages into a fund that paid unemployment benefits of between 50 and 75 per cent of the basic pay for a maximum of two years, depending on the period of employment and the amount of the contribution. At the onset, four kinds of workers were eligible for unemployment benefits. These were (a) workers in enterprises that had declared bankruptcy, (b) workers made redundant by enterprises that had received official notice of bankruptcy and were undergoing reorganization,

(c) contract workers whose contracts had expired or been terminated, and (d) workers who had been dismissed by their employers.

A revised regulation replaced the 1986 Regulation in 1993. The revised regulation changed the contribution rate to 0.6 per cent of workers' overall pay, which was a more realistic calculation of their actual income, as it includes bonuses and other payments as well as basic pay. It also revised the payment levels from 120 to 150 per cent of the local social relief rate and covered three more categories of jobless workers. These were (a) those who had been employed in enterprises that had been dissolved pursuant to relevant state regulations, (b) those made redundant by enterprises that had suspended operations in accordance with relevant state regulations, and (c) others who were eligible for unemployment insurance (Regulation on Unemployment (*daiye*) Insurance for Workers and Staff in State-Owned Enterprises 1993).

The existing unemployment insurance scheme is based on the Regulation on Unemployment Insurance (*shiye baoxian tiaoli*) (1999). This regulation has extended unemployment insurance coverage to employees of all kinds of urban firms. Both employers and employees contribute to it, with employers paying 2 per cent of their payrolls and employees paying at least 1 per cent of their wages. Only registered involuntarily unemployed workers who had contributed to the scheme for at least one year are eligible for its benefits, which last up to two years, depending on how long beneficiaries have contributed to the scheme. Its payments are set locally at levels above the local poverty line but lower than the local standard minimum wage. By the end of 2009, the scheme had covered more than 127 million people, with 2.35 million having received unemployment benefits through it, and its aggregated income had reached 152.4 billion RMB (Ministry of Human Resources and Social Security 2010).

Re-employment services centre

The PRC government launched a national programme called the Re-employment Project (*zai jiuye gongcheng*) in early 1995 to help laid-off workers to find jobs. It targeted unemployed people who had been unable to find work for six months and enterprises that could not afford to pay their employees a basic living wage. Its principal aim was to provide comprehensive services to help unemployed people find jobs quickly. It also required local governments to implement policies supporting and providing services for laid-off and unemployed workers who wanted to set up their own businesses (Tian 1999).

Shanghai, a key industrial city in China burdened with many overstaffed SOEs, was the first to implement the Re-employment Project in 1996 when it created the re-employment service centres (RSCs) in order to mobilize many social agencies to assist SOEs in helping *xiagang* workers. The RSCs' core functions were to look after the *xiagang* workers, to create re-employment channels for them and to combine the provision of minimal welfare for them with re-employment programmes. Their funding came equally from the state, society and the related industrial sectors, and paid for the *xiagang* workers' basic living costs, medical bills and social insurance premiums (Wong & Ngok 2006). The RSCs' success in averting serious discontent among redundant workers in Shanghai received wide publicity, and Shanghai's local experiences became a national policy in 1998, when the government required all enterprises with redundant workers to set up RSCs, which became an integral part of 'a social security system with Chinese characteristics' (Tian 1999: 1).

Xiagang workers and their firms' RSCs signed agreements that specified their mutual obligations. The RSC had the responsibility of providing an integrated package of services and benefits that included financial support, career retraining and job referrals. It contributed to the *xiagang* workers' social insurance premiums, such as those for pension and health insurance, and paid the cost of any medical treatment they may have needed in addition to paying them a basic living allowance. It also organized job training, vocational guidance and job introductions. It terminated the living allowance of any *xiagang* workers who twice refused to accept jobs to which the centre referred them. The centres were funded equally by the local government, the enterprise and social insurance funds, what the Chinese called the three-three-three system (Wong & Ngok 2006). *Xiagang* workers who failed to get a job after their maximum three-year period of trusteeship with an RSC could apply for unemployment benefits for a maximum of another two years. If that became exhausted, their last resort was the locally administered MLSS or social relief (Lee 2000).

As a temporary policy device designed to help disgruntled laid-off SOE workers in the context of mass privatization without a sound social security system, the RSCs were only temporary, and the government had phased them out by the early 2000s, after the large-scale privatization and downsizing of SOEs had come to an end. The Chinese authorities had made a great effort to improve the unemployment insurance and social assistance systems in order to provide unified social protection for unemployed people, whether they had been laid off from SOEs for the first time, dismissed by their employers after re-employment or lost their jobs due to the termination of their labour contracts. Their last resort in case they had difficulty making ends meet was still to become recipients of the MLSS (Leung 2006; Wong & Ngok 2006).

The MLSS

The MLSS, China's key social assistance policy, is a means-tested social assistance programme that the Shanghai municipal government initiated in 1993 to address the increasing urban poverty resulting from market-oriented economic reforms by providing a basic standard of living for its urban-registered residents. In 1994, recognizing the success of the Shanghai MLSS programme, the Ministry of Civil Affairs (MCA), which has responsibility for implementing national social assistance and social welfare policies, decided to extend the scheme to other cities in the coastal regions on an experimental basis. Based on the pilot cities' positive experiences, the MCA decided to extend the

MLSS nationally in 1996. The State Council issued its first document on the MLSS in 1997, which demonstrated the central government's determination to expand it further in response to the rapidly increasing number of *xiagang* workers caused by the economic reforms (Leung 2006; Ngok 2010).

The PRC government promulgated its first administrative regulations in regard to the MLSS in 1999, establishing its legal framework and establishing the right of urban-registered residents to social assistance. The regulation stipulated that urban residents with non-agricultural household registration status were entitled to material assistance from the local government for their basic life needs if the average income of their family members was below the local minimum standard of living (State Council 1999).

Because the MLSS is a means-tested programme, its beneficiaries are people in such socially disadvantaged groups in urban China as what are known as *three-nos* households, which have no means of livelihood, no work ability and no family support, unemployed workers and low-income households with non-agricultural household registration status and average family incomes below the local minimum standard of living, which local governments set according to the costs of such basic necessities as food, clothing and housing (Leung 2006).

Local governments are responsible for the MLSS's main expenditures. Such grassroots governing organizations as street offices and residents' committees are responsible for handling MLSS applications. Applicants must submit application forms together with supporting evidence to the street office or residents' committee where they live. Local governments have applied the MLSS's provisions differently for different kinds of beneficiaries and encourage able-bodied young beneficiaries to look for jobs in the labour market (State Council 1999; Tang *et al.* 2003).

The MLSS was serving four million people by the end of 2000, which was approximately 25 per cent of all impoverished urban people (Tang *et al.* 2003). The number of MLSS recipients rose to 11.7 million in 2001, more than 20 million by the end of 2002 and 22.47 million in 2003. The number of MLSS beneficiaries has since stabilized, indicating that it had entered a stage of consolidation (Ngok 2010). By the end of August 2010, the MLSS had benefited 229.36 million people in 11.32 million urban households throughout China, and its total fiscal expenditure had reached 30.23 billion RMB (Ministry of Civil Affairs 2010).

Workfare measures in China

Problems with the MLSS

The problem of long-term dependence on the MLSS has attracted widespread attention since its introduction, as many of its beneficiaries, although capable of working, have been permanently trapped in the scheme. A 2008 survey of its beneficiaries in six cities revealed that half of them had been on it since

2000 and that at least 40 per cent had never left the scheme during this time, which means that more than 80 per cent of them had been on the benefit continuously for eight years (Task Force on China Urban Minimum Living Standard Scheme Performance Evaluation 2008). In 2007, for example, 62.9 per cent of the 22.72 million MLSS beneficiaries were of working age, 939,000 of all beneficiaries, or 4.1 per cent, were in employment, 3.44 million, or 15.1 per cent, were in casual employment, 2.98 million, or 13.1 per cent, were retired people aged 60 or older, 6.27 million, or 27.6 per cent, were registered unemployed, 3.64 million, or 16 per cent, were unregistered unemployed, 3.22 million, or 14.2 per cent, were enrolled students and 2.23 million, or 9.8 per cent, were non-students aged 17 and younger (MCA 2008).

The number of those who are capable of working but who have been relying on MLSS benefits is clearly huge. It is worth noting that the general international definition of long-term welfare dependency is being on a benefit for a year or more (Freud 2010). Such studies as Hong (2005) have therefore concluded that the MLSS is creating a permanent low-income social class in China. The problem of the MLSS being a refuge for the lazy has received much media attention, which has provoked considerable criticism of the scheme (Guang 2003; Lai & Wang 2006; Wang 2006; Bi 2007). Within this context, the introduction of workfare measures has become particularly vital for both any future reforms of the MLSS and China's long-term strategy for developing its social security system.

The emergence of workfare in China

Owing to its economy being a transitional one, China's workfare initially involved policies that aimed to help *xiagang* workers to find re-employment. As the previous section explained, to help them to do this, the PRC government launched a national re-employment project in the mid-1990s that involved the national deployment of RSCs. As part of this process, it also implemented a package that included such re-employment initiatives as tax reductions, small loans and subsidies. The State Taxation Administration and the Ministry of Labour and Social Security, now the Ministry of Human Resources and Social Security, issued three policy documents in 2005 and 2006 in regard to using tax incentives to help *xiagang* workers to find re-employment or start self-employment. The small-loan policy aims to help them and other unemployed people to start their own small businesses and become self-employed by enabling those who have been out of employment for a set amount of time to apply for small loans from state-owned banks. It also subsidized the social insurance contributions of re-employed workers in newly created positions in the service sector (Wong & Ngok 2006; Ngok 2010).

As the preceding section explained, the government introduced the MLSS in the late 1990s as a new type of public assistance scheme with the clear purpose of pacifying such vulnerable social groups as *xiagang* workers, other unemployed people, retirees and poor farmers (Ngok 2010). Its original focus was mainly on lifting the average monthly income of impoverished people up to their local poverty thresholds without any explicit conditions or incentives with regard to work. During the twenty-first century, however, the PRC government has gradually introduced workfare measures as conditions for receiving MLSS benefits.

The first national administrative regulation with regard to the MLSS issued by China's State Council (1999)[2] stated that the scheme's guiding principles were to involve combining state guarantees with social support and to encourage self-reliance through employment (*laodong zijiu*). Although it emphasized the latter as a guiding principle, it mentioned only one work requirement for the scheme's beneficiaries, stipulating that 'urban residents of working age with the ability to work while jobless should take part in non-profit community social services organized by their local residents' committees when receiving a benefit'.

Community service does not involve paid employment, but is a means of reminding the beneficiaries that they need to make some contribution to the community in return for public assistance. It can be argued that participating in community service may to some extent stigmatize MLSS beneficiaries and impose some psychological pressure on them to seek re-employment and leave the scheme as soon as possible. We observed this in our fieldwork, as the members of the residents' committees used the requirement to participate in community service as a key technique for preventing MLSS beneficiaries from working at unregistered jobs, as many able-bodied MLSS beneficiaries work covertly without reporting it.

As Chinese culture has a strong work ethic and Chinese social policy is employment oriented, it seems strange that the MLSS had no strong workfare provisions from the start. One reason for this was the separation of China's labour market and social assistance policies. As explained earlier, the country was undergoing radical economic reforms that made vast numbers of jobs redundant when the PRC government introduced MLSS to mollify the millions of disgruntled *xiagang* workers, and its purpose was just to supplement the re-employment policy package by providing income maintenance. As the re-employment policies already included many workfare measures, the early policy documents with regard to the MLSS had paid little attention to workfare and neglected to make work a condition for receiving MLSS benefits (Leung 2006; Ngok 2010).

The situation changed in 2001, however, when the PRC government sought to combine the social protection policy for the *xiagang* workers with the unemployment insurance system and make the MLSS the key social safety net for all disadvantaged social groups. As an increasing number of *xiagang* workers left the RSC and social insurance system for the MLSS, the government began to strengthen the MLSS's workfare provisions (State Council 2001). Local governments' workfare initiatives had provided good information for the central policymakers and, in 2001, the State Council approved the social security reform proposal prepared by Liaoning province, declaring that:

the MLSS should both guarantee the subsistence of urban poor people and encourage them to look for jobs and realize self-reliance through employment. Residents who are able to work but refuse to participate in community services and who reject job offers two consecutive times without sufficient reasons are not eligible for MLSS benefits.

State Council (2001)[3]

About four months later, the General Office of the State Council issued a notice with regard to strengthening the work requirements for urban MLSS beneficiaries that emphasized the need to

change the MLSS recipients' mindset from being dependent on government relief and to encourage and help them to find jobs by themselves so they can earn their own living and improve their living conditions gradually.

General Office of the State Council (2001)

Although the MLSS's original policy framework had no clear-cut approach to workfare, the PRC government's changing attitudes expressed in subsequent policy documents began to encourage local governments to embrace workfare measures at their discretion. Local governments' fiscal pressures resulting from paying the costs of the MLSS also contributed to the widespread adoption of local-level workfare, especially in the prosperous coastal regions, although cash transfers from the PRC government are possible (Ngok 2010). Local governments have introduced a range of measures for implementing workfare, including work-first, training and financial incentives (Xiao & Leung 2010).

The PRC government has paid close attention to the workfare measures practised by local governments, as it has the explicit intention of augmenting the MLSS's workfare elements, which it has clearly demonstrated in its efforts to revise the scheme's current administrative regulations, to which end MCA officials have prepared drafts of proposed revisions. A draft revision that the MCA released for consultation in May 2010[4] contained many workfare measures. Its Item 16 stipulated that 'the Civil Affairs Department should reduce or terminate the MLSS benefits of beneficiaries who refuse to accept a referred job while not actively seeking jobs for six months, or who reject referred job offers three times'. Its Item 14 stipulated that 'families receiving benefits from the MLSS after making a report of a new appointment are eligible to receive its benefits for a certain period of time'. Its Item 17 focuses on the expenses incurred in starting a new job, stipulating that 'within a certain period of time MLSS beneficiaries who have accepted jobs when their incomes have been means-tested may deduct such costs as working expenses'. These changes clearly indicate the acceptance and introduction of the concept of workfare in MLSS policies. The new version of the MLSS regulation is expected in 2011.

Local workfare initiatives

Although the operative PRC government policy document on the MLSS does not provide explicitly for workfare, as do the policies on the re-employment of *xiagang* workers, an examination of the local policy documents with regard to the MLSS reveals that its local implementation involves considerable workfare. We compared local policy documents with regard to MLSS in such big cities as Beijing, Chongqing, Guangzhou, Shanghai, Shenzhen, Tianjin and Wuhan, and found that many local governments have indeed adopted workfare measures at their discretion. Table 2.1 provides a summary of these.

Work-first

Local governments have mainly implemented the work-first principle by either requiring beneficiaries to provide evidence of job-seeking or accepting job offers to which they refer them. All the cities in this comparison have introduced measures of this type, making the acceptance of job assignments a condition for the renewal of the MLSS benefit.

Guangzhou's local MLSS policy document states that 'the benefit will not be renewable if a beneficiary refuses to accept job assignments twice, to accept the job referral service, to take a job training course, or to participate in community service' (Guangzhou Government 2008). Wuhan refuses to renew the benefits of those who 'groundlessly refuse to accept referred jobs twice within a year' (Wuhan Government 2004). Tianjin similarly compels beneficiaries to work by implicitly assuming that those 'who refuse to accept job offers referred by the local branch of the Labour Bureau ... have earnings at the local MLSS threshold' and terminating their benefits (Tianjin Government 2001). Some cities, such as Shanghai, even provide job referrals before processing MLSS applications, thereby effectively making accepting job referrals a prerequisite for participation. As the first city to pilot the MLSS, Shanghai rejects any application from anyone 'who groundlessly refuses to take re-employment opportunities referred by the local branch of the Labour Bureau and therefore has no right of access to the unemployment benefit in conformity with the legal provisions' (Shanghai Government 1996). Making the MLSS benefit subject to termination upon refusal to accept employment sends a strong signal to beneficiaries that they must demonstrate a willingness to work. It is unmistakably clear that local authorities place much importance on these work-first measures.

Training

Training tends to be less popular with local governments than work-first. Not all the cities in our sample have introduced training programmes, and most of those that have adopted them have done so relatively recently. The Chongqing municipal government requires MLSS beneficiaries to 'register

Table 2.1 Local workfare measures in China

City	Work-first	Training	Financial incentives	Others
Beijing	Provide job-seeking evidence (2000); must accept referred job offers (2000, 2002)	Take training course (2004)	Progressively withdrawing benefit as income rises (2006)	Participate in community social service (2000)
Chongqing	Must accept referred job offers (2008)	Take training course (2008)	Financial support for re-employment (2008)	Participate in community social service (2008)
Guangzhou	Ineligible if refuse to accept job offer (1999); renewable upon accepting job assignment (2008)	Take training course (2008)	Top-up joballowance upon re-employment (2006)	Participate in community social service (2008)
Shanghai	Ineligible if refuse to accept job offer (1996)*	Take training course (1999)		Participate in community social service (1999)
Shenzhen	Must accept referred job offers (2008)	Take training course (2008)		Participate in community social service (2008)
Tianjin	Must accept referred job offers (2008)**			Participate in community social service (2001)
Wuhan	Must accept referred job offers (2004)			Participate in community social service (2004)

Sources: Beijing Government (2000, 2002, 2004, 2006); Chongqing Government (2008); Guangdong Government (1999); Guangzhou Government (2006, 2008); Shanghai Government (1996, 1999); Shenzhen Government (2008); Tianjin Government (2001a, 2001b); Wuhan Government (2004)

Notes:
* This is set up as a prerequisite in Shanghai, where former unemployment benefit recipients who refuse to take up referred job offers and thus lose such benefits will not be eligible to apply for the MLSS benefit either.
** Tianjin applies this measure slightly differently from other cities by assuming that recipients who refuse to accept referred job offers have earnings up to the local MLSS threshold.

their unemployed status with the local public employment service organisation and take part in community service and skills training courses arranged by local residents' committees' (Chongqing Government 2008). Their recent and apparently reluctant introduction indicates either that many local governments do not see training as an effective way to return unemployed people to the labour market or that they are reluctant to invest the resources necessary for providing it.

Financial incentives

Financial incentive programmes are even less popular with local governments than those for training, as only three cities have introduced them. One of these financial incentives involves the progressive withdrawal of people's benefits or allowances after they accept employment. Beijing, for example, allows the families of beneficiaries who have found re-employment to 'receive 100 per cent of their previous benefit for the first month [after starting their new jobs] and then 50 per cent for the second' (Beijing Government 2006). Guangzhou provides a top-up allowance, which this chapter will describe later. Although Beijing and Guangzhou have detailed procedures for implementing financial incentives, Chongqing's approach is ambiguous, as the local government requires only that the 'local branch of the Labour Bureau provide employment support in conformance with the relevant regulations' (Chongqing Government 2008), without specifying how or the source of the funding.

Local implementation of MLSS, therefore, relies heavily on work-first programmes and tends to ignore training and financial incentives. This appears to be the result of two main factors. One of these is that both training and financial incentives require local governments to expend additional resources and work-first programmes have minimal financial implications. As local governments have the principal responsibility for paying for the MLSS, they have a strong incentive to keep its budget down (Ngok 2010).

Furthermore, work-first programmes are all at the discretion of local governments' civil affairs bureaus, whereas providing training and financial incentives requires collaboration with national government ministries and departments, and the mechanisms for doing so are not always available. Local governments' preference for low-cost workfare programmes over extra-resources-needed and collaboration-required ones reveals the segmented structure of China's welfare institutions.

Impact of workfare: the case of Guangzhou

Guangzhou is the capital city of Guangdong Province, one of the wealthiest provinces in coastal China, and has China's third largest metropolitan economy (Statistics Bureau of Guangdong 2010). Having had many overstaffed SOEs, Guangzhou was among the first cities to introduce the MLSS in response to the large number of lay-offs from them in the late 1990s. As it has since gradually added extra conditions for local MLSS beneficiaries, Guangzhou is a good case of creeping conditionality in the scheme's local implementation.

Although Guangzhou has presented its workfare measures in a series of policy documents, one Guangzhou Government (2006) document summarizes them. It is notable for its supply-side labour incentives, particularly (a) the work-first termination of the MLSS benefit upon two rejections of job offers, (b) the financial incentive of top-up allowances for those accepting job offers, and (c) reductions and exemptions from municipal charges and fees for those accepting job offers.

The termination of the MLSS benefit upon two rejections of job offers is a punishment measure for those whom the authorities view as being unwilling to rely upon themselves. Guangzhou requires its MLSS beneficiaries who are able to work to accept job offers that their local branch of the Labour Bureau has referred to them and terminates their benefits if they reject two consecutive ones. They then need to reapply in order to restore their status as MLSS beneficiaries (Guangzhou Government 2006).

Unlike this punitive work-first measure, top-up allowances upon accepting job offers are a reward for those whom the authorities view as being cooperative by accepting job offers that their local branch of the Labour Bureau has referred to them. Former MLSS beneficiaries are entitled to receive top-up allowances, which were 530 RMB in 2006, after accepting job offers that result in the ending of their MLSS benefits. The local government deducts this allowance from the beneficiaries' household means tests rather than paying it to them directly, and only does so when the new jobs involve permanent or flexible employment contracts. Beneficiaries accepting casual employment without contracts are ineligible for this allowance, showing that the authorities clearly favour contract-based over casual employment. Reductions and exemptions from municipal charges and fees for those accepting job offers are another reward in addition to the top-up allowances. These entitle those receiving them to reduced rents if they live in public housing and exemptions from such municipal charges as sewage disposal and cleaning (Guangzhou Government 2006).

We have been conducting a longitudinal study of Guangzhou MLSS beneficiaries for the past two years. Our sample has included fifty households and our methodology has primarily involved interviews. We have found that these workfare measures have been overwhelmingly ineffective. The work-first measures in particular have been difficult for front-line bureaucrats to administer and unpopular with the beneficiaries. Our sample has included forty-nine people who are of working age and able to work. Eight of them have reported that they have never received any job referrals, and thirteen that they have accepted some casual jobs that the residents' committee and street office have referred to them. Eight of these thirteen asserted that accepting such jobs has been detrimental to them for various reasons, and only one stated that doing so has made him better off.

The primary reason for the acceptance of such job offers being detrimental has been mismatches between the people and the jobs. Most of the recipients are low skilled and middle aged, and most of the jobs either require some skills or are physically demanding. Beneficiary A, for example, is aged 45, has only finished junior secondary school and suffers from gallstones. A *xiagang* former SOE worker, he took an electrician training course provided by a voluntary organization and earned a junior certificate. Most of the employers with whom he has spoken, however, have told him that they are seeking younger electricians with higher qualifications. He explained in an interview that:

> I'm middle-aged – who wants me? Bosses can easily get someone younger than me. There are so many from outside Guangzhou – they have no household status – all looking for jobs. They ask for less, and have good qualifications, God knows whether genuine or not, but I'm just not competitive, you know.[5]
>
> Case 35

Another problem involves the nature of the jobs. Residents' committees and street offices find it difficult to find beneficiaries regular jobs with regular incomes. Beneficiary B is able to work, but the last job offer he received had been for a casual worker and had demanded more physical strength than he, a weak middle-aged man, had. The residents' committees and street offices therefore have trouble securing job offers for regular positions that pay a regular income, and they often fail to consider job offers on a case-by-case basis taking the beneficiaries' individual abilities into consideration. We asked Beneficiary B why he had not accepted a security post arranged by the residents' committee and he replied:

> Well, how should I put this? It's not that I refused it. It isn't a regular job, anyway. When they asked me to do it I just went, but there are times when I'd like to go but it isn't available. It isn't regular. In addition, most of the time it's night shift – staying up all night for only 800 RMB a month. I'm not in good health and staying up at night would just make my health worse. This money isn't enough for medical treatment, you see. I'd rather not earn this money.
>
> Case 28

Work-first measures are also inconsiderate of families with special needs. Some beneficiaries are the main carers for other members of their families, and work-first measures should not apply to them at all. Beneficiary C is a single mother who needs to look after both her daughter and her mother-in-law. Her case reveals the over-rigidity of the accept-jobs-or-else requirement for beneficiaries with different family responsibilities and the need to revise them and grant more discretion to those administering the scheme. We asked if her benefit would be taken away if she were to refuse to accept jobs. Her answer was:

Yes, they say that if I don't accept work they'll terminate my status. How could they do that? It's unjust that I have to take whatever they offer me! Well, you also need to think about if I'm able to take it or not. I have my daughter and mother-in-law to look after.

Interviewer: They insisted regardless?

Yes, I said I have reasons for not taking up their offer, but they just refused to listen and just said that my status will be terminated if I don't accept the job.

Case 17

Interestingly, we found little with regard to the existence of the training and financial incentive programmes, let alone their impact. The local policy documents stipulate that these measures should be implemented (Guangzhou Government 2006), but those in our Guangzhou sample report either not having been informed about them or not having been introduced to them. Many in our sample reported having received some training courses, but their former work units at the SOEs had mainly provided them, and did so before they began receiving their MLSS benefits. Many in the sample were also poorly informed about the top-up allowance formula that applied to their cases and therefore did not know whether they had received the proper amount for them. Furthermore, most of the jobs that they had accepted had been without formal labour contracts, making them therefore ineligible to receive any allowance. Without knowing what their entitlements were or having had any experience of them, the people in our sample were unable to help us to assess whether the training and financial incentive measures have been effective.

Our sample's perception that training and financial incentives are beyond their reach clearly indicates that work-first measures are the core of Guangzhou's workfare programme. We therefore conclude that the programme's impact has been generally unsatisfactory.

Discussion

This chapter's previous sections have discussed workfare in China with a policy review and empirical evidence. We have found that workfare ideas and measures are widely present in local government policy documents and practices, but that their implementation has been unsatisfactory. This raises the important questions of what the fundamental reasons are for the unsatisfactory implementation of these measures and even of the scheme as a whole, and what has driven the emergence of workfare in China.

The MLSS's flawed mechanisms

The MLSS is a means-tested income support scheme with the objective of assisting those in poverty. Its unit for delivering its benefits is households, unlike the income-support programmes in most developed countries, which work with individual people. The MLSS also aims to raise the average monthly income of each family member to locally established thresholds rather than pay eligible beneficiaries a set amount. The total amount of MLSS benefits to which a family is entitled is equivalent to the size of the family times the difference between the local MLSS threshold and the family members' average monthly income (e.g. Beijing Government 2000).

The formula for this calculation is $B = (T-AMI)N$, in which B is the total amount of the MLSS benefits to which a family is entitled, T is the local MLSS threshold, AMI is the family members' average monthly income, and N is the number of family members. $(T-AMI)$ is the actual amount paid to each family member, the average of which among local MLSS beneficiaries represents the local level of MLSS benefits. For a family of three, when the local MLSS threshold is 350 RMB and the family members' average monthly income is 200 RMB, the total amount of MLSS benefits for the family is 450 RMB.

As in any evaluation of a poverty relief scheme, it is necessary to take into account the three important factors of headcount, poverty gap and duration (Barr 2004). The poverty gap is how far those involved are below the threshold, more generally referred to as the poverty line. The MLSS mechanism's first flaw is that it creates a poverty trap by filling the poverty gap rigidly. This is particular interesting because the MLSS is a de facto gap-filling (*buchaxing*) style of income support scheme, with its main function being to ensure that members of eligible families can all live at a government-set income level equivalent to the local threshold. It withdraws its benefits, however, at the same rate as its beneficiaries' incomes rise when they receive employment, and most cities have rigidly set the replacement rate of benefits from earnings at 100 per cent. Some cities, such as Guangzhou, provide allowances to counteract this loss, but the requirement for contract-based employment has made this irrelevant, as most of the jobs offered to beneficiaries are casual ones. For beneficiaries, therefore, the poverty gap becomes a poverty trap because of this implicit tax rate on their earnings.

Another flaw is the real level of benefits attached to the status of being an MLSS beneficiary. In 2003, the State Council published a new document with regard to supporting measures for the scheme's implementation that provided for the gradual implementation of a range of supplementary allowances for health care, children's education, housing and heating in northern China (State Council 2003). This means that gap-filling benefits represent only the explicit and nominal part of the total benefits a family actually receives from the scheme. Remaining an MLSS beneficiary or leaving the scheme therefore means more than receiving enough to fill the poverty gap. This has also resulted in the emergence of marginal households, or families with incomes slightly above the local MLSS threshold. Members of such households can experience a variety of disadvantages. With regard to student financial support, for example, students from families receiving the MLSS benefit are automatically eligible for the national student loan scheme and have preferred standing when applying for a bursary (Chan 2009). Parents of such students therefore have an incentive to rethink whether to accept jobs. This also applies to those receiving such other supplementary allowances as supporting measures.

Yet another flaw is that the mechanism's assumption of equivalence elasticity does not reflect the reality of families of different sizes. Other things being equal, the living expenses of a couple are lower than those of two single people. For one thing, couples have no need to rent two flats. Equivalence elasticity, which can have a value between 0 and 1, is an indicator for measuring the equivalence of families of different sizes. Atkinson *et al.* (1995) distinguished four approaches to setting a value for this elasticity, which is never 1. The MLSS's design, however, assumes that equivalence elasticity is always 1 regardless of family size. The result is that the bigger the family, the more likely its benefits from the scheme are to be significantly higher than the average local income, and big families with only one employable person would have lower total incomes if that person were to accept a job.

Reaction to the illusion of welfare dependency

Governments usually introduce workfare programmes to address the problem of welfare dependence. This makes the question of whether any welfare dependence exists among China's MLSS beneficiaries one that requires thorough examination.

Welfare dependency refers to situations in which jobs are available and unemployed people who are able to work do not take them. Common Chinese arguments against all welfare benefits are that they destroy the work ethic and feed lazy people (*yanglanhan*). In order to prevent unemployed people from relying on welfare benefits, many developed countries have proposed or implemented social security programme reforms that use the key word *activation*, which refers to activating the incentive to work among unemployed people (Freud 2010; Xiao & Leung 2010).

It is important to be careful when comparing what has happened in the West and the reality in China, as MLSS beneficiaries engage extensively in unregistered employment. Lu and Tian (2008) found that 40.71 per cent of MLSS beneficiaries in Shanghai had more than five hours of such paid employment weekly, and their average monthly income from this unregistered employment was 1,208 RMB. Taking their family size into consideration, 96.12 per cent of the families with at least one member involved in unregistered employment had an average per capita monthly income that was higher than the local MLSS threshold. Welfare dependence within the context of an ineffectively administered scheme therefore involves a significant proportion of its beneficiaries simply trying to maximize their incomes by combining unregistered employment with their benefits. It provides a disincentive to participate in the official labour market and an incentive to participate in the unofficial one, a situation that refutes the perception of feeding lazy people.

This widespread unregistered employment among MLSS beneficiaries is clear evidence of flaws in its structural design, particularly the effectiveness of its means-testing methods, as well as its local administration, but two other factors influence the context in which these shortcomings occur.

One of these factors is that MLSS benefits are at the subsistence level, in most provinces at approximately merely 6 to 9 per cent of the average urban worker's salary. Table 2.2 illustrates this. To urban Chinese living in poverty, the MLSS benefit is only just better than nothing, meeting their food needs only. Without taking up unregistered employment, they would have no resources for meeting their personal development needs, which they need to do in order eventually to escape from their impoverished situations. Blocking unregistered employment, in this sense, would create a real danger for longer term welfare dependence.

Next, flexible employment has become a labour market norm. Globalization, international competition and large-scale labour migration from rural to urban China have all stimulated the emergence of new and flexible forms of employment. Part-time jobs, casual contracts, seasonal jobs and jobs at an hourly rate, rather than full-time jobs on permanent contracts, have become increasingly more common (Peng 2009; Xiao & Leung 2010). Flexible employment has facilitated the growth of the unregistered employment market and has also resulted in new challenges to China's anti-unemployment policies, which developed according to assumptions of formal employment within a Fordist economic structure. This is not to assert that unregistered employment does no harm to MLSS beneficiaries and other disadvantaged social groups, as these jobs tend to have little if any job security and provide neither stable and regular income nor sufficient or appropriate protection for workers (Peng 2009).

With the MLSS's low level of assistance and the changing nature of the labour market, welfare dependence in China is therefore more of an illusion than a reality. The creation of such an illusion in various ways has made a strong case for the introduction of workfare measures, which do not occupy the moral high ground. Local governments under fiscal pressure also have the motivation to introduce workfare measures as a way to control spending on the scheme. After more than a decade of implementation at local levels, some have argued that momentum has built up for national legislation establishing workfare programmes formally as national policy (Peng 2009).

Conclusion

Unemployment was new to China and the Chinese people in the 1990s when large numbers of SOE workers began to be laid off. The government introduced three lines of anti-unemployment policies as a policy response, of which the last one, the MLSS, has eventually become its main approach for looking after unemployed people's basic needs. Since the start of the twenty-first

Table 2.2 The MLSS in urban China, 2009

Region	Average monthly income of urban employees (RMB)	Average MLSS threshold (RMB)	Average monthly gap-filling benefits (RMB)	Average MLSS threshold as % of average monthly salary	Average monthly gap-filling as % of average monthly salary
Beijing	4,845.00	410	358	8.46	7.39
Tianjin	3,749.33	430	350	11.47	9.34
Hebei	2,365.25	245	152	10.36	6.43
Shanxi	2,372.42	213	132	8.98	5.56
Nei Mongol	2,558.25	241	215	9.42	8.40
Liaoning	2,592.00	272	166	10.49	6.40
Jilin	2,185.83	212	181	9.70	8.28
Heilongjiang	2,211.25	217	165	9.81	7.46
Shanghai	5,295.75	425	289	8.03	5.46
Jiangsu	2,990.83	310	184	10.37	6.15
Zhejiang	3,116.25	334	257	10.72	8.25
Anhui	2,471.50	234	163	9.47	6.60
Fujian	2,388.83	213	140	8.92	5.86
Jiangxi	2,058.00	194	162	9.43	7.87
Shandong	2,474.00	262	170	10.59	6.87
Henan	2,279.75	186	134	8.16	5.88
Hubei	2,260.58	214	156	9.47	6.90
Hunan	2,273.67	195	140	8.58	6.16
Guangdong	3,029.58	244	144	8.05	4.75
Guangxi	2,358.50	217	153	9.20	6.49
Hainan	2,077.83	243	201	11.69	9.67
Chongqing	2,580.42	231	200	8.95	7.75
Sichuan	2,380.25	196	151	8.23	6.34
Guizhou	2,353.75	170	152	7.22	6.46
Yunnan	2,249.33	199	150	8.85	6.67
Tibet	4,062.50	310	211	7.63	5.19

(*Continued on next page*)

Table 2.2 (continued)

Region	Average monthly income of urban employees (RMB)	Average MLSS threshold (RMB)	Average monthly gap-filling benefits (RMB)	Average MLSS threshold as % of average monthly salary	Average monthly gap-filling as % of average monthly salary
Shaanxi	2,515.42	192	386	7.63	15.35
Gansu	2,264.75	171	133	7.55	5.87
Qinghai	2,796.75	223	171	7.97	6.11
Ningxia	2,840.17	204	187	7.18	6.58
Xinjiang	2,312.75	172	162	7.44	7.00
National average	2,728.00	228	173	8.36	6.34

Sources: National Bureau of Statistics (2010); Social Assistance Division, Ministry of Civil Affairs (regular update available at http://dbs.mca.gov.cn/article/csdb/tjsj/ (accessed 16 February 2011)

century, however, many of those who have landed in the MLSS's safety net have been unable to escape from it. Much of the criticism of the scheme has focused on whether it has created a new long-term social group of low-income people who constitute the social phenomenon of welfare dependence.

This chapter has argued that welfare dependence is most probably an illusion in China, as the MLSS's benefits are at the subsistence level. As the work ethic is deeply rooted in Chinese culture and tradition, however, any sign of welfare dependence is likely to generate pressure for measures to counteract it. Within such a context, the idea of workfare, with or without the mentioning of it as a concept or the philosophy behind it, is certainly welcome at all levels of government.

Local authorities have adopted various types of workfare programmes since the 1990s. The activation approach, in particular the provision of training and financial incentives or both to assist unemployed people, has in practice lagged far behind such work-first policies as punishing those who refuse job offers or otherwise show an unwillingness to become re-employed. This creeping conditionality has resulted in the MLSS experiencing a complex shift from being a moderate protectivist scheme to an aggressively productivist one in some of China's major cities.

The implementation of such measures is far from satisfactory, however, as our study in Guangzhou has found that they are neither easy to implement nor acceptable or helpful to the unemployed people themselves. The problematic mechanism through which local governments deliver and withdraw benefits is clearly a major obstacle to the scheme's success. It therefore seems likely that China adopted workfare to address the problem of welfare dependence without it actually existing.

Notes

1 This paper is supported by the Research Project on the Challenges and Coping Strategies of Social Policy in China, sponsored by China's Ministry of Education, and the project on Building the Social Policy Framework for the Welfare Society in China, sponsored by Sun Yat-sen University, China.
2 Government documents cited in this paper are all obtained from official websites. These documents, available online, are all without exact page numbers.
3 All translations of Chinese documents are by the authors.
4 This is an unpublished document that the authors read as part of the consultation process.
5 The translations of the interview transcripts are by the authors.

Bibliography

Atkinson, A.B., Rainwater, L. and Smeeding, T.M. (1995) 'Income Distribution in European Countries', in A.B. Atkinson (ed.) *Incomes and the Welfare State: Essays on Britain and Europe*, Cambridge: Cambridge University Press.
Barr, N. (2004) *The Economics of Welfare State*, 4th edn, Oxford: Oxford University Press.

Beijing Government (2000) *Detailed Rules and Regulations on the Implementation of the Minimum Living Standard Scheme in Beijing*, Beijing: Beijing Government.
——(2002) *A Number of Suggestions on Perfecting the Minimum Living Standard Scheme in Beijing*, Document no. 19, Beijing: Beijing Government.
——(2004) *Provisional Measures in Establishing a Mechanism for Minimum Living Standard Scheme Recipients*, Beijing: Beijing Government.
——(2006) *Notice on Perfecting Our City's Urban Residents' Minimum Living Standard Scheme's Diversified Assistance System*, Issued on 27 June.
Bi, K. (2007) 'A Not-for-lazybones MLSS worth Generalising', *Legal Daily*, 27 April 2007.
Chan, C.K., Ngok, K.L. and Phillips, D. (2008) *Social Policy in China: Development and Well-being*, Bristol: The Policy Press.
Chan, W.K. (2009) 'Evaluating Student Loan Schemes in China: A Social Policy Perspective', *Journal of Public Administration* 2, 6: 156–75.
Chongqing Government (2008) *Chongqing Urban Residents' Minimum Living Standard Scheme Implementing Measures*, Document No. 18, issued on 25 July.
Feng, L.R. (1988) 'Youth Unemployment in China', *International Social Science Journal* 40: 285–96.
——(1991) 'A Comparison of the Two Unemployment Peaks in China during the Last Decade', *International Social Science Journal* 43: 191–207.
Freud, D. (2010) *Reducing Dependency, Increasing Opportunities: Options for the Future of Welfare to Work*, London: Department for Work and Pensions.
General Office of the State Council (2001) *The Notice on Strengthening Further the Work on the Minimum Living Standard Scheme for Urban Residents*, Official document, 12 November.
Gu, E.X. (2001) 'Forging a Labour Market in Urban China: the Legacies of the Past and the Dynamics of Institutional Transformation', *Asian Affairs* 28: 92–111.
Guang, W. (2003) 'Forty Percent of the MLSS Recipients are Able to Work, Be Aware of creating Lazybones', *Beijing Evening News*, 27 October.
Guangdong Government (1999) *Guangdong Province Urban (Rural) Residents' Minimum Living Standard Implementing Measures*, Document no. 52, Guangdong Government.
Guangzhou Government (2006) *Notice on the Diversified Assistances to the Extreme Poor in Our City*, Document no. 25, Guangzhou Government.
——(2008) *Suggestions on Furthering the Construction of the Social Assistance System of Our City*, Document no. 6, Issued on 7 August.
Hong, D.Y. (2005) 'When Moral Responsibility Transferred into Institutional Arrangements: The Outstretched Effects and Development of the Urban Minimum Living Standard Scheme', *Economic and Social System Comparison*, Issue 3.
Information Office of the State Council (2004) *White Book on Social Security in China*, Beijing: State Council.
Lai, Z.F. and Wang, F. (2006) 'Rather on the MLSS benefit: An Emergence of Young Lazybones', *Beijing Evening News*, 31 March.
Lee, H.Y. (2000) 'Xiagang, the Chinese Style of Laying Off Workers', *Asian Survey*, 40, 6: 914–37.
Leung, C.B. (2006) 'The Emergence of Social Assistance in China', *International Journal of Social Welfare* 15: 188–98.
Leung, C.B. and Xiao, M. (2010) 'Social Assistance Workfare Policy', Paper presented at the *Workshop on the Minimum Living Standard Scheme and Social Exclusion*, Sun Yat-sen University, June 2010.

Lu, M. and Tian, S.H. (2008) 'Explicit Unemployment or Implicit Employment: Evidence from a Household Survey in Shanghai', *Management World*, No. 1.
Ministry of Civil Affairs (2008) *China Civil Affairs' Statistical Yearbook 2008*, Beijing: China Statistics Press.
——(2010) *The Monthly Statistical Bulletin of the Development of Civil Affairs Undertakings*. Online. Available at http://files2.mca.gov.cn/cws/201009/20100920100993918.htm (accessed 10 October 2010).
Ministry of Human Resources and Social Security (2010) *The Statistical Bulletin of the Developments of the Human Resources and Social Security Undertakings in 2009*. Online. Available at http://w1.mohrss.gov.cn/gb/zwxx/2010-05/21/content_382330.htm (accessed 10 October 2010).
National Bureau of Statistics (2010) *China Statistical Yearbook 2010*, Beijing: National Bureau of Statistics.
Ngok, K.L. (2010) 'Social Assistance Policy and its Impact on Social Development in China: The Case of Minimum Living Standard Scheme', *China Journal of Social Work* 1: 35–52.
Peng, Z. (2009) 'The Minimum Living Standard Scheme and the Work Incentive of Recipients: The Chinese Style Welfare Dependency and its Reform', *Social Security Studies* 10: 163–74.
Shanghai Government (1996) *Shanghai City Social Assistance Implementing Measures*, Document no. 60, Shanghai: Shanghai Government.
——(1999) *Notice on a Number of Issues Concerning the Connecting Work in our City's Social Assistance Policy*, Document no. 37, Shanghai: Shanghai Government.
Shenzhen Government (2008) *The Implementing Measures of Urban Minimum Living Standard Scheme in Shenzhen City*, Document no. 189, Shenzhen: Shenzhen Government.
State Council (1999) *The Regulation on Guaranteeing Urban Residents' Minimum Living Standard*, Beijing: State Council.
——(2001) *The Written Reply on Agreeing the Implementing Proposal of the Social Security System Pilot Reform in Liaoning Province*, Beijing: State Council.
——(2003) *Notice on Further Strengthening Urban Residents' Minimum Living Standard Scheme*, Beijing: State Council.
Statistics Bureau of Guangdong (2010) *Guangdong Statistical Yearbook 2010*. Online. Available at www.gdstats.gov.cn/tjnj/ml_e.htm (accessed 20 October 2010).
Tang, J. et al. (2003) *The Final Safety Net: Poverty and the Scheme of Minimum Living Standard in Urban China*, Beijing: Huaxia Press.
The Task Force on China's Urban Minimum Living Standard Scheme Performance Evaluation (2008) *A Report on the Implementation of the Urban Minimum Living Standard Scheme in China*, Minimum Living Standard Scheme Section, Ministry of Civil Affair; School of Labour and Human Resources, Renmin University.
Tian X.B. (ed.) (1999) *The Establishing and Operation of the Reemployment Service Centre*, Beijing: China Labour Press.
Tianjin Government (2001) *Tianjin City Minimum Living Standard Implementing Measures*, Document no. 38, Tianjin: Tianjin Government.
Wang, B.X. (2006) 'The MLSS Benefit is for Good Reasons not for Lazybones', *People's Daily*, 13 April 2006.
Wong, L. and Ngok, K.L. (1997) 'Unemployment and Policy Responses in Mainland China,' *Issues & Studies* 33: 43–63.

——(2006) 'Social Policy between Plan and Market: Xiagang Off-duty Employment and the Policy of the Re-employment Service Centres in China', *Social Policy & Social Administration* 40: 158–73.

Wuhan Government (2004) *The Implementing Measures of Urban Minimum Living Standard Scheme in Wuhan City*, Document no. 63, Wuhan: Wuhan Government.

Xiao, M. and Leung, C.B. (2010) 'Social Assistance Workfare Policy', *Social Security Studies*, 11: 96–108.

3 Workfare in Hong Kong

Joe C.B. Leung

Introduction

Even though the global economy seems to be showing signs of recovery from the 2008 economic crisis, a recent annual employment report published by the Organisation for Economic Co-operation and Development (OECD) has warned that OECD economies are facing the daunting twin challenges of reducing high unemployment and unprecedented fiscal deficits (OECD 2010). The International Labour Organization (ILO) has also recently issued a report showing that global youth unemployment has reached its highest level on record (ILO 2010). Most governments therefore need to reinvigorate their labour policies in order to try to bring the most disadvantaged groups back into the labour market.

After appearing to recover from the Asian financial crisis of 1997 and 1998, Hong Kong maintained a 6–8 per cent economic growth rate from 2004 until 2008. Then, as a result of the global financial crisis, its gross domestic product (GDP) fell by 2.7 per cent in 2009. It has already started to bounce back, and its Financial Secretary (2010) has forecast that its GDP is likely to grow by 4–5 per cent in 2010.

This improvement in its economy has returned its government's budget to surplus for 2009–10, and unemployment rates have gradually declined. Hong Kong's government has always had less debt than others, and its exchange fund was US$194 billion and its foreign currency reserves were US$177 billion for the last fiscal year, ranking it seventh in the world (Census and Statistics Department (CSD 2010a). All these indicators show that the Hong Kong government's financial situation is sound and healthy.

According to the United Nations Development Programme's (UNDP) Human Development Index, Hong Kong is a region of 'very high human development', ranking twenty-fourth in the world in 2007. Life expectancy is 82.2 years, ranking it second globally; the combined gross enrolment rate in education from primary to university level is 74.5 per cent, ranking it eighty-eighth; and its per capita GDP adjusted for purchasing power parity is US$42,306, ranking it tenth (UNDP 2009: 171).

As a so-called productivist state, Hong Kong considers social policy to be a means of facilitating economic growth (Goodman et al. 1998; Holliday 2000;

Gough & Wood 2004). It therefore follows a model of residual or remedial welfare in which individuals and families are the major sources of social welfare. This policy is based on the ideology that active government intervention and provisions would erode the traditional Chinese values of self-reliance and social obligation (Chan 1996; Tang & Midgley 2002; Wong & Wong 2005; Chui *et al.* 2010). The government therefore plays a merely facilitative and regulatory role in social welfare (McLaughlin 1993; Chan 1996, 1998; Wildings 1997, 2007; Holliday 2000; Chow 2003).

When Hong Kong reunited with the People's Republic of China in 1997 as the Hong Kong Special Administrative Region (HKSAR), a newly constituted Basic Law replaced the colonial governmental structure. The Basic Law requires the HKSAR government to keep public expenditures in line with economic growth and to balance its budget. Under the principles of *big market, small government* and *market leads, government facilitates*, the government's role is to create the right conditions for markets to develop. These conditions include maintaining the rule of law, keeping taxes low, keeping tax laws simple, nurturing talent, investing in infrastructure and helping businesses to tap export markets (Financial Secretary 2010). Social policy development in Hong Kong has, however, not been just 'the product of a crude application of a laissez-faire ideology, but rather of the complex interaction of political, social and economic factors' (Wildings 1997: 245). The government has focused primarily on its broader goals of maintaining economic competitiveness and political stability.

Having a small government, Hong Kong's recurrent public expenditures in 2009–10 only made up 19.2 per cent of GDP. Public spending on education was 3.1 per cent, social welfare 2.4 percent and health 2.2 per cent of GDP, which is extremely low by international standards (OECD 2009; Financial Secretary 2010), yet social services still account for 58 per cent of recurrent government spending. Partly because Hong Kong's taxes are so low, social services spending takes up a higher proportion of tax revenue than in most OECD countries (Legislative Council (LegCo) Panel on Welfare Services November 2004).

The Basic Law requires that no major changes be made to Hong Kong's pre-reunification welfare system. Hong Kong has therefore tried to maintain its flexible labour market policy and its competitive economic advantages. It has no compulsory, publicly financed social insurance programmes for retirement, medical care or unemployment. Both the colonial and the HKSAR governments have maintained that the economy is the main engine of welfare and that full employment is the government's single most important welfare objective (Hong Kong Government 1996). In 2007, the HKSAR's then financial secretary affirmed that the welfare policy is one of self-reliance:

> The core principle of our poverty-alleviation policy is to help the disadvantaged move from welfare to self-reliance through promoting employment. In fostering economic development, we must also address

the needs of our workers who are unable to adapt to economic restructuring. We will do so by providing them with employment assistance and retraining opportunities, so as to help them achieve self-reliance and improve their livelihood, with a view to building a harmonious society.

Financial Secretary (2007: n.p.)

The government Commission on Poverty (2007: 1) also echoed the importance of employment as the core strategy for alleviating poverty and achieving self-reliance, claiming, 'Not only does employment improve economic well-being, it also enhances the self-respect of the individual, encourages social participation and instils a positive role-modelling for the young generation'.

Hong Kong government policy is based on the firm conviction that employment is the best form of welfare for the people, and that it is a key to social stability as well as a source of steady income and protection for individuals and families. The government has based its employment promotion strategy on the two basic policies that it assume the responsibility for facilitating the economic growth necessary for creating more employment opportunities and that it provide job-seekers with employment support and training to increase their competitiveness and motivation (Financial Secretary 2010).

The Hong Kong government therefore bases its social policy on the conviction that sustainable and balanced development results from policies that have the goal of equality of opportunity rather than equality of income. This means that it considers that the best way to help the disadvantaged is by giving them opportunities to move upwards. On its path to the ultimate goal of liberal welfare, Hong Kong social policy emphasizes individual reliance and family responsibility, with government intervention as a last resort.

After reviewing the background socioeconomic conditions and the analysis with regard to Hong Kong's social policy ideology, this chapter describes the economic transitions, demographic shifts and changing labour market structures that have contributed to the emergence of a polarized labour force with wide income disparities. Facing the challenge of ensuring sufficient employment opportunities, the government has initiated a broad array of programmes in the last decade designed to improve them and to help unemployed people get jobs. These employment services have mainly targeted young people, unemployed middle-aged workers and able-bodied recipients of social assistance. It has developed workfare programmes developed to both push and pull those in this third category back into the labour market. The effectiveness of these programmes is largely uncertain, as the government lacks objective evaluations of them, which it needs to inform further programme improvements.

The Hong Kong labour market

Hong Kong's population reached seven million in mid-2009. It continues to show moderate annual increases despite a low fertility rate, mainly due to Mainland migrants coming to reunite with their families. Life expectancy at birth in 2009 was 79.8 years for men and 86.1 years for women. In 2009, its population included 890,000 people aged 65 or older, accounting for 12.8 per cent of the total, an increase from 7.7 per cent in 1986 (CSD 2010a). The gradual retirement of the post-war baby boomers in 2014 will coincide with a rapid increase in the population aged 65 and older. The CSD (2010b) has projected that the elderly will make up 28 per cent of the population by 2039. It has projected further that the overall dependency ratio, which is the number of children aged 14 and younger and adults aged 65 and older divided by the number of people aged 15 to 64, will increase from 337 in 2009 to 625 in 2039. With an increasingly elderly society and low fertility rates, working people are overwhelmingly likely to constitute an increasingly smaller proportion of the population, projected to decrease from 75 per cent in 2009 to 62 per cent in 2039.

As Hong Kong's manufacturing industries have declined, their contribution to the HKSAR's GDP had shrunk to only 2.5 per cent in 2008. Tertiary industries now account for more than 92 per cent of its GDP. Of the 3.7 million workers in Hong Kong in 2009, 22.9 per cent had completed less than a primary school education, down from 26.3 per cent in 2004, and 25.2 percent had had some post-secondary education, up from 21.9 per cent in 2004 (CSD 2010a). These low educational levels can be attributed to migrants from the Mainland, as their educational levels have generally been low. People with inadequate education and skills have been finding it harder to find jobs with decent pay as Hong Kong has transformed itself into a financial centre.

Hong Kong's overall labour force participation rate, only 60.7 per cent in 2009, 69.4 per cent for men and 53.1 per cent for women, is low by international standards. This is lower than the average labour force participation in OECD countries, which was 70.6 per cent in 2009 (CSD 2010a; OECD 2011). Table 3.1 illustrates how the labour force participation rate has declined moderately in recent decades, particularly among men. Women, however, have experienced a minor increase.

Hong Kong has no mandatory retirement age, but the official retirement age for the civil service and large companies is usually 60. This is relatively early by international standards, and it is lower than might be expected, considering Hong Kong's long life expectancy. Increasing economic prosperity has led Hong Kong's elderly population to participate less in the labour market, with the rate dropping from 13 per cent of the labour force in 1991 to 9.8 per cent in 1996, 7 per cent in 2006 and 1.2 per cent in 2009. The elderly

Table 3.1 Hong Kong labour force participation rates (%) by sex, 1996–2009

Sex	1996	2001	2006	2009
Male	76.6	71.96	9.2	69.4
Female	49.2	51.6	52.4	53.1
Both sexes	62.8	61.4	60.3	60.7

Source: Census and Statistics Department (2010a)

work force also has a significant gender imbalance, being 11.6 per cent male and 3.1 per cent female in 2006 (CSD 2008).

This decline in employment among the elderly is consistent with the trend towards early retirement. A strong Confucian belief holds that older people should enjoy life and receive support from their children rather than have to work. Older workers face several types of discrimination, including negative perceptions about their ability, more expensive employment insurance and a lack of legal protection (*South China Morning Post* 12 May 2010: A15). Ethnic Chinese societies have much lower rates of economic participation for people aged 60–64 than the OECD average of 45.9 per cent. Urban Mainland China's rate is 25.4 per cent, Taipei's is 30.9 per cent, and Hong Kong's is 28.1 per cent (Herd *et al.* 2010).

For a long time, the Hong Kong authorities did not consider unemployment to be a critical problem, but two years after the outbreak of the severe acute respiratory syndrome (SARS) epidemic in 2002, Hong Kong's unemployment rate reached a high of 6.8 per cent. It then fell to 3.6 per cent in 2008, but rose again to 5.4 per cent from June to August 2009 as a result of the global financial crisis. The economy began recovering after that, however, and unemployment was back to 4.3 per cent in July 2010, the lowest since December 2008. Hong Kong's unemployment rate is low by international standards, however, with the average OECD unemployment rate having been 8.7 per cent in the first quarter of 2010 (OECD 2010).

Financial crises tend to affect the employment rates of different groups and industries differently. During economic recessions, such vulnerable demographic groups as women, the elderly, recent migrants, young people and poorly educated people make up an even higher portion of unemployed, underemployed and poorly paid workers. Unemployment rates tend to be high in construction and retail, whereas the low-wage jobs that remain tend to involve consumer or producer services. Manufacturing industries have laid workers off. These vulnerable people can expect to experience a prolonged period of joblessness, low pay and the harmful effects of social exclusion, low job satisfaction and poor health.

The global economic crisis had a particular impact on young people. The unemployment rate for the 15–19 age group reached 28.7 per cent from May to July 2009, then fell to 20.1 per cent by July 2010, still much higher than the overall unemployment rate. From 2004 to 2009, this age group experienced average unemployment rates 2.1 times larger than the overall unemployment rate (LegCo Panel on Manpower 14 December 2009; *South China Morning Post* 18 August 2010: C3). In comparison, the average unemployment rate for people aged 15–24 in the OECD was 19 per cent in 2009 (Scarpetta *et al.* 2010).

Facing a mounting employment crisis at the time, the HKSAR government announced its Initiatives for Wider Economic Participation in 2000. This included public works projects to create a wide array of temporary and low-skilled jobs. It extended these initiatives further during the SARS epidemic in 2003 and 2004, creating 73,000 short-term and temporary jobs and training opportunities with various government departments. During the global financial crisis of 2008–10, it also created temporary jobs in government departments and non-governmental organizations (NGOs) by expediting major and minor infrastructure projects, together with a job creation plan involving 60,000 positions (LegCo Panel on Manpower 12 February 2004a; Labour and Welfare Bureau 10 December 2008).

The term *working poor* refers to people who have gainful employment but do not earn enough to emerge from poverty. Approximately 7.5 per cent of Hong Kong's households are classified as working poor. Some 66 per cent of these households are made up of three or four people. Even though the number of working poor households remained stable from 1998 to 2005, these households have generally suffered a decline in monthly income over the years. It is noteworthy that the proportion of households with two members working has increased substantially and that the proportion of working women has also increased considerably. The working poor households tend to be located in such remote areas as Tuen Mun and Yuen Long and such old industrial areas as Kwun Tong and Kwai Chung. Most of the employed people in working poor households unsurprisingly have low-skilled jobs (Commission on Poverty 2007; Chan 2008).

Paid employment produced 78.6 per cent of Hong Kong people's incomes in 2006, with the incomes of 71.2 per cent derived only from employment and that of 7.4 per cent from both employment and other cash income. The median monthly income from individual people's main employment in the working population increased from HK$9,500 in 1996 to only slightly more at HK$10,000 in 2006. The median monthly household income fell slightly over the same period, however, from HK$17,500 to HK$17,250. The proportion of households earning less than HK$4,000 per month increased from 6.7 per cent in 1996 to 9.2 per cent in 2006, whereas the percentage of people earning more than $60,000 per month increased from 6.9 per cent to 8.3 per cent over the same period (CSD 2007). The declining wages of certain low-paid occupations and the rising incomes of such highly skilled employees as managers and administrators has aggravated the wealth gap. The monthly incomes of low-skilled workers declined from HK$6,000 a month in 1997 to only HK$5,000 in 2006 (*South China Morning Post* 27 April 2007: A2).

The CSD's (2007) household income distribution data show that Hong Kong's Gini coefficient has risen steadily, from 0.451 in 1981 to 0.476 in 1991, 0.518 in 1996, 0.525 in 2001 and 0.533 in 2006. If these figures were to include public expenditures for social services, however, these coefficients would be significantly lower. Adjustments for salary tax, public housing benefits and education benefits would lower the Gini coefficient to 0.427 in 1996, 0.421 in 2001 and 0.427 in 2006. Income disparity has, however, clearly become more critical and has created great concern about social instability, yet some have contested the interpretation of the impact of the rising figures. Rising income disparity has been largely the result of the polarization of the incomes of those with professional and low-skilled jobs and the increased number of households with elderly people (Commission on Poverty 2007). The government has emphasized that the way to address this problem is to create opportunities for those with low incomes to move up to jobs that pay more.

Assistance to the unemployed

Hong Kong's Labour Department provides unemployed people with a network of job centres, telephone employment service centres, an interactive employment service website, vacancy search terminals in NGOs and recruitment centres for the catering and retail industries. The department also occasionally organizes job fairs, particularly in remote districts. In 2008, it provided 146,308 placements, an increase of 8 per cent over 2007. It provides special employment assistance programmes targeting young people, the middle-aged and people with disabilities who lack high qualifications (LegCo Panel on Manpower 19 March 2009).

The Employment Programme for the Middle-aged helps middle-aged jobseekers to re-enter the labour market as early as possible. The government had launched a pilot re-employment training programme for the middle-aged in 2001 and extended it in 2003. Organizations employing this programme's participants provide them with on-the-job training for three months in return for a training allowance of HK$1,500 per month for each trainee they employ (LegCo Panel on Manpower 20 February 2003, 12 February 2004a).

The government established the Employees Retraining Board (ERB) in 1992. It serves unemployed people with low educational qualifications who are aged 30 or older. It relaxed the age criteria in 2007 to cover people aged 15 or older with education at the sub-degree level or below. It currently has eighty appointed training bodies with more than 350 training centres that provide retraining services to the unemployed. The Manpower Development Scheme now offers approximately 500 courses covering thirty industries it has identified as having market potential. It also provides such general training courses for enhancing employability as vocational languages, commercial numeracy and information technology (IT) applications. It also offers specially designed training courses and job placements for such vulnerable demographic groups as non-engaged youth, new arrivals, disabled people, victims of industrial accidents, ethnic minorities and offenders undergoing rehabilitation (ERB 2010).

In 2003, the government introduced a levy on the employers of overseas domestic helpers. It has used the revenue from the levy, which has amounted to nearly HK$5 billion, to fund the ERB. The retraining has focused on housekeeping and post-natal care courses. The board claims that more than 120,000 people have passed these courses over the years, but businesses are still having significant difficulty recruiting workers. An editorial in the *South China Morning Post* (7 April 2010: A12) claimed that 'it turns out that many trainees are housewives who join the courses for something to do and have pocketed the training subsidies, ranging from HK$1,500 to HK$2,000 for two weeks, without any intention of taking jobs'. However, the board is apparently reluctant to tighten the eligibility for job subsidies.

The government introduced the Youth Pre-employment Training Programme (YPTP), which provides pre-employment training to people without a degree aged 15 to 24, in 1999 and the Youth Work Experience and Training Scheme (YMETS), which provides on-the-job training to the same demographic, in 2002. The Labour Department administers the YPTP, which tries to make young people more employable by providing a wide range of modular training for such general employment skills and attitudes as leadership, job searching, interpersonal skills, computer applications and job-specific skills. The YMETS provides job placements with on-the-job training of 6–12 months that can turn into long-term employment. The government claims that the YPTP has trained more than 90,000 young people and that the YWETS has helped 62,200 young people secure employment between 2002 and 2008. More than 70 per cent of these programmes' participants were able to secure employment after receiving training from them (LegCo Panel on Manpower 14 December 2009).

In 2009, the youth-oriented programmes started to provide newly employed young people with continuous recruitment, personalized career guidance and counselling services for 12 months after they had found employment in order to help them adapt successfully to workplace difficulties and develop their job skills further. From time to time, they also organize new training programmes and projects that trainees can attend with the help of course fee reimbursements (LegCo Panel on Manpower 14 December 2009). Although enrolment in these two programmes declined between 2006–7 and 2008–9, evaluation studies found satisfactory placement and employment rates (Labour and Welfare Bureau 28 October 2009).

The Youth Self-employment Support Scheme started providing opportunities for young people to become self-employed in 2004. This programme commissioned NGOs to train its young participants to become self-employed in such fields as IT, multimedia applications, personal care and public performances (LegCo Panel on Manpower 12 February 2004b).

In 2007, the government entered into partnerships with NGOs to introduce the Youth Employment Start (YES) programme. Housed in two centres near popular gathering places for young people, YES provides one-stop personalized advice and support services with regard to employment and self-employment for people aged 15 to 29. These services include career assessment, career guidance, job search facilities, training and development programmes and self-employment support (LegCo Panel on Manpower 14 December 2009).

Hong Kong does not have an unemployment insurance or compensation scheme. Unemployed people are eligible to obtain assistance from a means-tested social assistance programme known as the Comprehensive Social Assistance Scheme (CSSA). The CSSA serves as a safety net of last resort for people who cannot support themselves financially. It was originally only for people who were unable to work. In 1977, the colonial government extended it to cover able-bodied people aged between 15 and 55 years. In 1996, the last full year of colonial rule, 77.4 per cent of the CSSA's cases were people unable to work, mostly those who were elderly, disabled and sick. However, the proportion of able-bodied recipients, who have been mostly single parents, low earners and unemployed people, increased from 18.4 per cent in 1998 to 29.6 per cent in 2008, and the proportion of working-age recipients, whom the government considers to be aged 15 to 59, increased from 26.3 per cent in 1996 to 42.3 per cent in 2008. CSSA expenditures also increased from HK$7.1 billion, or 5 per cent of total recurrent government expenditure, in 1996 to HK$18.6 billion, or 8.6 per cent, in 2008 (CSD August 2009) (Table 3.2).

In 2008, 51.4 per cent of Hong Kong's unemployment cases were living alone, 63.8 per cent were male, and 75.5 per cent were aged between 40 and 50. The median length of CSSA assistance was 5.1 years, and 66.6 per cent had been recipients for more than three years. The median length of CSSA assistance for single parents was 5.6 years, 56.4 per cent had been recipients for more than five years, and 69.2 per cent were relying entirely on CSSA without any other source of income. Finally, 79.2 per cent of low earners receiving CSSA assistance had been doing so for more than three years (CSD 2009). These groups of able-bodied recipients have been largely trapped in the welfare system.

The government introduced a pilot Transport Support Scheme (TSS) in June 2007 to provide a time-limited transport subsidy with the aim of encouraging needy job-seekers and low-income employees living in designated remote districts to find work in other districts. In response to public demand, the government enlarged the measure in July 2008 by relaxing the eligibility criteria and extending its duration (CSD 2009). From June 2007 to June 2009, it received 33,425 applications, of which it approved 97 per cent. Sixty-two per cent of the applicants were aged 41 or older and 8.6 per cent were aged 20 or younger, and 55 per cent had monthly incomes of between HK$5,001 and HK$6,500. Most lived in Yuen Long and Tuen Mun, and legislators have recommended that the scheme be extended cover other districts (LegCo Panel on Manpower 19 November 2009).

Table 3.2 Comprehensive social assistance scheme demographics (%)

	1996	*2004*	*2008*
Older people	59.5	50.7	53.4
Permanent disability	7.1	5.7	6.3
Ill health	10.8	7.8	8.6
Single parents	7.7	13.4	12.7
Low earnings	1.8	5.5	5.7
Unemployment	8.9	15.3	11.2
Others	4.2	1.7	2.2
Number of cases	159,937	295,694	284,569

Source: Census and Statistics Department (2009)

The HKSAR government is planning a series of major infrastructure projects, but the construction workforce is ageing, with more than a third of Hong Kong's construction workers being older than 50 and only 6 per cent younger than 25, so the industry expects to experience a shortage of workers. The government's 2010 budget therefore includes a plan to give training allowances to attract young people into construction. As preferences shift, more people, especially young ones, now prefer office jobs, which are in short supply. Fewer people are looking for jobs in retail, restaurants, catering, cleaning and security services, which have more vacancies. The government's new Pilot Employment Navigator Programme provides people who have worked continuously for three months after receiving intensive employment counselling and job-matching services with a job subsidy of HK$5,000 a month for three months (*South China Morning Post* 27 February 2010). The programme aims to encourage employment for people who have difficulty finding jobs and to address the mismatch between job market supply and demand. The three-month allowance is an incentive for people to get new jobs and to develop the habit of going to paid employment (Financial Secretary 2010).

Workfare

The government began to review the CSSA as early as 1997 with a focus on how to help unemployed CSSA recipients to rejoin the labour market and move towards self-reliance. The CSSA pays different amounts to different categories of recipients for meeting their normal day-to-day basic needs in order to discourage able-bodied people from becoming reliant on the subsidies, with higher amounts going to children, the elderly and people with disabilities or ill health. Elderly, disabled and sick people are also entitled to a number of special grants to meet their special needs. After a public consultation exercise, the government implemented the Support for Self-reliance scheme (SFS) in 1999 to provide active and personalized employment assistance for unemployed CSSA recipients. Its measures included (a) extending the provision of total disregard of the first month's income from a full-time job to employable able-bodied adults, (b) cutting down the types of special grants available to able-bodied recipients and lowering the standard rate of assistance for able-bodied recipients compared with such people unable to work as children and elderly, disabled and sick adults, and (c) reducing the standard rates for able-bodied people by 10 per cent in households with three able-bodied members and by 20 per cent in households with more than three able-bodied members, in recognition of larger households' economies of scale (LegCo Panel on Welfare Services 8 November 2004).

The government became concerned about the proportion of recipients who were able to work as well as the dramatic increases in CSSA cases. The caseload in September 2004 was 182 per cent higher than in 1994, an annual growth rate of 12 per cent and a 327 per cent increase in the total number of recipients. The proportion of recipients aged 60 or older decreased from 57.5 per cent in 1994 to 34.2 per cent in 2004, and the proportion of people between 15 and 59 had grown to 42.9 per cent of all recipients. This means that the proportion of cases involving people able to work such as the unemployed, low-income workers and single parents had increased from 11.3 per cent to 34.5 per cent over the same period. This resulted in the CSSA's budget increasing from HK $3.4 billion in 1994 to HK$17.9 billion in 2004 and from 3.2 per cent of total government recurrent expenses to 8.8 per cent over the same period (LegCo Panel on Welfare Services 8 November 2004).

The SFS initially responded to this increase in able-bodied cases with the Active Employment Assistance (AEA) and Community Work programmes. It required all CSSA unemployed and low-income recipients without full-time jobs to participate in AEA, which involved attending regular interviews with employment officers where they received employment information and developed action plans for job-seeking. It also required them to do community service work for one day or two half-days weekly (LegCo Panel on Welfare Services 14 June 2004).

The government also introduced two major short-term employment assistance schemes. It paid NGOs to conduct the Special Job Attachment programme (SJA) and the Intensive Employment Assistance Fund (IEA) starting in 2001. It then introduced the Ending Exclusion Project (EEP) in 2002 to help single-parent CSSA recipients find jobs (LegCo Panel on Welfare Services 14 June 2004). These programmes have the aim of helping able-bodied CSSA recipients to return to the labour market with job training, employment counselling, post-employment support and temporary financial aid.

The SFS initially seemed to be working, as the number of CSSA unemployment cases declined noticeably and continuously until early 2001. As the economy deteriorated, however, they increased by 96 per cent and expenditures rose by 118 per cent from April 2001 to April 2003 (LegCo Panel on Welfare Services 14 June 2004), increasing from 23,573 cases in 2000 to 50,118 in 2003. This led the government to conclude that the SJA, IEA and EEP workfare programmes were relatively ineffective, as only a limited number of CSSA recipients had been able to regain full-time employment, and most had only been able to secure part-time jobs (Tang 2009).

During the recession, the Basic Law required the government to cut its expenditures, including civil service salaries, resulting in CSSA benefits for larger families, for example, possibly becoming higher than the average market wage. This required further reform of the CSSA, so the government introduced a package of reforms in 2003 called the Enhanced SFS in order to intensify its workfare approach. These reforms included (a) an enhanced AEA programme, (b) intensive employment assistance projects (IEAPs), (c) increasing disregarded income, and (d) revamped community work requirements (LegCo Panel on Welfare Services 8 November 2004).

The enhanced AEA programme involved the introduction of such forms of targeted assistance as direct job-matching and post-placement services. It required government district offices to develop new job openings to provide more job opportunities. It also tightened the criteria for terminating CSSA payments to AEA participants failing to comply with their obligations without good cause (LegCo Panel on Welfare Services 8 November 2004).

NGOs operated the IEAPs, which provided employment assistance services to unemployed applicants whose resources rendered them marginally ineligible for the CSSA. Near-CSSA recipients could receive temporary financial aid and incentive payments. AEA-CSSA recipients could also receive referrals to these projects. The reforms also increased the maximum level of monthly disregarded earnings from HK$1,805 to HK$2,500 (LegCo Panel on Welfare Services 8 November 2004).

Furthermore, the SFS reforms required unemployed recipients to participate in community work within the first three months of receiving CSSA assistance rather than the previous six months. Long-term AEA participants had to perform community work three days weekly. They also expanded community work opportunities to include more government departments, NGOs and schools (LegCo Panel on Welfare Services 8 November 2004).

Approximately forty NGOs are responsible for running the IEAPs, with each having responsibility for at least 100 participants, a mix of seventy CSSA recipients and thirty near-CSSA recipients. Performance requirements stipulate that each programme:

> assist 28 CSSA participants and 12 near-CSSA participants to secure full-time employment, of whom 21 CSSA participants should be able to change their unemployment status to either off CSSA due to paid employment or CSSA low-earners for a period no less than three months.
> LegCo Panel on Welfare Services (14 June 2004: annex V: 1)

Evaluation studies of EEP, IEAP and the community work programme commissioned by the Social Welfare Department showed positive results, including improvement in social participation, motivation to seek employment and awareness of the need for self-reliance (Tang & Cheung 2007; Tang 2009).

Hong Kong has been relatively more lenient in enforcing work requirements and obligations on single-parent social assistance recipients than other developed countries (Finn & Gloster 2010). From its inception, the CSSA did not require its single-parent recipients whose youngest child was below the age of 15 to work. Faced with the rising number of single parents receiving assistance, however, the government introduced the Ending Exclusion Project from 2001 to 2006 to help single parents maximize their chances of participating in social and economic activities. The project was voluntary and supported participants by providing employment and childcare services (LegCo Panel on Welfare Services 14 December 2010).

The government then introduced the New Dawn project in 2006. Its aim has been to help single parents and family caregivers integrate back into the labour market and move towards self-reliance. It has required single parents whose youngest child is between the ages of 12 and 14 to actively seek paid employment of no less than 32 hours per month, and 17,448 CSSA recipients had participated by 2009. Of these, 5,203 had secured paid part-time or full-time jobs, a success rate of 29.8 per cent. They worked mainly as cleaners, service workers, shop sales assistants, domestic helpers and in other low-skilled jobs. A consultancy study commissioned by the Social Welfare Department reported that most of the project's participants said in focus groups and individual interviews that their participation had had a positive effect on family income, quality of life, self-confidence and self-esteem. Most also reported that employment had not hurt their parent–child relationships. Most of the general public also supported part-time work requirements for single-parent CSSA recipients, although they did not favour heavier sanctions for refusal to participate in the project (LegCo Panel on Welfare Services 14 December 2009).

In 2006, the government also introduced the Special Training and Enhancement Programme for young, able-bodied CSSA recipients aged 15–29 in three deprived districts. It includes counselling, structured motivational or disciplinary training and mandatory job placements (Social Welfare Department 2006). It also implemented district-based EAPs for long-term, middle-aged CSSA recipients in three deprived districts (Commission on Poverty 13 February 2007).

The colonial government originally introduced the disregarded earnings provision in 1978 as an incentive for CSSA recipients not required to work such as single parents and the elderly to earn incomes. It did not involve employable, able-bodied recipients. It extended it to able-bodied adults in regular employment in 1988, and in 1993 began pegging the maximum level of monthly disregarded earnings to 100 per cent of the standard rate for single adults. In 1995, the scheme began totally disregarding the first month's income earned by CSSA recipients who were not required to seek work, and in 1999, the HKSAR government extended this provision to employable, able-bodied adults who had not benefited from it during the previous two years (LegCo Panel on Welfare Services 13 April 2004).

The government then decided in 2003 to strengthen the disregarded earnings incentives for finding jobs by making all categories of recipients who had been on CSSA for at least three months eligible for their earnings to be disregarded. It relaxed this to two months in 2007. The time requirement was to prevent employed people with income levels higher than the CSSA level from becoming eligible for benefits immediately. The disregarded earnings provision had no time limit. The government increased the no-deduction limit for disregarded earnings from HK$451 to HK$600 in 2003 (LegCo Panel on Welfare Services 13 April 2004).

The disregarded earnings provision lifted the incomes of families with employment earnings above the basic need level that the CSSA had defined. However, the government was concerned that a more generous disregarded earnings provision could encourage people to remain on the CSSA without making a real effort to achieve self-reliance (LegCo Panel on Welfare Services

13 April 2004). The total amount of disregarded earnings spending increased from HK$298.9 million, or 2.1 per cent of total CSSA expenditure, in 2001–2 to HK$803.7 million, or 4.7 per cent of total CSSA expenditure, in 2005–6 (LegCo Panel on Welfare Services 13 April 2004). The ability of the disregarded earnings provision to promote employment has as yet received no objective evaluation.

Social enterprises

The Commission on Poverty (2007) studied the development of social enterprises, which Hong Kong's Chief Executive praised highly in his election campaign as a community-based approach to providing employment for disadvantaged demographics. One hundred NGOs and private companies were operating 284 social enterprise projects in Hong Kong by the end of May 2008. More than businesses and more than social services, social enterprises aim to achieve social objectives using entrepreneurial strategies. Successful ones generate income with business operations and reinvest their profits into their communities and with disadvantaged groups. They generate revenues in order to support their ultimate social missions rather than to maximize their profits (Hong Kong Council of Social Service and Hong Kong Shanghai Banking Corporation Social Enterprise Business Centre 2010).

The Commission on Poverty (2007) noted that social enterprises have remarkably diverse origins and modes of operation. They can be (a) run by charities or non-profit organizations, either directly or through subsidiaries, that have developed more entrepreneurial and integrated market operation approaches with some of their welfare programmes, (b) subsidiaries of for-profit businesses that run well-developed corporate social responsibility programmes alongside their business operations, or (c) from the result of projects supported by government seed funding. Most of them aim at long-term financial self-sufficiency, although they are currently operating at various levels of cost recovery.

Social enterprises may be any of thirty-seven types of businesses, including production and sales, domestic services, general cleaning services, catering services and such personal care services as health care for the elderly, escort services for patients and post-natal care. Seed money for social enterprise projects employing people from disadvantaged groups at the community level comes from the Enhancing Employment of People with Disabilities through Small Enterprise Project of the Social Welfare Department, the Enhancing Self-reliance through District Partnership Programme of the Home Affairs Department and the Community Investment and Inclusion Fund of the Labour and Welfare Bureau. These funds also encourage partnerships between NGOs and businesses. This conforms with the government policy to encourage the business sector to develop corporate social responsibility (Commission on Poverty 2007).

The current development of social enterprises includes (a) learning experiences from overseas, (b) enhancing the management capacity of NGOs by establishing training institutes and training support, (c) sharing good practice experiences, (d) facilitating the involvement of the business sector through mentorship and the provision of technical advice and information, (e) promoting public understanding through increased public education, (f) investigating how public procurement at the central and local levels can help more government contracts go to social enterprises, and (g) integrating the development of social enterprises with the work requirements of able-bodied recipients of social assistance (Commission on Poverty 2007).

The Commission on Poverty (2007) summarized social enterprises' positive contributions to the promotion of employment for the disadvantaged by noting that (a) the integration of social and commercial purposes in the delivery of goods, services or both creates a real work environment for members of disadvantaged groups and is conducive to raising their skill levels and employability, and (b) the business approach incorporated in social enterprises helps to secure progressive changes in the mindset of disadvantaged people and enhance their capacity for embracing challenges and uncertainties, which is essential for ultimate and long-term self-reliance.

The operation of social enterprises poses a formidable challenge and risk to the NGOs and the disadvantaged, however. Successful social enterprises require the NGOs to have a real enterprising spirit and widespread community support. Government policy needs to safeguard against unfair competition by not providing too much policy preference and exemptions to social enterprises over small and medium-sized for-profit enterprises. A government consultancy study on social enterprises underlined the need to promote public understanding, private sector involvement and supportive financing and training environments (Tang *et al.* 2008).

Conclusions

The unemployment rate in Hong Kong and the number of CSSA unemployment cases have both shown moderate improvement, dropping to 31,758 cases in May 2010 after reaching a high of 50,118 cases in 2003 (Social Welfare Department 2010). Low-earner and single-parent cases have also fallen. No urgent need to intensify the workfare programmes further is apparent.

Hong Kong's overall economy has been showing signs of recovery and growth in 2010. The government's fiscal budget has returned to surplus and the HKSAR has a large foreign exchange reserve. Unlike governments in other developed countries, Hong Kong's does not face a fiscal crisis and is not in debt. It is therefore capable of more extensive and proactive intervention to improve the well-being of its poorer citizens, whose situation remains critical, with 850,000 living below the social assistance level. Even though the unemployment rate is still low by international standards, more people than ever are trapped in long-term unemployment and are having difficulty finding employment (*Hong Kong Economic Journal* 4 September 2010). Hong Kong still has a sizeable population of vulnerable people such as new arrivals, school dropouts and older workers whose prospects of finding formal employment with decent pay are bleak.

Over the past decade, the Hong Kong government has shown increasing concern for strengthening the labour market and promoting workfare. It has introduced a broad array of workfare programmes and services, including retraining, target-oriented employment services, job subsidies, transport subsidies, work placements and experiences – which are apprenticeships – and business start-up support. Unlike those of other developed countries, Hong Kong's government is under no meaningful pressure to create public sector jobs, introduce short-term work schemes to preserve jobs or reduce employers' non-wage costs, such as social security contributions (OECD 2010).

Hong Kong's government support mainly emphasizes job-seekers' responsibilities and self-reliance. This means that it is hesitant to intervene directly in the labour market. Its approach so far has been to enhance the employability of those who are in the labour market. Its policy direction with regard to employment assistance has emphasized work first rather than activation. Its services have focused on encouraging people to get jobs first, even though the jobs may be poorly paid and temporary, rather than acquiring skills first and work later. It has recently moved towards developing job placement experiences and job subsidies, which, as with transport subsidies, lower employers' labour costs. All these policies and programmes reflect its productivist social policy orientation.

The Labour Department and the Social Welfare Department are the government departments in charge of providing employment services. The Labour Department's principal focus is the labour market situation. The Social Welfare Department's role has been to provide more personalized support to people in vulnerable populations needing jobs, usually by purchasing services from NGOs, but it has been preoccupied with the need to give CSSA recipients sufficient benefits to ensure that they can make ends meet, rather than to encourage them actively to seek jobs. By 2010, it has become crucial to determine how to integrate the work of the two departments in order to provide more coordinated one-stop services for those most vulnerable.

The Hong Kong government has apparently addressed its unemployment crisis better than those in other developed countries. It has provided a wide array of individualized employment services targeting different types of welfare recipients and people in different vulnerable demographics. These employment services have, however, often been segmented, overlapping, small scale, piecemeal and poorly coordinated (Wan 2006).

The Hong Kong government therefore faces the formidable challenge of having to figure out how to expand employment services that can enhance the human capital of its more vulnerable citizens. Its employment services require a more vision-based, long-term, comprehensive and coordinated labour market policy to replace its current short-term and reactive approach.

More importantly, it needs to provide more support to low-income people to enable them to work and be self-reliant rather than rely on welfare. It needs to enact such measures as introducing a minimum wage, strengthening retraining programmes, providing tax credits or subsidies to working-poor households and developing community economies (Subcommittee to Study the Subject of Combating Poverty February 2006). In addition to its lack of a long-term, comprehensive labour market policy, it also lacks a system for objectively evaluating its workfare employment services and programmes. Valid programme evaluation is vital for further improvements.

Bibliography

Census and Statistics Department, Hong Kong Special Administrative Region Government (2007) *Thematic Report: Household Income Distribution in Hong Kong*, Hong Kong: Government Printer.
—— (2008) *Thematic Report: Older Persons*, Hong Kong: Government Printer.
—— (2009) 'Statistics on Comprehensive Social Security Assistance Scheme, 1998–2008', *Hong Kong Monthly Digest of Statistics*, Hong Kong: Census and Statistics Department.
—— (2010a) *Hong Kong Statistics*. Online. Available at www.censtatd.gov.hk/hong_kong_statistics/statistical_tables/?charsetID=1&tableID=007 (accessed 1 December 2010).
—— (2010b) *Hong Kong Population Projection 2010–2039*. Online. Available at www.censtatd.gov.hk/products_and_services/products/publications/statistical_report/population_and_vital_events/index_cd_B112001504_dt_latest.jsp (accessed 1 December 2010).
Chan, C.K. (1998) 'Welfare Policies and the Construction of Welfare Relations in a Residual Welfare State: The Case of Hong Kong', *Social Policy & Administration* 32, 3: 278–91.
Chan, R. (1996) *Welfare in Newly-Industrialized Society: The Construction of the Welfare State in Hong Kong*, Avebury, UK: Aldershot.
Chan, W.K. (2008) *Low-income Workers in Hong Kong*, Hong Kong: Central Policy Unit, Hong Kong Special Administrative Region Government.
Chow, N. (2003) 'New Economy and New Social Policy in East and Southeast Asian Compact, Mature Economies: The Case of Hong Kong', *Social Policy & Administration* 37, 4: 474–91.
Chui, E., Tsang, S. and Mok, J. (2010) 'After the Handover in 1997, Development and Challenges for Social Welfare and Social Work in Hong Kong', *Asia Pacific Journal of Social Work and Development* 20, 1: 52–64.
Commission on Poverty, Hong Kong Special Administrative Region Government (2007) *Report of the Commission on Poverty*, Hong Kong: Government Printer.
—— (13 February 2007) *Progress Report on The Trial Project My STEP – Special Training and Enhancement Programme*, CoP TFCY Paper 2/2007. Online. Available at www.cop.gov.hk/eng/pdf/TFCY_02_2007E.pdf (accessed 1 December 2010).
Employment Retraining Board (2010) Website. Online. Available at www.erb.org (accessed 1 December 2010).
Financial Secretary, Hong Kong Special Administrative Region Government (2007) *2007 Budget Speech*. Online. Available at www.budget.gov.hk/2007/eng/budget16.htm (accessed 12 February 2011).
—— (2010) *2010–2011 Budget*. Online. Available at www.budget.gov.hk/2010/eng/speech.html (accessed 1 December 2010).

Finn, D. and Gloster, R. (2010) Lone Parent Obligations, a Review of Recent Evidence on the Work-related Requirements within the Benefit Systems of Different Countries, Department for Work and Pensions, Research Report no. 632. Online. Available at www.dwp.gov.uk (accessed 1 December 2010).

Goodman, R., White, G. and Kwon, H.J. (eds) (1998) *The East Asian Welfare Model: Welfare Orientalism and the State*, London: Routledge.

Gough, I. and Wood, G. (2004) *Insecurity and Welfare Regimes in Asia, Africa and Latin America: Social Policy in Development Contexts*, Cambridge: Cambridge University Press.

Herd, R., Hu, Y. and Koen, V. (2010) 'Providing Greater Old-age Security in China', Economics Department Working Papers, no. 750, Paris: Organisation for Economic Co-operation and Development.

Holliday, I. (2000) 'Productivist Welfare Capitalism: Social Policy in East Asia', *Political Studies* 48, 4: 706–23.

Hong Kong Council of Social Service and Hong Kong Shanghai Banking Corporation, Social Enterprise Business Centre (2010) Website. Online. Available at www.socialenterprise.org.hk (accessed 8 February 2011).

Hong Kong Economic Journal, 4 September, 2010: 2.

Hong Kong Government (1996) *Hong Kong: Our Work Together*, Hong Kong: Government Printer.

International Labour Office (August 2010) *Global Employment Trends for Youth*, Geneva, Switzerland: International Labour Office.

Labour and Welfare Bureau, Hong Kong Special Administrative Region Government (2008) *Creation of Employment Opportunities*, 10 December. Online. Available at www.lwb.gov.hk/eng/legco/10122008.htm (accessed 1 December 2010).

——(2009) *Youth Employment*, 28 October. Available at www.lwb.gov.hk/eng/legco/28102009_17.htm (accessed 1 December 2010).

Legislative Council Panel on Manpower (2003) *Action S4 – A Special Project for Vulnerable Trainees of the Youth Work Experience and Training Scheme*, LC Paper no. CB(2)1188/02–03(05), 20 February, Hong Kong: Legislative Council.

——(2004a) *Extension of Temporary Jobs in the Public Sector*, LC Paper no. CB(2)1219/03–04(03), 12 February, Hong Kong: Legislative Council.

——(2004b) *Youth Self-employment Support Scheme*, LC Paper no. CB(2)1219/03–04 (05), 12 February, Hong Kong: Legislative Council.

——(2009) *Employment Services of the Labour Department*, LC Paper no. CB(2)1078/08–09(04), 19 March, Hong Kong: Legislative Council.

——(2009) *Progress of the Review of the Transport Support Scheme*, LC Paper no. CB (2)276/09–10(05), 19 November, Hong Kong: Legislative Council.

——(2009) *Measures Taken by the Labour Department to Promote Youth Employment*, LC Paper no. CB(2)523/09–10(04), 14 December, Hong Kong: Legislative Council.

Legislative Council Panel on Welfare Services (2004) *The Provision of Disregarded Earnings under the Comprehensive Social Security Assistance Scheme*, Paper no. CB (2)1927/03–04(03), 13 April. Hong Kong: Legislative Council.

——(2004) *Progress of the Intensified Support for Self-reliance Measures under the Comprehensive Social Security Scheme*, Paper no. CB(2)2695/03–04(04), 14 June, Hong Kong: Legislative Council.

——(2004) *Comprehensive Social Security Assistance Scheme*, Paper no. CB(2)145/04–05(03), 8 November, Hong Kong: Legislative Council.

——(2010), *New Dawn Project*, LC Paper no. CB(2)450/09–10(05), 14 December, Hong Kong: Legislative Council.
McLaughlin, E. (1993) 'Hong Kong: A Residual Welfare Regime', in A. Cochrane and J. Clarke (eds) *Comparing Welfare States: Britain in International Context*, pp. 105–40, London: Sage.
Organisation for Economic Co-operation and Development (OECD) (2009) *Government at a Glance*, Paris: OECD.
——(2010) *OECD Employment Outlook, Moving Beyond the Job Crisis*, Paris: OECD.
——(2011) *Labour-force Statistics by Sex and Age, OECD*. StatExtracts. Online. Available at: http://stats.oecd.org/Index.aspx?DatasetCode=LFS_SEXAGE_I_R (accessed 12 February 2011).
Scarpetta, S., Sonnet, A. and Manfredi, T. (2010) 'Rising Youth Unemployment during the Crisis: How to prevent Negative Long-term Consequences on a Generation?' OECD Social, Employment and Migration Papers, no. 106, Paris: OECD.
Social Welfare Department (2006) *Service Specification on District Employment Assistance Trial (DEAT) Projects*. Online. Available at www.cop.gov.hk/eng/pdf/TFCY_02_2007E.pdf (accessed 1 December 2010).
——(2010) Online. Available at www.swd.gov.hk (accessed 1 December 2010).
South China Morning Post, 27 April 2007: A2.
——27 February 2010: A1.
——7 April 2010: A12.
——12 May 2010: A15.
——18 August 2010: C3.
Subcommittee to Study the Subject of Combating Poverty, Legislative Council (2006) *Report on Working Poverty*, LC Paper no CB(2)1002/05–06, Hong Kong: Legislative Council.
Tang, K.L. (2009) 'Welfare-to-work Reform in Hong Kong', in J. Midgley and K.L. Tang (eds) *Social Policy and Poverty in East Asia*, pp. 99–115, London: Routledge.
Tang, K.L. and Cheung, C.K. (2007) 'Programme Effectiveness Activating Welfare Recipients to Work: The Case of Hong Kong', *Social Policy & Administration* 41, 7: 747–67.
Tang, K.L. and Midgley, J. (2002) 'Social Policy after the East Asian Crisis: Forging a Normative Basis for Welfare', *Journal of Asian Comparative Development* 1, 2: 301–18.
Tang, K.L., Fung, H.L., Au, K., Lee, J. and Ko, L. (2008) *Social Enterprises in Hong Kong: Toward a Conceptual Model*, Hong Kong: Central Policy Unit, Hong Kong Special Administrative Region Government.
United Nations Development Programme (UNDP) (2009) *Human Development Report 2009, Overcoming Barriers: Human Mobility and Development*, New York: UNDP.
Wan, A. (2006) *From Welfare to Self-reliance, District Study on Employment Assistance*, Report for submission to Commission on Poverty, Hong Kong: Hong Kong Special Administrative Region Government.
Wildings, P. (1997) 'Social Policy and Social Development in Hong Kong', *Asian Journal of Public Administration* 19, 2: 244–75.
——(2007) 'Social Policy', in W.M. Lam, P. Lui, W. Wong and I. Holliday (eds) *Contemporary Hong Kong Politics, Governance in the Post-1997 Era*, Hong Kong: Hong Kong University Press.
Wong, S. and Wong, V. (2005) 'Hong Kong: from Familistic to Confucian Welfare', in A. Walker and C.K. Wong (eds) *East Asian Welfare Regimes in Transition: From Confucianism to Globalisation*, pp. 73–91, Bristol: The Policy Press.

4 From workfare to cash for all
The politics of welfare reform in Macau

Alex H. Choi and Eva P.W. Hung

In his policy address in 2004, Edmund Ho, the then chief executive of the Macau Special Administrative Region (MSAR) government, formally inaugurated the era of workfare by declaring that:

> ... we will put resources to retrain the unemployed to make them more employable ... To create the right social environment, we will put in place a workfare program. Some of the job opportunities [in this workfare program] will be created in the social service sector provided by social groups.
>
> MSAR Government (2004)

Again in the 2006 policy statement, Edmund Ho emphasized the importance of the workfare programme to address unemployment because it encourages 'people to be responsible for their own well being'. The message of a leaner and meaner approach to welfare could not be made clearer.

Nevertheless, the determination to pursue the workfare programme proved to be short-lived. Not only was the scheduled expansion of the workfare programme put on hold, the existing welfare system was given more resources to expand and new protections were added from 2007 onward: economic assistance for the poor was raised and new forms of subsidies targeting the working poor and those on the waiting list for public housing were put in place. On top of these, the government announced in 2008 a not insubstantial cash payment for every Macau citizen under the so-called Wealth Partaking Scheme, and it has been continued every year since then. Given this situation, it is not surprising that the term 'workfare' was no longer found in any policy address after 2006.

This chapter attempts to recount this episode of workfare experimentation in Macau. In so doing, it shows how the state used workfare to manipulate the labour market and to facilitate capitalist accumulation. Workfare was initially considered useful out of the unique circumstance of the liberalization of Macau's casino economy. Nevertheless, it was quickly found to be inappropriate when the political environment deteriorated. The examination of the rise and decline of the workfare experiment thus illuminates key sociopolitical processes in the ascendancy of Macau as the casino capital of Asia. It also illustrates that the 'welfare to work' process is not inevitable. In fact, local political contests and their indeterminate outcomes figure prominently in the construction of the welfare regime even in a business-dominated and highly globalized economy such as Macau.

Studies on the East Asian welfare regime tend to distinguish it as 'productivist', whereby social policies are subordinated to the imperative of rapid economic growth (Kwon 1997; Holliday 2000; Aspalter 2006). This productivist approach, however, takes no note of the legitimation function of the welfare system (Gough 2001: 180). In fact, in many other societies, social welfare plays a significant legitimation role for the political regime. The expansion or contraction of welfare thus becomes flexible and malleable, conditioned by prevailing political contests. In this sense, productivism is also to be mediated by the articulation of a growth-oriented discourse, which is subjected to debates and contests. A political approach to the study of welfare is therefore called for (Piven & Cloward 1993: 421; see also Peck 2001: 80). The challenge for the study of workfare in Asian societies is therefore to go beyond the welfare system approach and to look into local and global factors that brought workfare into the welfare system. In this regard, Macau serves as an interesting case study. In the first place, the workfare programme was put in place at a time when Macau's welfare system was undergoing rapid expansion. It seems that welfare and workfare programmes blend effortlessly together. The dynamics that push forward the workfare programme simultaneously also produced the welfare system in Macau. Second, the Macau case demonstrates that welfare is valued more for its legitimation function than for regulation. The conservative state in Macau has become generous in welfare provision because welfare can be used conveniently to sustain the migrant worker programme, which has become a key instrument for labour regulation and is taken to be a cornerstone for the casino economy to take off. Welfare and retraining programmes are put in place to patronize the poor and to hold them back from street demonstrations against labour importation. In turn, workfare is incorporated into the rapidly expanding welfare programme by giving the latter a facade of purpose and legitimacy and by making it more palatable for the business elite. Inevitably, the permeation of short-term political logic shapes the development of the welfare system in the direction of short-term fixes and makeshift changes. Ironically, even during the period of workfare, it is often the unemployed demanding serious measures from the government that can put them back to work.

The following discussion consists of three parts. The first part outlines the emergence of the welfare state in the 1980s and shows how the inception and development of social welfare was closely related to the history of labour opposition to the import of migrant workers. Social welfare served a unique legitimacy function for both the colonial political elite and the Chinese business interests in the dying days of Portuguese colonialism. The second part traces the attempt by the post-transition MSAR government to introduce workfare when the casino economy was liberalized in 2004. It analyses the programme's inadequate and contradictory design and how it has been rapidly sidelined and pre-empted by political events since 2007. The final section looks into the proliferation of cash allowance schemes and short-term wage subsidies as means of political management of the increasingly agitated public. The outcome is the creation of a so-called dependency culture among the unemployed. A genuine programme aiming to put these people back to work has to go beyond workfare to look into the underlying structural cause of unemployment during a period of rapid expansion of the job market.

Welfare, legitimacy and the colonial regime

The colonial regime in Macau had engaged in various forms of relief and social assistance for quite a while. These functions were eventually put under the aegis of a departmental level body, the Social Work Bureau, in 1980. But it was not until the setting up of the Social Security Fund in 1990 that a so-called welfare state developed. The Fund runs a contributory social insurance system providing retirement pension, unemployment insurance, disability allowance, etc. for working people. Several pivotal events in the contemporary history of Macau led to the emergence of the social security system.

First, the colonial state in Macau suffered a humiliating defeat in the so-called '123 Incident' in 1966 under a pro-Beijing anti-colonial movement that seriously undermined its confidence and determination to govern. The crisis reached a peak in the wake of the 1974 Portuguese revolution. The post-revolution socialist government in Lisbon pursued a decolonization policy and offered to return Macau to China, which China declined. Instead, the two parties reached a consensus: although China's sovereignty over Macau was recognized, Lisbon had the right to administer the territory for the foreseeable future. From then on, the Lisbon government granted more local autonomy to Macau in preparation for its eventual reunification with China. In 1986, negotiations between the two governments on the future of Macau began, and a deal was quickly made in the following year for Macau to return to China in December 1999. With few economic interests in Macau, Portugal's key concerns during this period of transition politics appeared to be perpetuating its cultural legacy and ensuring a glorious retreat. The latter was especially important given its painful and humiliating experiences in the withdrawal from Goa and East Timor. One of the elements in this glorious retreat from the last colonial outpost held by Lisbon was the setting up of a social security system demonstrating the colonizer's concern for and benevolence towards its subjects (Wu 1994: 26–27; Mok 2009: 77).

Second, the tax revenue of the colonial government soared in the 1980s due to a series of revisions of the gambling monopoly contract, raising the tax rate from 10.8 per cent to 30 per cent (Liu 2002: 305). Government acquiescence in the practice of subcontracting out casino VIP rooms to outside operators in 1984 substantially raised the volume of casino business, and hence also the tax revenue (Liu 2002: 414–15). Casino tax revenue as a percentage of total government income doubled from about 20 per cent in the early 1980s to 40 per cent in the early 1990s (Xu 1994: 178). This had provided the government with a foundation to take a more active role in the social sector.

Third, since the '123 Incident', the pro-Beijing social groups (*shetuan*) in Macau have risen in prominence not only because of their proven ability to destabilize the colonial regime but also because of their extensive penetration into the social sector. After Beijing normalized relations with Lisbon and reached a consensus over the future of Macau at the end of the 1970s, these social groups turned their antagonistic stance towards the colonial regime into one of collaboration in maintaining social and political stability during the period of transition. When the colonial regime widened the franchise of the directly elected seats in the Legislative Assembly to the local Chinese residents in 1984, these social groups actively participated in the election and took almost all the available seats. They thus became politically powerful because their support and collaboration were vital in making the colonial regime's governance effective (Wu 1994: 9).

However, it did not mean that the pro-Beijing social groups were homogeneous and equal. Instead, the business elite, as has been widely commented, enjoyed a higher status in the pro-Beijing network and had a stronger influence on the colonial regime. Neither did it mean that the colonial regime had degenerated into a puppet of these social groups. On the one hand, all these social groups received orders from Beijing, which had already defined their role during the transition to be supportive of political stability. Any action that might bring a face-off with the colonial regime and jeopardize stability was to be avoided. On the other hand, the social groups also had different constituencies to serve that could put their interests at loggerheads. Thus, whereas these groups had to act in unison according to the wishes of Beijing on paramount issues related to national interests, there could be considerable differences over local matters. Such differences might not be easily settled within the pro-Beijing system if they impinged on key interests that were vital to the constituencies that the social groups were supposed to represent. These social groups had to publicly demonstrate to their constituents that they had fought for their interests. These differences gave the colonial regime room to assert its own interests, either by playing off one group against the other or by taking the side of one group whose interests were closest to its own. The creation of the social security system in Macau can be said to fall into this category (see Mo 1994: 52, 57; Wu 1994: 4).

Fourth, the economy and society of Macau has experienced a rapid transformation since the late 1970s. Export-oriented industries set up by Hong Kong investors have quickly become the key economic pillars and the largest employers. These industries absorbed the Chinese migrants flooding into the colony since China opened up in 1978. The colonial government initially took a relaxed attitude to these influxes, but eventually an agreement was reached with China in 1983 to regulate the inflow by setting up a monthly quota of 120.

Despite this arrangement, illegal immigrants were still commonplace. Their illegality was rectified by periodic amnesties. By the end of the last amnesty declared in 1990, it was estimated that as much as 40 per cent of the population were recent immigrants (Ng 1990a: 191). The rapid industrial transformation of Macau coupled with the arrival of a significant immigrant population had put the society into considerable distress. The colonial government was hard pressed to devise appropriate social policies to smooth the industrial transition and migrant integration.

In response to the rise of the industrial class, the colonial government enacted the first Labour Relations Law in 1985 to provide workers with some basic protection.[1] A tripartite committee, the Standing Committee for the Coordination of Social Affairs (SCCSA), was set up in 1987 with members from two pro-Beijing groups, namely the Macau Chamber of Commerce and the Macau Federation of Trade Unions (MFTU), to advise on labour affairs. This committee, according to the government, heralded a new spirit of democratic collaboration between the colonial regime and the local society (Preto 1990: 510). The two key tasks entrusted to this committee for discussion were, not coincidentally, the import of migrant labour and the creation of a social security system.

For a few years, the business elite had demanded the import of labour citing labour shortages. But MFTU opposed it, claiming that it would hurt the interests of local workers. One month after the SCCSA's first meeting, the government issued a decree law (12/GM/1988) approving labour import (Zhao 1998: 117). Critics such as Ng Kuok Cheong (1990a: 192), a veteran legislator, branded this SCCSA the symbol of a 'conspiracy politics', where elite pro-Beijing groups in collaboration with the colonial regime ironed out their differences and imposed their will on Macau society. The capitulation of MFTU appeared to be a forgone conclusion because the Chinese government had earlier endorsed a development strategy based on the export of its surplus labour resources to overseas markets (Ng 1990b: 157; Mo 1994: 52). The MFTU was also averse to an open feud with the Macau Chamber of Commerce for fear of giving an impression of disunity among the pro-Beijing network (Mo 1994:57; Lam 1998: 41). Nevertheless, many angry grassroots workers claimed that labour import depressed wages and put them out of work. A handful of maverick Legislative Assembly members[2] continued to press the government on shelving the order, culminating in a Legislative Assembly debate in December 1988 (Ng 1990b: 160–61; Wu 1994: 21).

In the midst of this dispute, the government submitted a proposal to set up a social security system to the SCCSA for consideration. The proposal cited welfare as a right guaranteed under the Portuguese constitution. Similar to the Portuguese social security system enacted in 1984, it envisaged a comprehensive social security system that covered disability allowance, sickness allowance, unemployment insurance, old age pension, medical assistance, marriage and death allowance (Romao 1989; Tang 2003: 13).[3] The reference to the Portuguese constitution suggested that it was an attempt to extend the Portuguese system into Macau, and thus a glorious retreat project. However, the timing of the introduction of this proposal in Macau also indicated a short-term strategic value, namely to cool down the opposition to the importation of migrant workers by making concessions on boosting welfare protection for local workers (Lai 2009: 382; Mok 2009: 102–3).

But it turned out that the labour import dispute escalated and forced the MFTU to undertake a signature campaign against the importation of labour in August 1989. A total of 67,879 signatures had been collected (Mo 1994: 48–49). Although this mobilization of opposition did not result in a suspension of labour import, neither could MFTU be left empty-handed lest its effectiveness as the labour leader be undermined. In this situation, despite serious opposition from the business sector, the social security system was endorsed by SCCSA in the same month, and was allowed to pass into law by the end of 1989 (Lai 2009: 383). The Social Security Fund (SSF) began operation in the following year. The long-term demand by MFTU for old age protection was finally realized.

Even though the social security system appeared to provide a complete range of protection, it was hardly a generous system. Benefit payments were low, and qualification requirements were stringent. For instance, pensions were set at MOP300 per month, which represented a mere 12 per cent of the median wage of MOP2,585 in 1990. Workers had to make contributions for five years before they were entitled to the pension. Unemployment insurance was set at MOP600 per month, and the unemployed had to prove that they had been continuously employed for one year before they qualified for payment. Maximum length of payment was capped at two months in one calendar year. This low level of protection was to ensure that the social security system was affordable to employers. The most important guarantee, however, was on the method of financing this system. The contribution level was set at an extremely low level, MOP20 and MOP10 per month, respectively, for employers and employees.[4] Obviously, the social security scheme could not be sustained merely from these contributions and had to rely on government transfer, which comprised a regular allocation of 1 per cent of the government budget and various ad hoc grants. In effect, this supposedly contributory scheme has almost turned into a government programme supported out of general revenue. This arrangement appeared to be one of the primary means of securing the industrial elite's endorsement of the system.

There is little doubt that the social security system developed in the early 1990s in Macau was a minimal system designed to meet political contingencies with little concern for its long-run sustainability, or the real needs of its citizens. From its inception, it was a bargaining chip used to soften labour opposition to the migrant worker system. Although labour import was the primary instrument for labour regulation, the social security system was placed in a rearguard position to secure consent and to quell resistance by selectively doling out concessions on new benefits.

Subsequent key expansions of the social security system were intricately linked to the political imperative of containing the agitation against labour import.

For instance, in the mid-1990s, Macau entered a period of de-industrialization caused by a relocation of production facilities to mainland China. A high unemployment rate prompted the labour sector to demand curtailing labour imports to make jobs available to locals. In 1995, the government promised a freeze on *new* labour imports plus a sweetening in 1996 of the unemployment benefits by raising the benefit level to MOP60 per day, by relaxing the qualifying requirement to just nine months of work in the previous year and by extending the entitlement period from sixty to ninety days. However, in April 1997, the government succumbed to pressure from the employers by lifting the import ban when the unemployment situation had scarcely improved, causing an even bigger uproar from the labour sector (Zhao 1998: 127, 133–35; Lai 2009: 383; Mok 2009: 51).

At this moment, when the law and order of the colony was seriously undermined by the gangster war spun out of the casino VIP rooms, the colonial regime did not want any more industrial conflicts to poison the environment for a glorious retreat. It negotiated a special grant from the casino monopoly in 1998 to set up a 50 million dollar fund, run by the SSF, to render special assistance to the unemployed. One of its most well-known programmes, the literacy class, provided a daily allowance of MOP80 for the unemployed to attend classes on Macau history and culture, thus giving them access to better financial support without the restrictive qualification requirements associated with the unemployment benefit. In early 1999, an unemployment relief (UR) allowance was added to the original programme giving the unemployed a monthly allowance of MOP1,200 (Lai 2009: 179; Mok 2009: 52).[5]

In all, the emergence of the social security system in Macau came out of a unique situation in the early 1990s. The desire for a glorious retreat by the colonial state was certainly a factor, such that it would indeed take the trouble to carry out a controversial policy in the last days of its rule. The powerful business elite conceded to the new system not only because its financial contribution to the scheme was set at a nominal level, but also because it was almost regarded as a quid pro quo for the approval of migrant workers. Given that the social security system was created out of this political expediency, it could be seen as productivist because the benefit level was minimal so that it did not significantly raise costs that would hurt the profit margin of employers. But more importantly, it helped to contain opposition to the migrant worker system, which has become one of the most fundamental elements in maintaining the low-cost economy and the key grievances of the working class against the government. In this regard, the social security system has served an important legitimacy function.

From welfare to workfare

The political transition took place in December 1999 without a hitch. Edmund Ho, the son of the long-term leader of the pro-Beijing network, Ho Yin, was sworn in as the chief executive of the Macau SAR. Various leaders in the Macau Chamber of Commerce were recruited into his cabinet. Other pro-Beijing social groups and their leaders were given official and consultative positions in the government. But the economic situation was not very positive. The unemployment rate reached a record high of 6.8 per cent in 2000. This was complicated by the collapse of the property market putting many construction workers out of work. Several thousand Macau workers working in Taiwan were also sent home, thus adding to the ranks of the unemployed. But the number of migrant workers still remained high at 27,221, representing 13.9 per cent of the employed population (Choi 2006: 146). Starting in May 2000, local workers marched spontaneously in a series of demonstrations lasting for a few months on the streets of Macau calling for an end to the migrant worker programme and demanding jobs. Riot police reportedly used tear gas to disperse the demonstrators for the first time since the '123 Incident'.

After the incidents, the chief of the Labour Affairs Bureau promised to reduce the number of migrant workers to below 20,000. In addition, the government relaxed the qualification for UR, making it eligible to those 45 years old and below. It also substantially raised the level of payment for families with two or more members. For instance, a family of four's UR was raised from MOP3,150 to MOP4,800, representing an increase of 52.4 per cent. Expecting that the 50 million dollar fund was going to be exhausted, the government made fresh allocations to the Social Security Fund in April 2001 to extend the programme. UR recipients were required to attend literacy classes such as elementary English and local culture and history. The government also collaborated with three tertiary institutions in 2002 to provide a total of 4,000 full-time places for job training to those under 40 years old, who were seen as the most discontented with the government. Enrolees were entitled to generous allowance.[6] A total of MOP62.54 million was earmarked for this programme (Lai 2009: 181, 193). Considering that a total of 11,420 individuals and their families received UR and 3,917 individuals were under job training in the tertiary institutes in 2002 (Social Security Fund 2002: 41), these programmes had covered almost all the jobless.

Once again, the Social Security Fund was turned into an instrument for the government to fix its political problem. Temporary programmes and special allocations were put in place to douse the agitation of the unemployed against the importation of migrant workers. Rather than aiming for better protection and training for the jobless, these programmes were improvised to provide the government with political stability. This point was candidly admitted by the head of the Labour Affairs Bureau:

> The literacy classes provided the government with 3 years of precious breathing space [free from labour conflicts] to concentrate on handling the thorny issues of casino liberalization. ... Frankly speaking, foreign investors will not be interested in investing in a place where there is daily labour demonstration and a lot of political instabilities, right? ...
>
> *Macao Daily* (20 January 2004)

Indeed, Macau announced its intention to liberalize the casino sector in July 2000, three concession holders were chosen in February 2002, and the construction of the first new casino, the Sands, was close to completion by the end of 2003. Moreover, China opened the flood gate for tourists to visit Macau in 2003 in response to the economic damage inflicted by the severe acute respiratory syndrome (SARS) epidemic. By the end of that year, it appeared that the economy of Macau had finally emerged from a long period of recession. Unemployment rates began to decline. It was in this context that Edmund Ho announced in his policy statement the termination of the literacy class programme and its replacement by workfare.

Economic recovery was cited as the reason. Beyond this, these literacy classes were widely seen as ineffective in preparing the unemployed for work and did not target their needs. Many workers went to the classes simply because a good attendance record was required to maintain their benefit status. It was also said that the programme carried a strong disincentive to work and resulted in a dependency culture, as the amount of allowance was often higher than one could earn in the job market. Many middle-aged housewives were also said to be lured to join the training (see, for example, *Macao Daily* 21 November 2003, 22 December 2003, 10 April 2004, 2 July 2004). But an abrupt termination of the benefits for the 5,983 people attending the literacy classes would be too politically risky (*Jornal Va Kio* 24 April 2004). Workfare was seen as an instrument in weaning the unemployed from receiving generous subsidies and allowances. In this sense, workfare could be regarded as a fix to a problem, which was, in turn, the undesirable byproduct of a fix to an earlier political crisis. From this perspective, it is not incomprehensible for the government to restrict the workfare programme with allowance to former literacy class enrolees only (*Macao Daily* 20 January 2004, 25 April 2004, 23 July 2004).

Workfare in Macau formally began in mid-2004. Initially, it comprised two components. The first component, the Employment Assistance and Training Course (EATC), was jointly run by the Labour Affairs Bureau and the SSF. This programme lasted for a maximum of one year. Participants were restricted to students of the former literacy classes. The training was said to target the needs of the lowly educated and middle-aged to help them change career from manufacturing to the expanding service sector. Language training took two-thirds of their time. The rest was assigned to skill training in, for example, cleaning, waiting and cooking in hotel and restaurants, general office assistance, domestic work and property management. Trainees were entitled to a daily allowance of MOP80 with a maximum monthly allowance not exceeding MOP1,800. Most importantly, the training allowance was detached from family support. If the trainee's family needed welfare support, they had to make a separate application to the Social Work Bureau for the means-tested economic assistance programme. The training allowance would be deducted from the total benefit provided by the Social Work Bureau (*Macao Daily* 20 January 2004, 2 February 2004).

The second component, the Workfare – Community Based Employment Assistance Programme (WCEA), is run by the Social Work Bureau.[7] The programme is open to all recipients of economic assistance, and participation was said to be voluntary. According to the 2004 Annual Report of the Social Work Bureau, the goals of the programme are to help participants 'to experience the earning of income through work, ... to rebuild the confidence and habit of working, ... to increase their employability, ... and to increase their sense of social responsibility' (Social Work Bureau 2004) through working in job positions provided by social organizations. These participants were regarded as volunteers and were not regarded as employees of the social organizations. The total working hours were twenty-four hours per week. They were entitled to an allowance of MOP700 on top of their normal economic assistance benefit. A quarterly bonus of MOP1,000 would be issued if work performance was satisfactory. Participants in this programme would be able to continue to receive economic assistance payment for three months after they successfully found a regular job (*Jornal Va Kio* 8 February 2004).

The EATC was patently intended to reduce allowances in order to push workers back into the labour market. Those who exhausted the training allowance were channelled into the WCEA, which helped the unemployed to find work by giving them some hands-on work experience. The EATC was the easier part, and a significant number of former literacy class members took the retraining and applied for economic assistance from the Social Work Bureau. But the WCEA was a resounding failure. Initially, the Social Work Bureau announced a quota of 500 for the WCEA scheme. Job openings would come from key pro-Beijing social groups. In the end, fewer than 200 positions were available. Only a handful of WCEA participants managed to find regular work.[8] According to the Social Work Bureau, WCEA was supposed to create independence; ironically, it was in fact creating dependency on the programme (*Macao Daily* 18 August 2005, 18 February 2006). A number of WCEA participants expressed the wish for WCEA to continue indefinitely because they had stable work while enjoying a higher level of benefits (*Macao Daily* 13 January 2007; Tian & Zhang 2006: 173).

To counter this trend of dependency, the Social Work Bureau introduced an 'Active Life Service Scheme' (ALSS) in April 2006 to try to remove the disincentive to work inherent in the existing economic assistance system. The economic assistance system was based on a minimal subsistence index that increases with the size of the family. Any person whose total income falls below the index is entitled to economic assistance from the Social Work Bureau. However, as any earned income will be deducted dollar for dollar from the economic assistance, it leaves the welfare recipients with no real benefit from working. ALSS tempers this disincentive by allowing the recipients to keep a proportion of income within a range and over a maximum period of one year so that working is rewarded rather than penalized.[9] In addition, all recipients of economic assistance were to be assessed for their ability to work. For those identified as able and available for work, they would be either encouraged to take part in ALSS, or they would be placed in WCEA to prepare them to be eventually transferred to ALSS (*Jornal Va Kio* 27 April 2006).

Despite the initial fanfare of billing WCEA and ALSS as key programmes in returning people to work, their outcome has never been significant. Table 4.1 shows the new cases and the return to work rate between 2006 and 2009 for both WCEA and ALSS. The number of new cases enrolled into both programmes never represented more than 7.5 per cent of total welfare cases, and they never managed to return more than 170 unemployed persons to work in any one year. Moreover, both cases and return to work numbers have fallen precipitately since 2008. In 2009, there were about 206 cases, representing only 3.3 per cent of the total welfare cases. Only thirty-two people returned to work under the programmes.

Several factors explain the lack of success of the programme. The central issue is the failure of the programme to address key concerns of the welfare participants. Both programmes aim to increase confidence and train up the 'habit' of programme participants to work. It assumes that, given the right kind of assistance and inducement, welfare participants will finally be awakened to the benefits of working. Thus, unemployment is a deficiency squarely placed on the shoulders of the unemployed. However, programme participants often told very different stories. They said they had been trying really hard to look for work, but employers were only interested in young, compliant and low-wage migrant workers, and did not bother to give them any opportunities (*Macao Daily* 2 July 2004, 23 July 2004). Even if they managed to get work, they were often fired as soon as their employers got the migrant worker quota from the government. Thus, they usually languished in unstable and short-term jobs, which made them feel frustrated and hopeless (*Macao Daily* 18 February 2006). Moreover, market wages were so low that it made better economic sense for them to stay in the economic assistance system (*Macao Daily* 25 November 2005).

Table 4.1 WCEA and ALSS, 2004–09

Year	WCEA		ALSS		Economic assistance	
	Total cases(a)	Return to work (times)	New cases(b)	Return to work (times)	Total cases(c)	% of WCEA and ALSS*(d)
2004**	183	15	n.a.	n.a.	8,196	n.a.
2005	152	n.a.	n a.	n.a.	10,285	n.a.
2006	150	37	399	124	7,345	7.5
2007	170	12	233	150	6,530	6.2
2008	156	4	140	50	6,180	3.3
2009	110	7	96	25	6,278	3.3

Source: Social Work Bureau, Annual Report (various years)
Notes:
* d=(a+b)/c.
** June to December figure.
n.a., not available.

Thus, the real barrier for them to return to work is the structural condition of low-wage and insecure work imposed on them by the migrant worker programme.

However, the real reason for a steep decline in WCEA and ALSS probably lies more in a change of political attitude. Despite the commitment of the Social Work Bureau to make WCEA and ALSS mandatory for all ready-for-work welfare recipients (*Macao Daily* 30 June 2006), the threat was never actualized. Joining WCEA and ALSS remained voluntary. The drop in ALSS cases since 2008 probably indicates a relaxation in pressure on pursuing the workfare agenda.[10] As the next section will argue, the change in the approach to workfare reflects a major shift in the prevailing political climate.

From workfare to cash for all

The years 2006 and 2007 marked the watershed of the Edmund Ho government in terms of popularity and credibility. His government was rocked by a series of incidents, leading to questions of his effectiveness in maintaining social stability during a period of rapid economic growth. One of these issues, not unexpectedly, was the importation of migrant workers. Starting in 2005, the government has allowed the importation of migrant workers to soar. By 2006, the number of migrant workers had almost tripled from the level of 2002, reaching a total of 64,673 (see Table 4.2). Even though the number of unemployed workers has declined from a peak of 14,000, it still hovered at the 10,000 mark. The most damning issue with the migrant worker programme, however, was the government's insensitivity to workers' demands to put some limits on the programme, such as a maximum import quota, occupational restrictions and minimum wages. The government claimed that it would not allow the import of labour to hurt the interests of local workers, but this rang hollow because workers witnessed an inundation of non-locals into the labour market taking their jobs. The first post-2000 labour demonstration against the import of migrant workers took place in 2006, ending with a skirmish of demonstrators with the police in the main business district. By the end of the

Table 4.2 Migrant workers, unemployed population and unemployment rate, 2001–09

	Migrant workers	*Unemployed population (000)*	*Unemployment rate (%)*
2001	25,925	14.0	6.4
2002	23,460	13.7	6.3
2003	24,970	13.1	6.0
2004	27,736	11.2	4.9
2005	39,411	10.3	4.1
2006	64,673	10.4	3.8
2007	85,207	9.5	3.1
2008	92,161	10.1	3.0
2009	74,905	11.7	3.6

Source: Labour Affairs Bureau (2010)

year, the government was rocked by the Ao Man Lung, a high-ranking government official, corruption case, seriously damaging its integrity. In the wake of the Ao case, an even bigger anti-migrant workers and anti-corruption demonstration took place on May Day 2007. The demonstration was turned into an international news story when a policeman fired a series of warning shots into the air. Since then, May Day demonstrations have turned into a ritual for the independent labour movement to flex its muscles. Open calls for the resignation of Edmund Ho were no longer taboo.

The Edmund Ho government was under serious pressure to tackle the social contradictions. In his 2007 policy statement, Edmund Ho recognized that there were 'deep-seated structural problems' created in Macau during the process of rapid development, and promised to make 'pragmatic and timely responses' to solve these problems. Similarly, in the 2008 policy statement, he admitted that 'social contradictions have rapidly accumulated ... and [the government] has not made enough efforts in their prevention and remediation' (MSAR Government 2008).

Notwithstanding this acknowledgement, the government's policy response to these problems was often feeble, improvised and grossly inadequate. It has tried meticulously to avoid making any structural changes that might hurt the interests of the business elite. The preferred solutions appeared to be the use of the abundant supply of casino tax revenue to provide subsidy-based temporary relief that might achieve the greatest short-term political impact for the ruling regime.

April is the month for this form of politics to flourish in Macau. A rush of measures would be announced in this month in order to prevent a huge turnout for the May Day demonstration. Its origins could be traced to the so-called 'Ho's Nine Measures' announced on 8 April 2007. These measures include: lowering the pensionable age to 60 years old; the construction of 19,000 public housing units within five years; a wage hike for civil servants; improvements in public bus services and the construction of the mass transit system; the setting up of a government-subsidized central provident fund, the supply of a free computer for every school teacher and an increase in availability of more student loans and grant (*Jornal Va Kio* 9 April 2007). Over the years between 2006 and 2008, the government has put in place a series of cash schemes to address the concerns of residents, including:

a) Drinking water subsidies for people receiving welfare in view of the salinity problem;
b) Bus fare subsidies for passengers in the face of complaints of poor bus services and traffic congestion;
c) Subsidies for electricity to counter high fuel prices and inflation;
d) Rental subsidies for people complaining of long waiting times for public housing;
e) Medical vouchers for all permanent residents to purchase medical services from the private sector

(Chan & Lee 2011: 310–12).

These schemes might temporarily lower people's grievances but are not helpful in resolving the issues that caused the grievances in the first place. The medical voucher is a case in point. This scheme might divert demand-driven pressure away from the public health care service, but it did nothing to address the issue of the quality of services per se, such as the qualifications of medical personnel and the standard of courtesy services in the public health system. Moreover, the scheme failed to target the needy and caused a lot of wastage. With little use of the vouchers, healthy individuals and people with private insurance found ways to spend it on, for instance, supplements and healthy food, within the one-year expiry period. This scheme thus gives the impression that it is created to increase the political popularity of the regime more than addressing the medical needs of the people.

The government has adopted a similar approach to placate the agitation against the import of migrant workers. Since April 2006, the government has started to inject money into the welfare system to address issues of unemployment, low pay and poverty. The minimum subsistence index was raised four times in three years between 2006 and 2008, giving an overall increase of 65 per cent (Tang & Chan 2009: 223), compared with an increase of 19 per cent in the overall medium wage during the same period. In 2008, the entitlement of a four-person family (MOP7,970) was almost at par with the median wage. On top of these increases was the payment of the thirteenth monthly bonus to welfare recipients since 2007.

Facing the demands for a minimum wage to address the issue of working poverty, in September 2007, the government started to enforce a minimum wage of MOP21 per hour (or MOP4,368 per month) on cleaning and security-related jobs outsourced to private subcontractors. In January 2008, a wage subsidy scheme was also put in place to top up the income of full-time workers aged 40 years or older to MOP4,000 per month. Then in April 2008, Edmund Ho dropped a bombshell by announcing cash payments for every Macau citizen, young or old, rich or poor, in the name of sharing the wealth created in the years of rapid economic growth. Permanent residents were entitled to MOP5,000, and non-permanent residents to MOP3,000. This scheme, now known as the Wealth Partaking Scheme, has been repeated every year since then.[11] The budget for the 2008 scheme was a total of MOP2,600 million, which is many times the cost of the literacy classes (*Jornal San Wa Ou* 24 May 2008).

With all these facilities under way, in 2009, the government started the process to enact the migrant worker law, which was one of the promises of the 2007 'Ho's Nine Measures'. However, the new law merely reconfirms the status quo. Key demands from the labour groups, such as a maximum quota, occupational restrictions and a minimum wage, were brushed aside. Instead, three minor changes were put in place. First, the law imposed a migrant worker levy, which is currently set at MOP200 per month.[12] The levy, originally promised in the 2006 annual policy statement, was supposed to be paid by employers. However, without a minimum wage, there appears to be no mechanism to prevent it from being transferred to the migrant workers via a lowering of their wages. Second, a six-month ban was enforced on migrant workers who voluntarily quit their existing jobs. This ban thus in effect made it even more difficult for migrant workers to change employers. Finally, violation of the law became a criminal offence. However, the penalties for this crime are largely restricted to monetary fines.

Conclusion

Workfare was introduced by the government in 2004 to push unemployed workers back to the labour market when economic growth appeared to be picking up. Nevertheless, it had quickly become obsolete by 2008, not because the economy went back into decline, but because the political instability generated by the migrant workers programme had forced the government once again to resort to the money approach to fix political problems.

The decline in workfare epitomizes the impasse of Macau politics. The undemocratic system gives the local capitalist class a monopoly of political power. This monopoly is cloaked under a veneer of nationalism, and won the blessing of Macau's overlord in Beijing. One of the most visible symbols of this political power is its access to an almost unimpeded supply of cheap and compliant migrant workers. The political regime is left with the task of political management to maintain social stability. In this regard, the political regime is endowed with a privileged weapon – the tax windfall from the casino sector. This windfall makes it possible for the political regime to throw money at social problems without raising the tax rate. Many of the so-called independent labour groups are adept at playing this game of money politics. They realize that migrant workers are the hot-button issue that can mobilize the poor and unemployed on to the streets because the immigrants ostensibly take away their jobs and threatened their livelihood. The higher the turnout and the intensity of the conflict, the greater the pressure on the government to throw money at resolving social instability. This strategy, deliberately or not, perpetuates the deep divisions between local and migrant workers, and unwittingly contributes to the continuation of the migrant programme.

The discussion of welfare–workfare in Macau therefore cannot be isolated from discussion of the migrant worker system. In its history of development, the welfare and social security systems were often used to maintain the stability of the migrant worker programme, which has been the key instrument of labour regulation. Welfare–workfare is assigned a largely legitimacy role. More generous welfare measures are usually granted to soften agitation. Harder workfare measures are introduced when industrial peace returns. Both are necessary to guarantee the continuance of the present system of accumulation. Workfare may have receded now. But the piling up of cash subsidies might eventually prove to be too costly and too damaging to the work spirit of the working class. At that moment, workfare might be invoked again to tackle the crisis.

Notes

1 The law also outlawed the hiring of illegal immigrants (Zhao 1998: 115).
2 The Legislative Assembly was dominated by Macanese and pro-Beijing groups. However, this monopoly was broken in 1984 when a local middle class candidate who campaigned to protect the well-being of the common people won a single seat; hence, the 'Livelihood faction' of the Legislative Assembly. In the 1988 election, two more seats were won by this faction (Wu 1994: 10–11).
3 The proposal was described by Romao (1989), who was a senior official in the colonial government advising the governor on welfare policy. Before she moved to Macau, she worked as the deputy secretary for social welfare in the Lisbon government.
4 The contribution level was raised once in 1998 to MOP30 and MOP15, respectively, for employers and employees. It is still at that level as of now (2010). Total employer–employee contribution as a percentage of total income of the SSF never exceeded 36 per cent. In 2008, it represented a mere 7.42 per cent. The average figure between 1990 and 2008 was 17.8 per cent. The primary source of income for social security comes from government contributions (Mok 2009: 64–65).
5 To qualify for UR, workers had to be jobless for at least three months, aged 45 or above and with a household income below the Social Welfare Bureau's minimum subsistence index. The size of payment of UR varies with family size: a one-person family is entitled to MOP1,200, and a maximum of MOP4,190 for a six-person or larger family (Lai 2009: 179–80).
6 If the attendance record and performance in class were satisfactory, the trainees would be granted an average of MOP3,000 per month (Lai 2009: 206).
7 To facilitate this programme, rules on welfare recipients were finally changed in 2007 compelling those with the ability to work to register with the Labour Affairs Bureau, to receive job training and to accept Labour Affairs Bureau job placement (*Jornal San Wa Ou* 10 September 2003, 23 March 2007).
8 It was reported in July 2004 that Caritas Macau provided ninety workfare positions, neighbourhood associations sixty and the MFTU thirty (*Macao Daily* 21 July 2004). The Women's Federation of Macau provided twenty-two positions and helped six people to find job (see *Macao Daily* 18 April 2005).
9 The actual welfare payment depends on the 'assessed household income' (AHI). AHI is, in turn, the difference between the individual's work income and an exempted amount, which is calculated by reducing the individual's work income by MOP500, and then dividing the rest by half. This exempted amount is capped at a maximum of MOP2,000. The actual welfare payment is the difference between the pre-income welfare payment and the AHI. The reduced welfare payment starts from the second month a welfare recipient begins work, and will be terminated after one year if the recipient's work income exceeds the pre-income welfare payment (*Jornal Va Kio* 27 April 2006, 23 March 2007).
10 It is reported that welfare recipients were pressured into joining the programme. Social workers have considerable leverage on welfare recipients because all welfare cases are subjected to an annual review. Their consistent application of pressure might generate high enrolment numbers (Lai 2009: 234–35).
11 The value of the cash payment was increased to MOP6,000 and MOP3,600 for permanent and non-permanent residents, respectively, in 2009.
12 Employers of migrant domestic workers were exempted from the levy. Employers of manufacturing workers paid the levy at a 50 per cent discount (Social Security Fund 2010).

Bibliography

Aspalter, C. (2006) 'The East Asian Welfare Model', *International Journal of Social Welfare* 15: 290–301.

Chan, K.W. and Lee, J. (2011) 'Social Welfare Policy: A "Flexible" Strategy?', in N. Lam and I. Scott (eds) *Gaming, Governance and Public Policy in Macao*, Hong Kong: Hong Kong University Press.

Choi, A.H. (2006) 'Migrant Workers in Macao: Labour and Globalization', in K. Hewison and K. Young (eds) *Transnational Migration and Work in Asia*, London and New York: Routledge.

Gough, I. (2001) 'Globalization and Regional Welfare Regimes: the East Asian Case', *Global Social Policy* 1, 2: 163–89.

Holliday, I. (2000) 'Productivist Welfare Capitalism: Social Policy in East Asia', *Political Studies* 48: 706–23.

Jornal San Wa Ou, various dates (in Chinese).

Jornal Va Kio, various dates (in Chinese).

Kwon, H. J. (1997) 'Beyond European Welfare Regimes: Comparative Perspectives on East Asian Welfare Systems', *Journal of Social Policy* 26, 4: 467–84.

Labour Affairs Bureau of Macau SAR Government (2010) *Data on Labour*. Online. Available at www.dsal.gov.mo/chinese/otherstat.htm (accessed 15 October 2010).

Lai, W.L.D. (2009) *Macao's Social Welfare Model: A Prototype of a Regulatory Regime*, unpublished doctoral dissertation, University of Hong Kong.

Lam, O.I.A. (1998) *Social Welfare Policy of Macau during the Transitional Period*, unpublished Master's thesis, University of Hong Kong.

Liu, P.L. (2002) *Gaming Industry in Macau*, Hong Kong: Joint Publishing Ltd (in Chinese).

Macao Daily, various dates (in Chinese).

Macau SAR Government (2004) *2004 Policy Address*. Online. Available at http://portal.gov.mo/web/guest/info_detail?infoid=150 (accessed 11 September 2010).

——(2008) *2008 Policy Address*. Online. Available at http://portal.gov.mo/web/guest/info_detail?infoid=2750 (accessed 11 September 2010).

Mo, R.T. (1994) 'Political Development in Hong Kong and Macau: A Social Movement Perspective', in H. Yee (ed.) *Politics and Public Policy in Macau*, Macau: Macau Foundation (in Chinese).

Mok, S.I. (2009) *An Analysis of the Social Security Fund in Macau*, unpublished Master's thesis, University of Macau (in Chinese).

Ng, K.C. (1990a) 'Macau's Economic Policy and the Regional Dynamics of the Pearl River Delta', *Administration* 3, 1: 187–207 (in Chinese).

——(1990b) *The Democrats*, Hong Kong: Ching Man.

Peck, J. (2001) *Workfare States*, New York: The Guildford Press.

Piven, F. and Cloward, R.A. (1993) *Regulating the Poor: The Functions of Public Welfare*, updated edition, New York: Vintage Books.

Preto, A.R. (1990) 'Standing Committee for the Coordination of Social Affairs', *Administration* 3, 2/3: 507–13 (in Chinese).

Romao, M.C. (1989) 'An Analysis of the Social Welfare System in Macau', *Administration* 2, 3/4: 213–44 (in Chinese).

Social Security Fund of Macau SAR Government (2002) *Social Security Fund 2002 Annual Report*. Online. Available at www.fss.gov.mo/chn2/Pages/yearly/2002/chapter3.pdf (accessed 9 October 2010).

——(2010) *Frequently Asked Questions on Migrant Worker Levy*. Online. Available at www.fss.gov.mo/chn2/Pages/qa3.htm (accessed 16 October 2010).

Social Work Bureau of Macau SAR Government (2004) *Annual Report*. Online. Available at www.ias.gov.mo/stat/rept2004/index.htm (accessed 13 October 2010).

Tang, Y.W. (2003) *Social Welfare and Social Insurance in Macau*, Macau: Macau Social Security Association (in Chinese).

Tang, Y.W. and Chan, K.S. (2009) *Social Security Reform: Tenth Anniversary of the Macau Social Security Association*, Macau: Macau Social Security Association (in Chinese).

Tian, B.H. and Zhang, C. (2006) 'The Development of Social Welfare in Macau: A Workfare Perspective', in W.C. Ieong (ed.) *The Development of Social Welfare in Macau: Trends and Characteristics*, Macau: Centre for Macau Studies (in Chinese).

Wu, C.C. (1994) 'The Limitations of Party Politics and Democratic Development in Macau', in H. Yee (ed.) *Politics and Public Policy in Macau*, Macau: Macau Foundation (in Chinese).

Xu, Z.G. (1994) 'An Analysis of Public Expenditure and Revenue of Macau, 1983–92', in H. Yee (ed.) *Politics and Public Policy in Macau*, Macau: Macau Foundation (in Chinese).

Zhao, L.P. (1998) 'An Analysis of the Migrant Worker Policy in Macau', *Journal of Macau Studies* 8: 97–149 (in Chinese).

5 Workfare in Taiwan

From social assistance to unemployment absorber

Chin-fen Chang

Introduction to Taiwan

Located geographically in the Pacific Ocean south of Japan and Korea, Taiwan, officially the Republic of China (ROC), has been known as one of Asia's four tigers with highly developed economies since the 1980s, with the other three being Hong Kong, Korea and Singapore. Its population was about 23 million in 2009, which was less than half of Korea's but much greater than Hong Kong's and Singapore's, both of which have fewer than 10 million people. Its per capita gross domestic product (GDP) in 2009 was US$17,927, which was less than Korea's at US$20,265, Hong Kong's at US$31,407 and Singapore's at US$40,336. All four countries experienced negative effects from the global financial crisis that began in 2008. Taiwan had the four tigers' highest unemployment rate in 2009, with 5.9 per cent, followed by Hong Kong's at 5.1 per cent, Korea's at 3.7 per cent and Singapore's at 3.0 per cent. Its unemployment rate, however, had remained mostly less than 4 per cent over the previous few decades as its economy has steadily developed (International Monetary Fund (IMF) 2010).

The Human Development Index is a composite statistic that the United Nations (UN) uses to rank the degree of general social and economic development among its member countries or regions annually. The index's components include life expectancy, adult literacy, gross enrolment in school and per capita GDP. Taiwan is ranked twenty-fifth, which is in the same cluster as Hong Kong, Singapore and Korea (DGBAS 2007). As Taiwan does not belong to the UN, the Directorate-General of Budget, Accounting and Statistics (DGBAS) of the ROC's Executive Yuan calculates its ranking according to the UN's equation. Japan's ranking is much higher than that of the four tigers, and China's is considerably lower than that of all of them (DGBAS 2007). Taiwan has therefore achieved notably high human development during the past few decades.

Welfare state: Taiwan's version

The establishment and general features of Taiwan's welfare system are related to the political and democratic changes that have occurred there during the past twenty years. Taiwan had been ruled by the Nationalist Party (NP), also known as the Kuomintang (KMT), since 1945 until it lost its first presidential election to the Democratic Progressive Party (DPP) in 2000. The DPP was then the ruling party for eight years until the NP regained the presidency in 2008. Using the protection of national security as an excuse, the NP ruled under martial law from 1949 to 1987. This prohibited Taiwan's people from exercising such rights as those to gather freely, organize political parties or go out on strike, among many other restrictions. Criticism against the regime or any political unrest could result in imprisonment or worse. This authoritarian rule, combined with a lack of the imagination and knowledge of a modern state, made its development of a welfare state lag far behind its economic performance (Lin 1991).

Lee and Ku (2007) categorized Taiwan's welfare regime as conservative and productivist developmental. The backbone of its social security net is various forms of social insurance, which accounted for 47.8 per cent of its social security budget in 1996, increasing to 54.8 per cent in 2004 (Ku 2000; DGBAS 2006). Its largest social insurance programme is national health insurance, followed by labour insurance and insurance for military personnel, public servants and public school teachers. Ordinary citizens and employees make significant contributions to Taiwan's social security system. Employers also have to pay a significant portion of the premiums for the labour insurance fund. The amount that the state contributes, however, is limited. Most of the social insurance measures are by occupation. It is officially necessary to be employed in order to participate in an insurance programme. According to the Labour Insurance Act (passed in 1958 and revised many times since), workers pay 30–70 per cent of the premiums, depending on their employment status.

Figure 5.1 shows the types of social insurance and assistance Taiwan provides and the government agencies that administer each. National health insurance, administered by the Department of Health, is the only universal measure; all the other programmes are for specific groups. The Ministry of the Interior administers the farmers' insurance programme, the Council of Labour Affairs (CLA) the labour insurance programme for workers, the Ministry of National Defence insurance for military personnel, and the Ministry of Civil Service insurance for civil servants and teachers. All these programmes include compensation for medical expenditures and pensions. The National Pension, which provides only pensions, is for those not covered by any of these occupation-specific programmes. The Public Assistance Act of 1980 mainly assists low-income families. Some of its recipients have to attend workfare programmes. This chapter will discuss this in detail later. All of Taiwan's other workfare initiatives have also provided material relief to unemployed people.

This chapter next discusses the economic and political context in which Taiwan's various workfare measures became established. It then discusses the Public Assistance Act's citizen-based workfare programme, followed by the workfare programmes provided for unemployed people and the evolution of Taiwan's unemployment insurance policy. It concludes with a discussion of

80 *Chin-fen Chang*

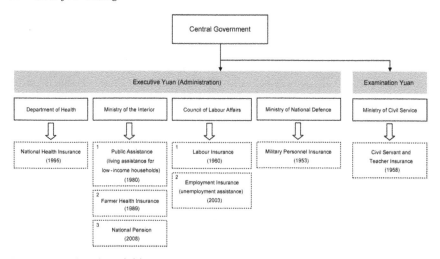

Figure 5.1 Taiwan's social insurance programmes
Sources: Compiled and drawn by the author
Note: Dates in parentheses are the years of implementation

temporary workfare programmes for victims of natural disasters and those with the aim of reducing unemployment.

Economic and political background of workfare measures

Economic background

The ROC has created many different workfare programmes over the years. Most of these have had similar content, with only minor changes with regard to who has qualified for them. Some of them have even shared similar titles. Increases in unemployment have generally been the most important factor influencing the establishment of most of them, as the state has tended to respond to rising unemployment by enacting new measures to show its determination to combat unemployment and help the unemployed.

Figure 5.2 illustrates Taiwan's economic trends from 1978 to 2009. Although not free from turmoil, the economy grew rapidly until 1990. The economic growth rate has remained below 8 per cent since then, and below 6 per cent during the twenty-first century, and real earnings generally increased steadily until 2000. The most volatile indicator, however, has clearly been the unemployment rate (DGBAS 2010a).

Globalization has played an important role in the development of Taiwan's economy since the 1970s, as it is particularly vulnerable to global trends because of its heavy reliance on exports. Advances in production, communication and transportation technology have made adapting the international division of labour to suit market demand easier. New information technology has also made

Workfare in Taiwan 81

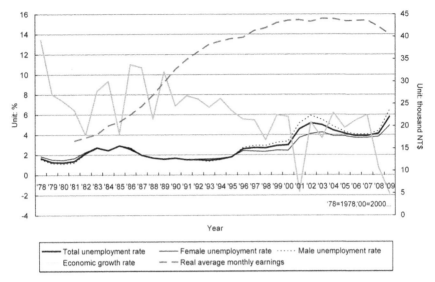

Figure 5.2 Taiwan economic statistics, 1978–2009
Source: DGBAS (2010a, 2010b)

it easier for investors to make complex transactions across national borders in seconds. All of these closer production, marketing and financial relationships have also meant that all of the countries and regions involved in global markets have shared risks when major investors or markets have had problems.

The two oil crises in 1972 and 1979 struck the first blows to Taiwan's economy, as it depends heavily on imported oil. When China opened its doors to foreign investors in the 1980s, Taiwanese businesses quickly moved there to build their factories. Part of this migration was in response to the demands of major Western buyers to reduce the costs, and part was to gain a foothold in China's consumer market. This capital flight took jobs with it, as many factories on Taiwan closed or significantly reduced production, and thousands of manufacturing workers rapidly lost their jobs (DBGAS 2010a).

Such events in the United States (US) as the bursting of the dot-com bubble in 2000, the 9/11 incident in 2001 and the 2008 financial crisis all had immediate effects on the global economy. The recession that followed the 2008 crisis caused many factories and shops to close in both the US and countries such as Taiwan that rely on it as a major export market.

The ROC government has proposed many of its economic recovery and welfare plans, including workfare measures, in order to alleviate the economic hardship of business failures and record high unemployment resulting from the external economic turmoil of the first decade of the twenty-first century. The unemployment rate began increasing in 1996 and reached more than 4 per cent in 2001. It then rose to more than 5 per cent in 2008 and remained there until late 2010. The recession has hurt manufacturing more than the service sector and has resulted in higher unemployment rates among men than among women (DGBAS 2010a).

Changes in macroeconomic conditions have played a crucial role in forcing the state to revise previous programmes and to propose new temporary relief measures. Ku and Finer (2007) pointed out that Taiwan's government, as with those in many other developed economies, has been facing a dilemma as a result of globalization. It has to avoid taxing businesses so heavily that it affects their competitiveness in world markets and also respond to pressure from an increasing social welfare budget sensitive to the effects of global economic instability on job opportunities. Both trends create fiscal difficulties for it. As most workfare measures are either temporary or only for those on low incomes, however, expenditures on them take up but a small share of its social welfare budget.

Political background

Still determined to retake the mainland, in the early decades of its rule, the NP spent a large proportion of its budgets on defence at the expense of such other needs as welfare programmes (Goodman & Peng 1996). Tsai and Chang (1985) argued that, as the NP is basically conservative with regard to welfare provision, it enacted all early legislation such as that addressing labour insurance and public assistance reluctantly as a way to respond to such external political conditions as pressure from the UN or the 1980 diplomatic crisis resulting from the US's normalization of relations with China.

Lin (1991) noted that, even though the NP enacted the labour insurance system in the 1950s, it was more of a political gesture than a result of welfare-oriented thinking. Since the 1960s, the ROC has devoted most of its initiatives and budget to infrastructure for economic development and defence. Furthermore, NP politicians delayed recognition of the need for welfare reform due to their conservative ideology. Lin (2005) reported that Hau Pei-tsun, a former NP premier, remarked in 1992 that Taiwan would never become a welfare state and that everyone should be responsible for their own lives. That the Commission on Human Security (2003) praised Taiwan for simultaneously achieving both economic growth and security for poor people seems to imply that market success automatically improves the economic welfare of most people.

Taiwan's welfare system has focused on social insurance and, more recently, social assistance. The labour insurance scheme, for instance, has the three main purposes of providing workers with medical insurance, maintaining victims' minimum living standards and providing workers with retirement pensions. The DPP became the country's main advocate of welfare policies when it was the opposition party before 2000. It had originally advocated many of the welfare policies and measures that the NP regime eventually enacted, including raising pensions for farmers and the national health plan (Ku 2000). Taiwan is the only one of the four tigers to offer universal health insurance for both citizens and migrant workers, which is the result of a DPP proposal (Ku & Finer 2007).

Taiwan's Legislative Yuan has passed most of the workfare measures with little objection from either party. In 2002, the then ruling DPP party proposed an employment promotion programme including workfare to the Legislative Yuan with the objective of reducing unemployment. The implementation of the Plan for Expanding Employment through Public Service, usually called the Public Service Employment Programme, however, resulted in a serious conflict between the legislature and the administration. The employment promotion budget was about 6.4 billion NTD, out of a total social welfare budget of 287.6 billion NTD. As the majority party in the Legislative Yuan, the NP created obstacles to its being passed. The DPP government responded by announcing the plan publicly to bring public pressure to bear on the NP legislators, and it passed (*The Epoch Times* 5 January 2003).

The 2008 financial crisis severely affected Taiwan's export economy and raised unemployment to another record high. The then NP administration responded quickly by proposing measures to create job opportunities for the unemployed and new university graduates. The budget for the workfare and vocational training plan was about 7.1 billion NTD for the first year (2009). As the NP was also the majority in the Legislative Yuan, the administration faced little resistance to the bill being passed (Taiwan Think Tank 2010).

Workfare policies and programmes in Taiwan

This section divides workfare programmes into the two categories of regular and emergency, based on the state's objectives. Regular workfare programmes represent those proposed as ordinary ones for those who need them. The government has also proposed several ad hoc ones to provide allowances for people affected by such natural disasters as earthquakes and typhoons or in severe economic recessions. The state has generally been more concerned with the outcomes of these emergency programmes than with the regular ones, as the public can examine their effectiveness easily. The difference also concerns the eligibility of the applicants. For the emergency workfare measures, only the local victims of the natural disasters are eligible to apply.

Regular workfare measures

Workfare on the basis of residential status

This was the first type of workfare programme introduced in Taiwan to assist low-income households regardless of the applicants' employment status. The local Taipei City Government instigated it by passing the Measure of Residents' Temporary Job Assistance in 1968. This has provided workfare to low-income households or poor individuals who have lived in the city for at least six months. The job duties include cleaning the streets, parks, schools and graveyards, as well as performing social services. It is still effective in 2010.

Taiwan's first national workfare policy was the Public Assistance Act (PAA) (1980). It stipulates that low-income households with at least one member able to work can apply for an allowance if their able-bodied member or members accepts arrangements for vocational training, employment assistance, aid in starting a small business or assigned work. Its purpose is to 'help them to depend on themselves' (Article 15). In order to be accepted to take part in this programme, the average monthly income per person in a household has to be below the minimum cost of living, and total family assets cannot exceed a certain amount (Article 4). The standards for minimum cost of living and total family assets vary with the economic conditions of each locality and are determined by the local government.

Unlike the workfare measures monitored by the CLA, which this chapter will discuss later, the PAA's (1980) work-and-relief programme did not require a specific employment status. People withdrawing from the labour market or who had no paid employment experience could also apply for the relief. Local government agencies decide the nature of the work, which includes planting, street cleaning, collecting recycled materials or being assigned to work for a non-governmental organization (NGO). Unlike the practices in other countries such as the US, therefore, Taiwan's workfare recipients did not work as cheap labour for profit-oriented businesses, and their work schedules were light. They could do most jobs within half a day and could look for other ways to increase their earnings during the remaining part of the day. This situation changed in the late 2000s, which this chapter will discuss later.

Workfare based on employment status

Taiwan's first social security measure for the unemployed was the 1958 Labour Insurance Act, which stipulated that eligible applicants could continue to pay their labour insurance premiums when unemployed in order to prevent their insurance tenure from being affected. They were, however, unable to receive any allowances or other assistance. The assistance it provided was therefore obviously limited.

The Ministry of the Interior governed labour affairs until the establishment of the CLA in 1987, which began a new era in the central government's approach to addressing labour policies. The CLA instituted the Programme on Promotion of Employment Stability (1989) to demonstrate its determination and capacity to execute employment policies successfully. It is a comprehensive measure covering almost all dimensions of employment security, including establishing a job training system and providing unemployed people with loans and workfare possibilities.

The Employment Services Act (1992) is an important law designed mainly to legalize and institutionalize the employment of foreign labour. Anticipating criticism that the importing of foreign workers compromises local workers' job opportunities and lowers wage standards, it also includes measures to promote the employment of Taiwanese by stipulating that public employment institutions should help laid-off workers get re-employment according to their orientations and work abilities. It mandates further that the CLA provide other measures to help unemployed workers actively and requires employers hiring foreign workers, whether businesses or households, to pay monthly fees into an employment security fund that has become the source of most employment promotion and unemployment relief programmes and activities. The fund had accumulated about 10 billion NTD by 2010, or about US$310 million at the current exchange rate (DGBAS 2009).

The 1993 enactment of the Employment Promotion Measure of Unemployed Workers Due to Plant Closure or Shutdown, also called the Employment Promotion Measure (EPM), was a response to that of the Employment Services Act and its related stipulations (Guo 1994). The promotion measure provided workers laid off because of plant shutdowns or closures with a monthly allowance of 6,000 NTD, or about US$188 at the current exchange rate, provided they receive job training and meet other requirements. In order to receive a higher allowance, they have to accept work duties assigned by government agencies (EPM). This was the beginning of workfare or work-for-welfare programmes for the unemployed in Taiwan. Subsequent revisions or new programmes have generally been based on this measure.

The EPM derived its revenue from the Employment Security Fund. The CLA estimated that it would help 1,700 people (*Economic Daily News* 6 September 1995), but was initially afraid that a huge crowd of workers would apply and the programme's budget would be unable to meet the demand. They turned out to be overly pessimistic, however, as no one applied to participate in it, even though hundreds enquired about it. In order to save face, the CLA revised the measure several times between 1993 and 1995, but attracted only one applicant (*Economic Daily News* 6 September 1995), apparently due to the rigid eligibility conditions.

For one thing, only previous manufacturing workers were eligible for the EPM, and the unemployment rate was below 2 per cent in the early 1990s. As most of the news about labour management disputes and employment security was about layoffs due to plant shutdowns or closures in the manufacturing industry, the CLA had designed the programme for production workers only, and they constituted less than one-third of the total workforce at that time (DGBAS 2010a).

The EPM's applicants, furthermore, had to have worked in a plant that had officially admitted being closed or shut down. It required them to show proof of the plant closing, which could be difficult to obtain as many manufacturers closed plants without advance notice, leaving the workers with no way of finding their former bosses and therefore of obtaining proof. The measure also disqualified from eligibile workers who had received more than three months of severance pay, required them to have worked for the same employer for at least one year before filing their application and to prove that they were their families' breadwinners. They also had to wait for two weeks after filing their applications to be accepted (EPM).

After going through all the trouble of getting approval, they could receive an allowance, which was inadequate, for a maximum of only four months. The Labour Standards Act stipulates the minimum working conditions for the employed in Taiwan. Its Article 21 requires employers to pay no less than a basic monthly wage to their employees, the level of which is decided by a committee. The basic monthly wage in 1993 was 13,350 NTD, or about US$417 at the current exchange rate, and the average monthly income for manufacturing workers in 1993 was about 29,000 NTD, but the EPM's monthly allowance was only 11,125 NTD. Workers could probably have easily earned that much or more doing temporary jobs, as the job market was promising at the time (DGBAS 2010b). Figure 5.2 illustrates this.

The CLA's director explained that the eligibility requirements were so high and the allowance was so low by asserting publicly that there is no such thing as a free lunch. He explained further that the EPM would not encourage workers to become lazy and stop looking for jobs, but that they should consider the assistance to be a temporary subsidy rather than unemployment relief. The director concluded by saying that workers should count on themselves to provide the means to support themselves and their families eventually (*United Daily News* 10 September 1993).

The CLA, however, was still embarrassed that almost no one had applied for the programme, so it modified the conditions several times. Most of these changes were insignificant and attracted few additional applicants. For instance, one of the modifications increased the upper age limit from 60 to 70 years. Another extended eligibility to those who had received severance pay if it had been a designated amount less than their wages would have been. As the other requirements remained the same, however, fewer than ten people applied for the programme before the last revision in 1995 (*Economic Daily News* 6 September 1995).

Workfare became a formal policy with the CLA's 1995 implementation of the Unemployment Assistance Measure (UAM), usually called the Assistance Measure. Its purpose was also to help laid-off workers earn an allowance through workfare. Unlike the EPM, however, the Assistance Measure had no limitation on the industry in which its applicants had worked, and it retained only three of the previous scheme's conditions. These were the requirements of a two-week waiting period after filing the application, of having worked for the same employer for at least a year and of being aged between 16 and 60 (UAM).

Although applicants had to accept whatever work the government agencies assigned to them while receiving their allowances, they could have two days off each week to search for real jobs. They could refuse their job assignments or assigned job-training programmes only if they had such acceptable reasons as their new job's earnings being less than two-thirds of what they had earned in their previous jobs, the new jobs being incompatible with their educational backgrounds or skills and the commuting distance to the new jobs or training places being more than 30 kilometres (UAM).

Those participating in the programme could receive a 600 NTD daily allowance for as many as twenty-five days a month, making their maximum monthly income initially 15,000 NTD, more than the EPM had offered and closer to the official basic wage, which had increased to 15,840 NTD by 1995. They could still only obtain the assistance for a maximum of four months, and had to go to their local public employment agencies to confirm their unemployment status in order to receive their monthly allowance (UAM).

Taiwan's economy began to experience change in 1996. The unemployment rate increased to 2.6 per cent, which is not high by Western standards but was a record high for Taiwan. The CLA responded to public pressure by proposing the Measure for the Implementation of the Employment Promotion Allowance, generally called the Measure of Employment Promotion (MEP) in 1998, which was introduced into the Legislative Yuan in 1999 and passed in 2002. It opened the era of legislated workfare for the unemployed in Taiwan.

The MEP had more differences from than similarities to the previous programmes. It did not restrict eligibility for workfare, training or transportation allowances to laid-off workers, but also included family breadwinners, physically disabled people, aboriginal people and those earning low incomes. It also included no age limitations, excluding only retired people receiving pensions (MEP). The most important difference was that it allowed the state to provide workfare and other forms of allowances to those who needed it depending on economic conditions, the unemployment rate and the budget.

The MEP therefore went beyond the Public Assistance Act and previous measures based on employment status by expanding the pool of eligible applicants and providing flexibility for the state to act in response to changes in external conditions. It became an instrument for the state to use to reduce the number of unemployed people and thereby improve its statistics, and therefore no longer required previous employment experience and included such minority groups as people with physical disabilities and aboriginal people. It did, however, retain a time limit, albeit extended to six months. The highest amount participants could receive was 17,600 NTD monthly (MEP).

Special workfare measures

In addition to the Public Assistance Act and various workfare-related measures for assisting the poor and the unemployed, the state enacted some temporary measures to meet the urgent needs of people affected by natural disasters and severe economic recessions. The recipients still needed to work to obtain the allowance, but the requirements were less rigorous than for the existing measures.

Restoration programmes after the 921 Earthquake in 1999

Taiwan experienced a 7.6 magnitude earthquake on 21 September 1999 that particularly affected the central part of the island. It killed more than 2,000 people and destroyed or seriously damaged 100,000 houses or apartments.

Many affected families and individuals experienced immediate economic hardship because of losing their jobs or having to leave their jobs in order to help their families or repair their homes (Shieh 2008).

The state appropriated part of the Employment Security Fund to provide allowances for those affected and others living in the affected areas based on a temporary programme called the Measure of 921 Earthquake Restoration Employment Services, Vocational Training and Temporary Work Allowance (ERES). Applicants for this allowance had to meet certain conditions such as the damage to their residences had to be more than a specified amount and one of the members of their families had to have participated in labour insurance previously. Those who qualified had to help with the restoration work in the affected areas and to work at least three days weekly to receive the weekly allowance (ERES). Some of those affected complained about this, but a local official defended the measure by pointing out that it was intended as workfare and not a social allowance (Huang 2000). The CLA also instructed this programme specifically to provide re-employment opportunities for the unemployed in the affected areas during 2004 and 2005 (ERES).

Employment promotion programmes in response to global recessions since 2001

The DPP's victory in the 2000 presidential election marked the beginning of a new era in Taiwan's politics. However, it took office as economic conditions were deteriorating, with the unemployment rate soon reaching close to 3 per cent. The 11 September 2001 attacks on the World Trade Center seriously affected the American economy and therefore the global one as well, including Taiwan's. Its unemployment rate reached 4.6 per cent in 2001 and more than 5 per cent in 2002 (DGBAS 2010a). Figure 5.2 illustrates this.

The CLA implemented two workfare measures to provide material relief to the unemployed, the Sustainable Employment Plan in 2001 and the Multi-Employment Promotion Programme in 2002. As unemployment remained high, in 2003, the DPP enacted the Plan for Expanding Employment through Public Service, called the Plan for Expanding Employment (PEE), which lasted until 2004. Unlike the earlier two programmes, the Council of Economic Planning and Development mainly organized the 2003–04 plan (Lin 2006).

As this chapter has indicated earlier, the jobs that the various workfare programmes provided had been mainly in the social service sector, the employers being either government agencies or non-profit organizations. The government expanded the pool of possible workfare jobs after 2000 to include ones in other government departments and agencies, as the job opportunities in the social service sector could only absorb a small proportion of the increasing number of unemployed people. The PEE, for example, required various government agencies to create specific numbers of jobs. Nine ministries and departments participated, the CLA providing about 22,000 jobs and the Environmental Protection Administration 1,300 (Executive Yuan 2004). The plan received funding from various sources, mainly such government-sponsored funds as the Employment Security Fund and the Recycling Fund, and partly from the government budget (PEE).

The criteria for benefiting from the Plan for Expanding Employment were less rigid than those for previous workfare programmes, as its participants did not have to come from low-income households or be family breadwinners, but they did have to be between the ages of 35 and 65 and to have worked for at least six months during the previous three years (PEE). It was, therefore, clearly targeted at unemployed people in the active, middle-aged workforce.

Employment promotion programmes in response to the 2008 financial crisis

The administration of former president Chen Shui-bian faced severe economic conditions after the DPP took power in 2000. To stimulate the economy and reduce unemployment, the state introduced such workfare programmes for the unemployed as a Sustainable Employment Plan, a Multi-Employment Promotion Programme and a Plan for Expanding Employment. The NP was forced to react even more quickly to the consequences of the 2008 global financial crisis, which affected Taiwan in the same year that the NP's Ma Ying-jeou won the presidential election. The decrease in export orders forced many factories and companies to shut down or even go out of business, resulting in several hundred thousand workers being laid off or forced to take unpaid leave. When the unemployment rate exceeded 5 per cent, the state reacted by providing another workfare measure, similar to the earlier ones, which is called the Employment Promotion Programme (EPP) in 2009 (Executive Yuan 2010).

Among its various efforts to promote employment, the EPP offers three types of workfare allowances. One provides an allowance for doing temporary work. It is similar to previous measures in which the applicants had to do jobs assigned by government agencies to obtain assistance. The highest monthly earnings are 17,600 NTD and these jobs last for up to six months. Another initiative provides employers with a stipend of 10,000 NTD for each unemployed worker they hire full time and employ for at least one month and 100 NTD per hour for each new part-time worker. It also continues the previous administration's Multi-Employment Promotion Programme (EPP).

The EPP has therefore extended the workfare policy further to include the private sector. While helping unemployed people to get jobs and maintain reasonable economic conditions, it also helps to reduce the participating private businesses' labour costs with state funds. The government plans for it to last from 2009 to 2012 with a total budget of 33 billion NTD, and has estimated that it will reduce unemployment by 0.3 per cent over that period by helping more than 200,000 people to find jobs (Executive Yuan 2010).

Although the government encountered little objection to enacting this programme, it received severe public criticism for another workfare measure. People aged 15 to 24 have always had higher unemployment than other age groups. Although Taiwan's unemployment rate was 4.1 per cent in 2008, 5.9 per cent in 2009 and 5.2 per cent in July 2010, the unemployment rate for young people in this age group has exceeded 10 per cent during that time (DGBAS 2010a). Concerned that upcoming graduations would flood the job market with young people and therefore increase the unemployment figures and make the government look incapable of handling the economy, the Executive Yuan instructed the Ministry of Education to devise a programme to subsidize fully the hiring of university graduates by private businesses (Executive Yuan 2010).

Working with the CLA and other ministries, the Ministry of Education matched applicants with available employers and subsidized their employment by 22,000 NTD monthly for up to a year. The media later ridiculed the programme as the 22K plan, and the graduates receiving the subsidy came to be called 22K receivers (*Apple Daily* 19 July 2010). The private sector has hired more than 30,000 college graduates through this programme, which the government extended to 2011, the unemployment rate still being more than 5 per cent in mid-2010. It did, however, reduce the monthly subsidy to 10,000 NTD and the time limit to six months (Central News Agency 5 July 2010).

Restoration programmes after Typhoon Morakot in 2009

On 8 August 2009, Typhoon Morakot struck the mountainous areas of southern Taiwan causing mudslides and flooding that killed more than 600 people and damaged more than 1,700 homes. The government provided some help to the affected families and individuals after a slow start, a cabinet reshuffle under tremendous public pressure. The CLA implemented a temporary work relief programme that has been in effect since 30 August 2010 (CLA 2009).

The work involved is related to the restoration of the affected areas. Those applying for this relief have had to prove that they were victims of the typhoon or living in affected areas at the time and demonstrate that they have the ability and intention to work. They have not, however, had to prove that they cannot find work, as unemployed people and those who have temporarily withdrawn from the labour market are both eligible. Recipients receive 100 NTD per hour up to 17,600 NTD monthly, which is somewhat more than the basic wage of 17,280 NTD. This programme therefore has fewer rigid requirements for participation than other workfare measures and relief through the Employment Services Act (CLA 2009).

Review of the effectiveness of the workfare system

The importance of political and economic factors

Taiwan's workfare-related policies and acts have tended to be passive, ad hoc and overlapping. The government initially used them as social welfare measures limited to poor people, then began to de-emphasize the requirement to work for welfare, but retained it as a signal that the state was not encouraging poor people to rely on government benefits. It did not become a way to help unemployed people survive temporary periods of hardship until the 1990s.

The state at that time had a primarily neoliberal perspective and treated unemployment as an individual problem. It asserted that even workers who had been laid off because of plant closures could find new jobs if they were willing to do so and justified this confidence by noting the low unemployment rate. Even when the state began implementing workfare programmes for laid-off workers in the 1990s, therefore, it made the qualifications for receiving benefits rigorous and the assistance period short. Unemployment rose and remained high after 1996, however, so the state began to accept the reality that it is a structural, enduring problem and to evaluate the effectiveness of workfare measures more seriously. This led to it gradually relaxing the requirements for participating in workfare programmes.

Table 5.1 summarizes the major past and still existing programmes and laws with regard to workfare, their main content and the unemployment rates in the corresponding years. It clearly shows that most of the programmes and their revisions came into effect after the late 1990s, when unemployment rates reached a then record high of 2.6 per cent and kept increasing during the new century. The state continued to enact more workfare programmes and unemployment benefits as the aggregate economic situation deteriorated and the unemployment rate remained high.

Political factors also influenced the enactment of various programmes to stimulate the economy, employment or both. For example, as Taiwan's elections usually take place at the end of the year, the state has tended to roll out new packages of programmes or policies to stimulate the economy, increase expenditure on social welfare or both during election years. Table 5.1 shows how workfare programmes with new titles came into effect in years that had legislative elections such as 1995, 1998 and 2001.

The substance of these programmes has not differed significantly. Even their titles have tended to use the same words, such as implementation, promotion and assistance. Changes in the ruling parties, premiers of the Executive Yuan, which is the ROC's cabinet, and even the ministers of the CLA apparently justified changing the programmes' titles. The new incumbents tried to avoid being perceived as imitating their predecessors or letting them take too much credit for initiating the programmes, but the basic tenets, requirements and benefits remained similar.

Workfare's effectiveness

Figure 5.3 shows the number of people receiving workfare assistance or instances of this and the total amount distributed. As government statistics do not provide earlier data, its data relate to the period between 1999 and 2009.

Table 5.1 Conditions at times of workfare and unemployment measures' implementation in Taiwan

Year	Measure or act	Description	Election	Unemployment rate (%)
1968	Measure of Residents' Temporary Job Assistance by Taipei City Government	Workfare for low-income households registered in Taipei City		*
1980	Public Assistance Act	Workfare for low-income households		1.23
1989	Programme on Promotion of Employment Stability (annulled)	Workfare for the unemployed	Legislative	1.57
1993–95	Employment Promotion Measure of Unemployed Workers due to Plant Closure or Shutdown	Workfare for laid-off manufacturing workers		1.45 1.56 1.79
1995–98	Unemployment Assistance Measure	Workfare for laid-off workers	Legislative	1.79 2.60 2.72 2.69
1998–2002	Implementation of the Employment Promotion Allowance	Workfare for laid-off workers	Legislative	2.69 2.92 2.99 4.57 5.17
2000–06	Measure of 921 Earthquake Restoration Employment Services, Vocational Training and Temporary Work Allowance	Workfare for those affected by the 921 Earthquake or residents of the affected areas		*
2001–02	Sustainable Employment Plan	Government agencies hiring unemployed	Legislative	4.57

Table 5.1 (continued)

Year	Measure or act	Description	Election	Unemployment rate (%)
		workers temporarily		5.17
2002	Employment Insurance Act	Legalize unemployment assistance without workfare		5.17
	Measure for the Implementation of the Employment Promotion Allowance	Legalize 'Implementation of the Employment Promotion Allowance'		
	Multi-Employment Promotion Programme	Promote local workfare projects		
2003–04	Plan for Expanding Employment through Public Service	Workfare for the unemployed	Legislative	4.99
	Programme on Expanding Employment Service in Areas Affected by the 921 Earthquake	Workfare for the residents of the affected areas	Presidential	4.44
2009	Measure for Implementation of Restoration and Temporary Work Allowance after Typhoon Morakot	Workfare for victims or residents of the affected areas		*
	Employment Promotion Programme	Workfare for the unemployed, including working in private business		5.85

Notes:
Measures or programmes not specified as annulled or for a specified time frame are still in effect
The author has translated the titles of the measures and acts from Mandarin Chinese
* These measures are not targeted to the unemployment rate

94 *Chin-fen Chang*

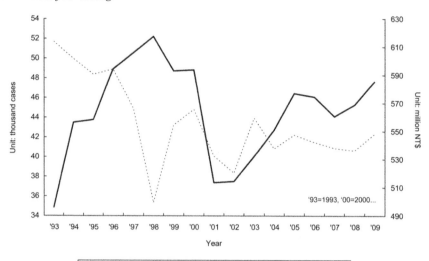

Figure 5.3 Scale of Taiwan workfare, 1993–2009
Source: Ministry of the Interior (2010)

The trend generally corresponds to that of the unemployment rate. When the unemployment rate dropped from 1998 to 2000 and from 2004 to 2007, the number of cases also decreased in the same years or with a one-year time lag. Although no evidence is available that shows whether workfare significantly relieves the financial needs of unemployed people and their families, the comparisons in Figures 5.2 and 5.3 show a strong correlation between job losses and the demand for workfare assistance (Ministry of the Interior 2009).

Lee (2007) characterized Taiwan's workfare and unemployment insurance programmes as rigid, ungenerous and individualistically oriented. In comparison with similar measures in Nordic and Western European countries, Taiwan's workfare has had strict requirements and low benefits. Lee noted further that Taiwan's waiting period between accepting applications and paying benefits is fourteen days, whereas in most European countries, it is three to seven days. Taiwanese workers therefore need to have more savings to help them endure hardship after losing their regular earnings, as their workfare benefits can be only 60 per cent of their previous earnings for no more than six months at most. In Europe, however, unemployment compensation beneficiaries may receive from 70 to 80 per cent of their previous earnings for up to one year to indefinitely. Taiwan extended the length of the compensation period only when the government could not lower the unemployment rate at the end of 2010.

Hsu (2001) found a mismatch between jobs and job-seekers in the 921 earthquake restoration programme. Most people in the affected areas had worked as farmers or service workers for restaurants, hotels or recreational enterprises before the earthquake. The restoration plan, however, required mostly people with construction and manufacturing skills. The programme was able to help the affected people make it through their temporary economic difficulties but not enhance their long-term job prospects.

Fu (2006) found the Public Service Employment Programme's effects to be mixed. About two-thirds of its participants were still jobless after it ended, as most of them were from the labour market's more disadvantaged demographics and the workfare failed to increase their chances of finding employment. The 32 per cent who did find regular jobs after participating in the programme, however, received mostly higher incomes than the programme's benefits, and the programme did provide them with a buffer after losing their previous jobs.

However, Fu's survey (2006: 135) also showed that 67 per cent of workfare recipients could not find jobs after their eligibility expired. Among them, over two-thirds tried but failed in their job search. Besides, close to 29 per cent of the respondents never worked before receiving workfare subsidy. Thus, the Public Service Employment Programme is better treated as an absorber of the unemployed and the most disadvantaged working class rather than as a buffer. For most recipients, workfare did not serve as a transitory plan between unemployment and re-employment. Their chances of being re-employed are not high.

Conclusions

Taiwan's workfare was more welfare oriented than work oriented before the start of the twenty-first century. Its recipients had to work only half days in order to receive their benefits, and they could use the remaining time to earn money by doing some other paid work or looking for full-time employment. This approach of more welfare than work, however, did not mean that Taiwan's authorities adhered to a Nordic-style welfare ideology or approach. They were instead acutely concerned about the possible abuse of its workfare programmes and enforced rigid eligibility standards while paying small benefits for limited periods. The subsequent relaxation of some of the qualifications involved only technical modifications, and Taiwan's workfare has still excluded many people in need of assistance from either the citizen-based or the unemployment-based programmes.

Although Taiwan's establishment of workfare policies has resulted in debate about whether they discourage workers from seeking real jobs and if they increase the government's deficit unnecessarily, their strict eligibility requirements and limited benefits have resulted in fewer participants than expected, so their impact on the fiscal budget has been limited. They have also not become a burden on the government's budget because most of the unemployment-based workfare programmes, such as the assistance and promotion measures, rely on the Employment Security Fund to supply their revenue.

Furthermore, the Employment Security Fund's role in providing assistance to laid-off workers has become a minor one since the passage of the

Employment Insurance Act (2002), the purpose of which is 'to improve the ability of workers to find employment, to promote employment, and to guarantee workers job training and basic living requirements for specified periods of unemployment' (Article 1: translated by the author). The act enables the state to provide unemployed people with subsidies such as unemployment benefits, early re-employment incentives, vocational training, living allowances and National Health Insurance premium subsidies. It does not, furthermore, require them to work in exchange for their benefits any more if they have participated in the labour insurance programme for a certain period of time.

Even though workfare has become gradually disconnected from providing unemployed people with assistance and work since the institutionalization of unemployment insurance, events in global markets have frequently pushed the state to institute temporary workfare programmes to alleviate unemployment problems. Overseas economic disturbances hurt Taiwan severely and immediately because of its great reliance on foreign markets for economic growth and being embedded in the global financial and trading network, so high unemployment has become a constant problem for it during the past decade.

Ku (2002) concluded that politics has been the most important force behind the development of Taiwan's welfare institutions, with both the DPP and the NP advocating various ways of reducing unemployment. Workfare has been an important political gesture to show the state's concern for people's difficulties and an instrument for stabilizing social uncertainty. It has been a more effective method than others for reducing unemployment when the politicians needed to produce a rapid policy result. The cost of workfare has become a political issue as the increasingly unstable global economy has brought Taiwan consistently high unemployment

Such studies as that by Sun (2009) have noted that workfare had not been essential to the operations of capitalism in Taiwan until the 2008 financial crisis. Sun also pointed out that its looseness has resulted from the lack of coordination between the CLA and the Ministry of the Interior. However, it is commendable for the workfare measures as workfare participants did only public service work for state agencies and NGOs but not for any private firms, and most of their duties did not require long hours or high labour intensity.

Even though the continuation of workfare measures to the less advantaged groups should continue in Taiwan to alleviate the commoditization of labour, providing the subsidy to highly educated job-seekers to lower the unemployment rate seems to lack legitimacy. Needing to curb the high unemployment rate over the past few years, however, the NP government has adopted a new workfare plan and has subsidized private businesses to hire new graduates or the unemployed. The state claimed that the workfare plan was effective during its first stages in 2009 and 2010, during which time businesses hired approximately 40,000 university graduates through the programme and about 62 per cent found their own jobs later (Central News Agency 5 July 2010). Whether tax money should be used to subsidize private businesses does, however, remain an issue, and as people with higher education tend to experience less unemployment than those with high school or only junior high school educations, assistance for the more advantaged demographic seems to miss the target and make conditions for disadvantaged people even more unfavourable during the economic recession.

Acknowledgements

The author wishes to thank Yuen-wen Ku and Chak Kwan Chan for their valuable comments. Also, I deeply appreciate the assistance of Yi-ping Chang. The author is responsible for any errors presented here.

Bibliography

Apple Daily (2010) 'No Shame to Receive 22K, Better than Being a Parasite at Home', 19 July. Online. Available at http://tw.nextmedia.com/applenews/article/art_id/32672071/IssueID/20100719 (accessed 13 November 2010) (in Chinese).
Central News Agency (2010) 'Subsidy to the Measure of Practical Training for College Graduates Decreased to Ten Thousand Dollars per Month', 5 July. Online. Available at http://www.cna.com.tw/SearchNews/doDetail.aspx?id=201007050249&q=%E5%A4%B1%E6%A5%AD%E7%8E%87 (accessed 7 September 2010) (in Chinese).
Commission on Human Security (2003) *Human Security Now*, New York: Commission on Human Security.
CLA (Council of Labour Affairs) (2009) 'Measure for Implementation of Restoration and Temporary Work Allowance after Typhoon Morakot', Online. Available at http://law.moj.gov.tw/News/news_detail.aspx?id=58389 (accessed 13 November 2010) (in Chinese).
DGBAS (Directorate-General of Budget, Accounting and Statistics) (2006) 'Summary of Social Security Expenditure in Taiwan', *Topic Report of Statistics* 13 June 2006, Taipei: Executive Yuan, ROC. Online. Available at http://www.dgbas.gov.tw/public/Data/661316404871.pdf (accessed 9 August 2010) (in Chinese).
——(2007) 'International Comparison of Human Development Index (HDI) in 2005', *Monthly Bulletin of Statistics* 12 December 2007, Taipei: Executive Yuan, ROC. Online. Available at http://www.dgbas.gov.tw/public/Data/712121616871.pdf (accessed 9 August 2010) (in Chinese).
——(2009) 'Sheet of Income, Expense and Balance of the Employment Security Fund in Taiwan, 2009'. Online. Available at http://win.dgbas.gov.tw/dgbas02/seg1/98l/98%E6%94%BF%E4%BA%8B-pdf/SF98-14.pdf (accessed 2 November 2010) (in Chinese).
——(2010a) 'Time Series Database of Manpower Survey in Taiwan'. Online. Available at http://www.dgbas.gov.tw/ct.asp?xItem=17144&ctNode=3246 (accessed 2 November 2010) (in Chinese).
——(2010b) 'Time Series Database of Employees' Earnings Survey in Taiwan'. Online. Available at http://www.dgbas.gov.tw/ct.asp?xItem=1135& ctNode=3253 (accessed 2 November 2010) (in Chinese).
Economic Daily News (1995) 'Relax Qualifications for Unemployment Compensation Application: Non-Primary Earners May Apply, the Amount of Subsidy Increase Too', 6 September, p. 9 (in Chinese).
Executive Yuan (2004) 'Press Release of Premier Yu chaired the Fourth Meeting of the Committee of Plan for Expanding Employment through Public Service of the

Executive Yuan'. Online. Available at http://www.cepd.gov.tw/dn.aspx?uid=5165 (accessed 10 February 2010) (in Chinese).

——(2010) 'Subsidized Amount and Persons of the Employment Promotion Programme in Taiwan, 2009–12', Taipei: Council for Economic Planning and Development, Executive Yuan, ROC. Online. Available at http://www.ey.gov.tw/public/Attachment/0181158971.pdf (accessed 2 November 2010) (in Chinese).

Fu, T.H. (2006) 'Effects of Public Service Employment Measure on Re-employment: The Perspective of Active Labour Market Policies', *Social Policy and Social Work* 10, 1: 115–49 (in Chinese).

Goodman, R. and Peng, I. (1996) 'The East Asian Welfare States: Peripatetic Learning, Adaptive Change, and Nation-building', in G. Esping-Andersen (ed.) *Welfare States in Transition: National Adaptations in Global Economies*, pp. 192–224, Thousand Oaks, CA: Sage Publications.

Guo, Z.C. (1994) 'Analysis of Unemployment Compensation System: Application in Taiwan', unpublished doctoral thesis, Graduate Institute of National Development, National Taiwan University (in Chinese).

Hsu, C.M. (2001) 'Exploration of Employment Service Problems in the Reconstruction Areas of the 921 Earthquake in Taiwan', paper presented at the Conference on Unemployment Problems at Present in Taiwan, Institute of Ethnology, Academia Sinica, Taipei, Taiwan, 16 March (in Chinese).

Huang, M.R. (2000) 'Aggressive Consideration of the Workfare System as an Employment Service Measure in Taiwan', *Employment and Training* 18, 1: 10–12 (in Chinese).

International Monetary Fund (IMF) (2010) *World Economic Outlook (April 2010): Rebalancing Growth*. Washington, DC: International Monetary Fund. Online. Available at http://www.econstats.com/weo/V021.htm (accessed 9 December 2010).

Ku, Y.W. (2000) 'Social Development in Taiwan: Upheavals in the 1990s', in K.L. Tang (ed.) *Social Development in Asia*, pp. 39–59, Dordrecht, Netherlands: Kluwer Academic Publishers.

——(2002) 'Towards a Taiwanese Welfare State: Demographic Change, Politics, and Social Policy', in C. Aspalter (ed.) *Discovering the Welfare State in East Asia*, pp. 143–67, Westport, CT: Praeger Publishers.

Ku, Y.W. and Finer, C.J. (2007) 'Developments in East Asian Welfare Studies', *Social Policy and Administration* 41, 2: 115–31.

Lee, Y.J. (2007) 'Unemployment Security Policies and Systems in Taiwan', in C.K. Wong, K.L. Tang and N.P. Ngai (eds) *Social Policy in Three Chinese Societies: Theory and Practice*, pp. 347–71, Hong Kong: Chinese University Press (in Chinese).

Lee, Y.J. and Ku, Y.W. (2007) 'East Asian Welfare Regimes: Testing the Hypothesis of the Developmental Welfare State', *Social Policy and Administration* 41, 2: 197–212.

Lin, W.I. (1991) 'Labour Movement and Taiwan's Belated Welfare State', *Journal of International and Comparative Social Welfare* 7, 1&2: 31–44.

——(2005) 'The Development of Social Welfare in Taiwan in the 1990s: A Retrospect and Prospect', *Community Development Journal (Quarterly)* 109: 12–35 (in Chinese).

——(2006) *Taiwan Social Gazette: Volume on Social Welfare*. Nantou, Taiwan: Taiwan Historica, Academia Historica (in Chinese).

Ministry of the Interior (2009) *Summary of Report on the Survey of the Low Income Family's Life Status in Taiwan Area in 2008*. Taipei: Executive Yuan, ROC. Online.

Available at http://www.moi.gov.tw/news_history_detail.aspx?type_code=01&sn=2701 (accessed 15 July 2010) (in Chinese).
——(2010) *Database of the Monthly Bulletin of Interior Statistics in Taiwan*, Online. Available at http://sowf.moi.gov.tw/stat/month/list (accessed 10 February 2010) (in Chinese).
Shieh, J.C. (2008) 'Review of 921 Post-Earthquake Housing Reconstruction Policies'. Online. Available at http://tw.myblog.yahoo.com/twjcshieh/article?mid=687&prev=702&next=-1 (accessed 13 November 2010) (in Chinese).
Sun, C.C. (2009) 'A Preliminary Analysis of the Linking between Work and Welfare: From "Workhouse Test" to "Workfare" and "Make Work Pay"', *Taiwanese Journal of Social Welfare* 8, 1: 119–47 (in Chinese).
Taiwan Think Tank (2010) *The Examination of the Mid-term of Ma Ying-Jeou Government: How Good Are You, Taiwan? (Taiwan Think Tank, Volume 6)*. Online. Available at http://www.taiwanthinktank.org/page/chinese_attachment_5/1426/201004s.pdf (accessed 13 November 2010) (in Chinese).
The Epoch Times (2003) 'The Premier Yu Shyi-kun Appeals to the Ruling Party and Opposition for Attention on the Unemployment Problems and Approved the Belated Budget', 5 January. Online. Available at http://www.epochtimes.com/b5/3/1/5/n262735.htm (accessed 3 November 2010) (in Chinese).
Tsai, W.H. and Chang, L.Y. (1985) 'Politics, Ideology, and Social Welfare Programmes: A Critical Evaluation of Social Welfare Legislation in Taiwan', *National Taiwan University Journal of Sociology* 17: 233–62.
United Daily News (1993) 'Tryout the Policy of Unemployment Compensation for One Year since September 16', 10 September, p. 6 (in Chinese).

6 Workfare in Japan

Shogo Takegawa

From privatization to workfare

The administration of United States (US) President Richard Nixon first popularized the word *workfare*. The concept has subsequently spread with globalization and neoliberalism to other countries, and it is now used as an umbrella term for social security programmes that include work requirements, with social security benefits strongly related to employment of some kind.

Margaret Thatcher was elected prime minister of the United Kingdom (UK) in 1979 and Ronald Reagan was elected president of the US in 1981. Both pursued vigorous neoliberal agendas, particularly with regard to their economic and social policies, promoting financial deregulation and economic globalization. As the neoliberal ideology's influence on governments throughout the world grew enormously, it became known as the Washington Consensus. Neoliberalism insists on the importance of relying completely on market mechanisms. Its agenda involved deregulation and privatization in every field of public activity in order to allow markets to function with maximum freedom. The welfare state had been under attack as the main cause of what people called big government even before the rise of neoliberalism. Traditional supporters of the welfare state saw the attack from neoliberalism to be a crisis for it (OECD 1981).

It later became clear, however, that although successful as an economic policy, privatization did not necessarily work well with regard to social policy because the demand for goods and services that social policies supply emerges intrinsically as a result of market failure and because the purpose of social policy's regulations is to prevent market dysfunction. Neither full privatization nor complete elimination of regulation is therefore possible with regard to social policy. The results of the neoliberal social experiments in its pioneering countries in the 1980s showed clearly that only partial privatization is possible with regard to social policy. This involves outsourcing some social services to private companies and promoting competition between them. Such markets created through partial privatization are called quasi-markets (Le Grand & Bartlett 1993).

The idea of workfare, which combines employment with welfare, has attracted attention as a neoliberal social policy, either as a replacement for privatization and deregulation or in addition to them. Governments initially regarded workfare as a way to solve technical problems in providing public assistance, in particular to avoid the poverty trap, which involves public assistance beneficiaries receiving insufficient incomes when they move into paid employment because of high effective marginal tax rates. Workfare's rationale is that requiring people to work in order to receive social benefits prevents those benefits from being a disincentive for work. It is also intended to avoid the unemployment trap of paying benefits higher than the minimum wage (Miyamoto 2002; Society for the Study of Social Policy (SSSP) 2006; Uzuhashi 2007).

Although privatization and deregulation are factors in general social policies covering such programmes as those addressing employment and housing, workfare is limited to such individual income maintenance programmes as public assistance and unemployment compensation. Workfare does, however, share with them the neoliberal ideology of the recommodification of labour. It is therefore necessary to address the power of the influence of neoliberalism in Japan in order to understand Japanese workfare.

Japan: a latecomer to neoliberalism

The UK entered the age of neoliberalism in 1979 with Margaret Thatcher and the US followed in 1981 with Ronald Reagan. Yasuhiro Nakasone was Japan's prime minister from 1982 to 1987 and, under the influence of neoliberalism, the Nakasone government privatized previously state-owned companies in such industries as telecommunications, the railways and tobacco. Although the neoliberal ideology had become the basis of Japan's economic policies, Japan differed from such neoliberal countries as the UK and the US in that it limited its neoliberalism to economic policies and did not attempt to privatize and deregulate social policies such as those involving housing, pensions and health care in the same way as the English-speaking countries had (Papadakis & Taylor-Gooby 1987; Kawakami & Masuda 1989; Johnson 1990).

Neoliberalism only started to affect social policies in Japan from the late 1990s to the early 2000s (Takegawa 2009a). The UK began privatizing its public pension plan in 1985, but an advisory committee of the Japanese government only proposed the privatization of Japan's employee pension plan in 1999. The UK initiated an agency system based on new public management theory in the late 1980s and, once again, Japan only institutionalized its independent administrative institution, which is analogous to the UK's agency system, in 1999. In 2004, Japan finally allowed temporary employment in the manufacturing sector in order to facilitate labour market flexibility, as the influence of neoliberalism peaked during the Koizumi government of 2001–5, which applied it to such areas as medical care, welfare services, education and housing (Papadakis & Taylor-Gooby 1987; Johnson 1990; Niki 2007; Osawa 2007).

Japan introduced neoliberalism into its social policies later than the other developed countries, partly because it had instituted its welfare state well after

102 *Shogo Takegawa*

they had done so in the mid-twentieth century, with the 1950s and 1960s being the welfare state's golden age in the West (Flora 1986). Japan, however, was then still reconstructing itself from the Second World War and did not have the well-organized socioeconomic conditions necessary to establish a welfare state (Takegawa 1999, 2005, 2009b).

Japan was a developing country economically with a much younger population than it has had in the twenty-first century. These two factors allowed Japan to enjoy the so-called demographic dividend, and its traditional family structure still flourished. This began to change in the early 1970s, and Japan began to develop a welfare state. Just as Japan's welfare state was about to enter its golden age, however, the other developed countries began to experience welfare state crises and entered their age of neoliberalism. This made it impossible for Japan to expand its welfare state in a context of high growth, as had the others. When Japan was in the initial stages of developing its welfare state, the government exercised considerable influence over social policy and its etatism prevented privatization and deregulation from informing its social policies (Shindo 1996; Takegawa 1999, 2005; Niki 2007).

Neoliberalism therefore began to affect Japan's social policies ten to fifteen years after it had affected such advanced welfare states as the UK and the US. It was only several years after the beginning of the twenty-first century that workfare became the subject of discussion among Japan's policy decision-makers.

Workfare under the Koizumi government

Neoliberalism's influence on Japan's economic policies reached its peak under the Koizumi government, and it also became pervasive with regard to social policy at that time. The Koizumi government adopted a basic reform programme that it called the *Honebuto no Hoshin*, or large-boned policy, at a yearly cabinet meeting. Neoliberalism was clearly the major influence on the 2003 large-boned policy, which established twelve experimental programmes that included lifting a ban on private for-profit hospitals and medical treatment that combined health insurance coverage with private medical treatment at the patients' own expense, deregulating pharmaceutical sales, operating public schools via private consignments, managing agriculture with for-profit companies and managing social and welfare facilities with a for-profit company. Although these policies were mostly unsuccessful, they clearly revealed the government's ideology (Council on Economic and Fiscal Policy 2003; Niki 2007; Takegawa 2009a).

The Koizumi government seldom used the Japanese word for workfare in its pronouncements, calling it instead *jiritsu-shien*, or self-reliance support. It anticipated that this concept would contribute to the curtailment of social security costs (SSSP 2006; Uzuhashi 2007). The first self-reliance support measure targeted single mothers. Table 6.1 shows how many were living in Japan from 1995 to 2008. The Ministry of Health, Labour and Welfare's (MHLW) (2002) published guidelines for this programme emphasized the

Table 6.1 Japanese single-parent households

Year	Thousands
1995	483
1998	502
2001	587
2004	627
2005	691
2006	788
2007	717
2008	701
2009	752

Sources: MHLW (2009)
Online. Available at www.mhlw.go.jp/toukei/saikin/hw/k-tyosa/k-tyosa06/1-1.html, http://www.mhlw.go.jp/toukei/saikin/hw/k-tyosa/k-tyosa09/1-1.html (accessed 5 December 2010)

importance of self-reliance support being based on employment and obtaining child support payments from irresponsible fathers. It stipulated specifically that single mothers were to receive lectures on employment support, subsidies for vocational training and loans for living expenses during the training period. The MHLW was to assist them with job placements, subsidies for education and training in self-reliance and employment information, and employers of single mothers were to receive employment incentives. As a result of these initiatives, the government revised the Welfare of Mothers with Dependents and Widows Act in November 2002, reducing the income maintenance programmes for single mother families. It also reduced the child care allowance, a benefit for single mothers, by half for those who had been receiving it for more than five consecutive years, and provided for this allowance to be suspended if they did not engage in job-seeking activities (Welfare of Mothers with Dependents and Widows Act 2002).

The next measure involved self-reliance support for homeless people. The Special Measures Concerning Assistance in Self-Support of the Homeless Act (2002: n.p.) clarified the country's responsibility for promoting self-reliance among homeless people and providing living support to prevent them from becoming street people. Although this law's original intention was to cover the securing of their housing, medical treatment and welfare, its first priority was to assist them with 'securing stable employment and employment opportunities by developing their occupational skills'.

The law charged each local government with the responsibility of enforcing it (Special Measures Concerning Assistance in Self-Support of the Homeless Act 2002). The Tokyo metropolitan government formulated a self-reliance support system for homeless people that provided a three-step programme for returning them to society. Its welfare office began by accommodating them in emergency temporary protection centres for a month, improving their health, consulting with them and deciding on the direction of their ongoing treatment. It then provided them with accommodation in a self-reliance support centre

104 *Shogo Takegawa*

for two months and with vocational training. The last step involved returning them to society and providing them with support in restarting their lives and seeking employment (Iwata 2006).

The next measure involved self-reliance support for young people. The increasing number of them who did not participate in the labour market had become a social problem in Japan as well as in other developed countries. Table 6.2 illustrates the extent of the problem from 1992 to 2002. In the UK, they are called not in education, employment or training (NEET) young people, and the Japanese have taken up the same term. The NEET in the UK tend to include those who are engaged in job-seeking activities, but Japan's NEET tend not to be. Japanese authorities define NEET as unemployed people between the ages of 15 and 34 who are neither students nor domestic workers (Kosugi 2006). Kosugi estimated that Japan had approximately 650,000 NEET in 2005, and their numbers had been increasing, leading the government to seek effective employment measures for them.

The government responded with Cabinet Secretariat (2003), a plan reflecting its recognition that failing to resolve what it saw as a desperate situation would result in serious future trouble. The concrete measures included careers education, which is basically vocational schools, what it called a Japanese-style dual system, which is an integrated learning system that combines on-the-job training with vocational education, and what it called job cafes, which were one-stop shops that provided NEETs with job placements and such employment services as internships. It then published Cabinet Secretariat (2004), a plan extending its employment support for NEETs by establishing what it called youth independent cram schools in 2005, in which about twenty young people at a time participated in three-month camps to acquire training in work skills and a work ethic in order to help them to move on to employment or training.

The government then introduced self-reliance support for those receiving public assistance benefits. Table 6.3 details how the problem grew from 1990 to 2008. The Japanese refer to public assistance as *livelihood protection*. The Large-Boned Policy (2003) called for the revision of Japan's livelihood protection system's standards, so the government established the Special Committee on the Livelihood Protection System inside the Social Security Council, which

Table 6.2 Unemployed Japanese aged 15–34 years (000)

Year	All unemployed aged 15–34			NEET		
	Male	Female	Total	Male	Female	Total
1992	593.2	714.0	1,307.2	325.5	342.8	668.3
1997	819.1	890.6	1,709.7	344.7	371.8	716.5
2002	1,120.3	1,011.5	2,131.7	410.2	437.0	847.2

Source: Cabinet Office (2005)
Online. Available at www8.cao.go.jp/youth/kenkyu/shurou/chukan.pdf (accessed 2 November 2010)

Table 6.3 Households receiving livelihood protection

Fiscal year	Total beneficiary households	Percentage of all households
1990	7,485,054	15.5
1991	7,208,368	14.8
1992	7,031,662	14.2
1993	7,033,277	14.0
1994	7,144,889	14.2
1995	7,223,101	14.8
1996	7,357,272	14.0
1997	7,577,856	14.1
1998	7,956,725	14.9
1999	8,448,659	15.7
2000	9,015,632	16.5
2001	9,662,022	17.6
2002	10,451,173	18.9
2003	11,295,238	20.6
2004	11,986,644	21.6
2005	12,498,099	22.1
2006	12,909,835	22.6
2007	13,263,296	23.0
2008	13,785,189	24.0

Source: MHLW (2010)
Online. Available at www.ipss.go.jp/s-info/j/seiho/seiho.asp (accessed 2 November 2010)

published a report at the end of 2004. In response to this report, the government reduced several benefits. One of these was additional support for single mother families, which it reduced because 'the standard amount of livelihood support for a supported single-mother family with the extra allowance [¥23,310 in April 2003] is higher than the living costs of a standard single-mother family' (Special Committee on the Livelihood Protection System 2004, n.p.). In 2005, the government reduced the maximum age of children eligible for the extra allowance from 18 to 15. It later abolished the extra allowance it had provided according to the children's age in incremental steps (Miyamoto 2009; MHLW 2010).

As the national government was reducing these benefits, local governments were proposing the introduction of self-reliance support programmes for welfare beneficiaries and creating a self-reliance promotion system for them. These were composed of programmes addressing employment, daily life and social life. The employment one involved workfare, which involved the welfare office and the public employment security office cooperating to refer jobs to selected recipients of public support who had the will and ability to work, to provide them with vocational training and education in manners and to place them in trial employment with subsidized wages (Uzuhashi 2007; Miyamoto 2009).

Table 6.4 Japanese people with disabilities (10,000s)

Type of disability	Total	Living at home All	Living at home Aged 18–64	Institutionalized	Employed
Physical	351.6	332.7	124.1	18.9	36.9
Intellectual	54.7	41.9	27.5	12.8	11.4
Mental	302.8	267.5	174.4	35.3	1.3
Total	709.1	642.1	326.0	67.0	49.6

Source: MHLW (2007)

It then introduced a self-reliance support programme for people with disabilities. Table 6.4 details the size and nature of Japan's population of people with disabilities in 2009. The Services and Supports for Persons with Disabilities Act (MHLW 2005) stipulated that the government provide welfare services appropriate to whether they had physical, intellectual or mental disabilities. Although the Koizumi government legislated this act, it was not implemented until the Abe government took office in 2006. The MHLW (2005) stressed that its primary objective was to make society friendlier for workers with disabilities.

It implemented two projects to achieve this objective. The Employment Transfer Promotion Project directed the vocational centres to provide training in living and vocational skills to those who wished to be employed by a company or to establish a company at home, and later to provide them with employment opportunities in cooperation with the public employment security office. The Work Continuance Support Project provided employment opportunities to people with disabilities who could not get employment despite their ability to work, and also provided work opportunities without employment contracts to those who had difficulty finding employment (MHLW 2005).

When providing these types of employment support, the government required those receiving them to bear 10 per cent of the usage fee. This was in keeping with the philosophy of fair payment for the services that they used, with the monthly payment being based on their incomes (MHLW 2005).

Five-year plan to move from welfare to employment

As the previous section explained, Japan introduced a series of self-reliance support policies for single mothers, homeless people, NEETs, public assistance beneficiaries and people with disabilities. These mostly involved employment support and had the objective of helping unemployed people to earn income and stop being dependent, whether latently or manifestly, on public assistance and welfare services. Receiving employment support, however, rarely involved the entitlement requirement for public assistance and welfare services, but it was workfare in the sense that the government offered employment support and reduced benefits as a package with the intention of reducing welfare dependence by promoting employment.

The Fukuda government of 2007–8 implemented a five-year plan at the end of 2007 to promote moving from welfare to employment, which utilized the employment support policies enacted in the first half of the 2000s. Because welfare-to-work policies had begun in the late 1990s in most other developed countries, this means that Japan took up the approach about ten years after most of the rest of the Organisation for Economic Co-operation and Development (OECD) countries. This plan's objective was to

> improve as much as possible through employment the self-reliance and living conditions of people with disabilities, households on welfare, and such people who receive public assistance as those in single-mother households, while securing the safety net.
>
> MHLW (2007: preface)

The planned period was the five years from 2007 to 2011, and the plan designated its first three years as the period for intensive efforts (MHLW 2007).

Numerical targets characterized this plan. It projected that the number of people with disabilities who were employed would increase from 496,000 in 2003 (MHLW 2004) to 640,000 by 2013 (MHLW 2007). The government also instructed the public employment security office to find employment for 240,000 people with disabilities and to transfer 9,000 of them from welfare to general employment annually by the 2011 fiscal year. It further instructed all local governments to implement the employment programme for households on welfare by the 2007 fiscal year and to increase its employment rate to 60 per cent by the 2009 fiscal year (MHLW 2007).

The plan mentioned only the objective of to 'keep promoting the permanent employment' of single mothers without setting numerical targets (MHLW 2007: 3). This was because single mothers' rate of permanent employment was 42.5 per cent in the 2006 fiscal year, which was higher than that for single mothers in other advanced countries. Most single parents in Japan have been unable to make a living without working full time because the government's income maintenance programmes for them were insufficient and because they experienced social pressure to do so (MHLW 2007; Uzuhashi 2007; Miyamoto 2009).

The programme for realizing these goals has four parts. The first is to develop a community-based national employment support system that includes, for example, establishing centres for employment and living support for disabled people in every local authority jurisdiction and increasing the number of participants in vocational training by 30 per cent by the 2011 fiscal year. By 2006, 59.8 per cent of Japan's local governments had introduced the self-reliance support programme, and the government was endeavouring to achieve 100 per cent participation by the 2007 fiscal year (MHLW 2007). The programme also planned to establish employment and self-reliance support centres in all localities and to implement the Single-Mother Self-Reliance Support Programme fully, the objective being to have every local government implement a self-reliance programme (MHLW 2007).

The next part of the employment support action plan called for the programme's implementation to be accomplished through collaboration between the public employment security office and the welfare office. The subsequent part involved improving Japan's employment promotion laws for people with disabilities, and included short-term employment as part of the computation of the mandatory permanent employment quota for people with disabilities that each company must meet, as the previous law calculated only permanent employees and provided insufficient incentives for those who employed people with disabilities for short periods of time. Japan's employment quotas for workers with disabilities are 1.8 per cent for private companies and 2.1 per cent for government agencies. The plan's final part involves raising the consciousness of those responsible for implementing its objectives with educational campaigns so that every public agency could achieve its employment quota for people with disabilities by the 2012 fiscal year (MHLW 2007).

Neoliberalism setback and a change in government

It is necessary to note that the government published the five-year plan to move from welfare to employment in 2007 because, as neoliberalism's influence on social policy was already undergoing a setback, the workfare policy's continuation had become problematic. Neoliberalism's influence on social policy had been gradually dwindling after peaking in the late 1990s and the first half of 2000. Its first setback was with regard to pensions. The Obuchi government had published the proposals of an economic strategy meeting that advocated privatizing employee pensions. The debate, however, shifted from that to how to maintain a balance of pension financing based on the assumption that public pensions would continue (Takegawa 2009a).

The Koizumi government's 2003–4 large-bone policy was the most radically neoliberal proposal in Japan's history, but subsequent governments made no effort to pursue it. The efforts to make the labour market more flexible peaked with the removal of the prohibition on temporary workers in manufacturing industry in 2004. The Diet rejected the Abe government's 2007 draft of a bill exempting white collar workers from statutory labour standards in 2007 because of strong public opposition. The Koizumi government's policy of curbing social security expenditures had gradually eased under the Liberal Democratic Party (LDP) governments of Abe, Fukuda and Aso. These reversals for neoliberal social policies came about because problems resulting from neoliberal economic policies such as unemployment, poverty and inequality made it hard to maintain social integration. The 2008 global financial crisis also caused Japanese people to lose trust in neoliberalism (Takegawa 2009a).

Japan experienced a change of government in September 2009. Although such changes are common in democratic countries, it was a big political event for Japan, as the LDP had maintained one-party control of the Diet since 1955, with only one brief interval out of power. The Democratic Party of Japan (DPJ) government that replaced the LDP was, furthermore, critical of the neoliberal ideology that the LDP had promoted since the Koizumi government (Takegawa 2009a). It was inevitable that it would review existing workfare policies, including the five-year plan to move from welfare to employment.

The review resulted from the DPJ's general election manifesto promise to end the Koizumi government's attack on single mother households. The DPJ government restored single mothers' extra livelihood support allowance that the previous government had abolished and promised to abolish the system of reducing the child care benefits of single mothers who had been receiving them for more than five years. It also abolished the Services and Supports for Persons with Disabilities Act's workfare content and promised to improve the law so that it could ratify the United Nations Convention on the Rights of Persons with Disabilities (DPJ 2009).

The DPJ also promised to improve public assistance by establishing a vocational training system with a ¥100,000 monthly benefit as a second safety net between livelihood protection and employment insurance, replacing the previous policy of providing only employment support. It also promised to continue employment support and announced the introduction of an employment support benefit of ¥30,000 per month for young people. It promised further to implement the 2002 self-reliance support law for homeless people, partly because it had been based on a DPJ proposal (DPJ 2009).

In order to ameliorate the LDP's regressive tax system, the government planned to abolish some income deductions for dependent families and introduce three kinds of refundable tax credits. One of these is an in-work tax credit, which is similar to what are generally called earned income tax credits, to stimulate employment by increasing the amount of tax deductions with benefits in proportion to increases in time spent in employment, so that beneficiaries' final incomes increase more than their total wages (DPJ 2009).

Most of the workfare policies enacted by the LDP governments after Koizumi's provided for a package of social security benefit reduction and employment stimulation, but the DPJ has characteristically tried to provide employment incentives by offering benefits without reducing employment stimulation itself. It has not, however, been able to enact all of the policies it proposed in its manifesto. It restored livelihood protection to single mothers in the form of an extra allowance immediately after it took power, but it has not abolished the system of reducing single mothers' child care benefits. It has frozen them by administrative ordinance instead, but the possibility of reducing the benefits of mothers not searching for employment remains. It has also not gone beyond reforming the cost of welfare services for people with disabilities and has made no progress in reforming vocational training with benefits and the employment support benefit for young people or the working tax credit (DPJ 2009, 2010).

It is unclear in the second half of 2010 what direction the DPJ's new policies will take. It only assumed power in 2009, and some reform policies are still at the preparation stage. The prospects for some policies being enacted, however, appear to be unlikely due to overoptimism with regard to finance at the time it published its manifesto.

Effects of employment promotion

Workfare is part of the strategy for the recommodification of the work force and constitutes an important part of neoliberal social policy. Its objective is to promote the latent and actual employment of welfare beneficiaries and to discontinue their dependence on public benefits. Japanese workfare advocates call this self-reliance support, and have used various techniques for achieving this objective, generally by offering cash benefits and such benefits in kind as vocational training in various combinations in exchange for labour. The ultimate criterion for judging whether such policies are effective is how well they promote employment. It is too early to make an overall judgement of Japanese workfare in the 2000s, but a partial evaluation is possible.

The number of employed people with disabilities has been increasing since the mid-2000s, rising from 2,230,000 in 2000 and 2,220,000 in 2004 to 2,510,000 in 2007. Their rate of employment also increased: the percentage of organizations achieving the legal employment quota in 2007 was 97.4 per cent for government agencies and 45.5 per cent for private firms. These figures may be overestimated, however, because the method of statistical calculation has changed since the 2006 fiscal year (MHLW 2010).

Employment promotion's effectiveness has, however, been limited for beneficiaries other than those with disabilities. Some welfare offices, for example, had still not implemented the self-reliance support programme by 2008, and most of those that had had done so on a limited basis only (Ministry of Internal Affairs and Communications (MIC) 2008). Few public assistance beneficiaries utilize the employment support project, however, although the employment rate of those who did take part in the Employment Support Project was 41.1 per cent in the 2005 fiscal year and 60.6 per cent in 2006. Only twenty-two of the 9,129 people who took part in the employment support project in the 2006 fiscal year utilized the trial employment for the promotion of permanent employment programme; only five of these twenty-two achieved permanent employment (MIC 2008). Miyamoto (2009: 122) noted that 'it created much temporary and unstable employment and was consequently unhelpful in supporting self-reliant employment'.

Iwata (2006) noted that the self-reliance support of homeless people programme in Tokyo achieved its objective with only about a quarter of those who stayed in the emergency temporary support centre, and that those sleeping rough in the parks and by the river showed no interest in the programme. She added that this was because it failed to attract them. The number of NEETs has remained at approximately 630,000 since 2002 (MHLW 2010), a clear indication that the government's employment promotion programmes for them have been ineffective. Kosugi (2006) observed that the independent youth cram schools for NEETs and the one-stop employment support centres for them had difficulty in attracting participants, partly because young people felt a stigma attached to attending these institutions. The new government discontinued the cram school programme in 2010, having judged it to be ineffective (Government Revitalization Unit 2009; MHLW 2010). The employment rate among single mothers, already high, has remained relatively stable throughout the 2000s (MHLW 2007; Uzuhashi 2007; Miyamoto 2009).

Japan's workfare programmes have therefore failed to increase employment significantly among single mothers, homeless people, unemployed young people and public assistance beneficiaries, although they did achieve some success with regard to the employment of people with disabilities.

Conclusion

The effects of Japan's workfare programmes for homeless people and NEETs were clearly limited. It is, however, necessary to note that homeless people and NEETs became a problem within the context of the labour market flexibility that resulted from globalization. Such supportive policies as workfare could by themselves have but a limited effect in enabling their employment. A comprehensive employment policy that includes job creation is necessary.

Workfare has not increased the employment rate for single mothers because they already tended to be employed in Japan, and because the measures to reduce employment support have worked well. The employment rate for single mothers was 89.4 per cent in 1998, 83.0 per cent in 2003 and 84.5 per cent in 2006. It has remained relatively stable throughout the 2000s (MHLW 2007; Uzuhashi 2007; Miyamoto 2009). It is notably higher than it tends to be internationally, and it is worth noting that, although workfare basically started as a policy to address single mothers' welfare dependency in the US, this has not been a problem in Japan.

The same is true of public assistance beneficiaries. In other advanced countries, one of the reasons for promoting workfare has been to enable unemployed people to become independent of public assistance. Japan's benefit system, however, is not only for those who are structurally unemployed, as its livelihood protection form of public assistance also covers people who are able to work. Most Japanese public assistance beneficiaries, however, more than 80 per cent in 2005, were old people and people with disabilities and illnesses, which makes Japan different from other advanced countries with regard to its need for workfare (Uzuhashi 2003). The workfare that the Koizumi government introduced tended to be ineffective because Japanese social policy had already been employment oriented. Uzuhashi (1997) insisted that welfare in Japan was already intrinsically a workfare system.

The slogan 'from welfare to employment' became much less prominent after the change in government, and has no longer appeared in the minutes of the Diet, as it makes no sense to say it to working people. What matters to them is the type of employment they have. It also makes no sense to say it when few employment opportunities are available. In August 2010, the unemployment rate was more than 5 per cent and the job–offer ratio was less than 0.6. If the government were to offer employment promotion independently of welfare, it would be highly unlikely to be effective. A combination of employment and welfare is important, instead. The relationship between welfare and employment in Japan has apparently entered a new stage as the country's experiment with neoliberalism has ended.

Bibliography

Cabinet Office, Government of Japan (2005) *Jakunen Mugyosha nikansuru Chosa* (Survey of NEET). Online. Available at www8.cao.go.jp/youth/kenkyu/shurou/chukan.pdf (11 February 2010).

Cabinet Secretariat (2003) *Wakamono Jiritsu Chosen Plan* (Challenge Plan for the Independence of Youths). Online. Available at www.meti.go.jp/topic/downloadfiles/e40423bj1.pdf (4 March 2011).

——(2004) *Wakamono no Jiritsu Chosen notameno Akushon Puran* (Action Plan for the Independence and Challenge of Youths). Online. Available at www.meti.go.jp/topic/downloadfiles/e60117aj1.pdf (4 March 2011).

Council on Economic and Fiscal Policy (CEFP) (2003) *Keizai Zaisei Unei to Kozo Kaikaku nikansuru Kihon Hoshin* (Basic Policies for Economic and Fiscal Management and Structural Reform 2003). Online. Available at www5.cao.go.jp/keizai-shimon/cabinet/2003/0627kakugikettei.pdf (accessed 23 November 2010).

DPJ (Democratic Party Japan) (2009) *Manifesto 2009*.

——(2010) *Manifesto 2010*.

Flora, P. (ed.) (1986) *Growth to Limits*, 5 vols, Berlin and New York: Walter de Gruyter.

Government Revitalization Unit (2009) *Dai 2 WG Hyoka Komento* (Budget Screening Report). Online. Available at www.cao.go.jp/sasshin/oshirase/h-kekka/pdf/nov11-kekka/2-7.pdf (accessed 23 November 2010).

Iwata, M. (2006) 'Fukushi Seisaku no Nakano Shuro Shien' (Welfare and Workfare in Social Policies for the Poor), *Shakai-Seisaku Gakkaishi* (*Journal of Social Policy and Labor Studies* 16.

Johnson, N. (1990) *Restructuring the Welfare State: A Decade of Change*, Hemel Hempstead: Harvester Wheatsheaf.

Kawakami, T. and Masuda, T. (eds) (1989) *Shinhoshushugi no Keizai Shakai Seisaku* (Neoconservative Economic and Social Policy), Tokyo: Hosei Daigaku Shuppankyoku.

Kosugi, R. (2006) 'Shokugyoseikatsu eno Ikoshien to Fukushi' (School to Work Transition and Social Welfare), *Shakai-Seisaku Gakkaishi* (*Journal of Social Policy and Labor Studies*) 16.

Le Grand, J. and Bartlett, W. (1993) *Quasi-Markets and Social Policy*, Basingstoke, Hampshire: Macmillan Press.

Ministry of Health, Labour and Welfare (MHLW) (2002) Boshikateitou Jiritsu Shien Taisaku Taiko (Guideline on Self-Reliance Support for Single-Mother Families). Online. Available at www.mhlw.go.jp/topics/2002/03/tp0307-3.html (4 March 2011).

——(2004) *Shogaisha Jittai Chosa* (Survey on Employment of Persons with Disabilities). Online. Available at www.mhlw.go.jp/houdou/2004/10/h1019-1.html (accessed 5 December 2010).
——(2005) *Shogaisha Jiritsu Shienho* (The Services and Supports for Persons with Disabilities Act). Online. Available at www.mhlw.go.jp/topics/2005/02/tp0214-1.html (accessed 23 November 2010).
——(2007) *On the Scheme of Employment Quota*. Online. Available at www.mhlw.go.jp/bunya/koyou/shougaisha/04.html (accessed 23 November 2010).
——(2007) *The Five-Year Plan to Promote 'From Welfare To Employment'*. Online. Available at www.kantei.go.jp/jp/singi/seichou2/dai4/siryou3.pdf (23 November 2010).
——(2009) *Kokumin Seikatsu Kiso Chosa Heisei 20 nen* (Comprehensive Survey of Living Conditions of the People on Health and Welfare, Heisei 20), Tokyo: Kosei Tokei Kyokai.
——(2010) *Rodo Keizai Hakusho* (White Paper on the Labour Economy), Tokyo: Nikkei Insatsu.
——(2010) *Kihon Goishi* (Basic Agreement on Single Mother Addition). Online. Available at www.mhlw.go.jp/stf/houdou/2r98520000005gqy-img/2r98520000005gsg.pdf (accessed 23 November 2010).
——(2010) 'Heisei 21 nen 6 gatsu 1 nichi Genzai no Shogaisha no Koyojokyo nituite' (Employment Situation of Persons with Disabilities as of June 1, 2009). Online. Available at www.mhlw.go.jp/stf/houdou/2r98520000002i9x-img/2r98520000002ibf.pdf (4 March 2011).
——(n.d.) *On the Abolishment of Youth Independent Cram Schools*. Online. Available at www.mhlw.go.jp/bunya/nouryoku/jiritsu/ (accessed 23 November 2010).
MIC (Ministry of Internal Affairs and Communications) (2008) 'Seikatsuhogo ni Kansuru Gyosei Hyoka Kanshi Kekka ni Motozuku Kankoku: Jiritsu Shien Proguramu wo Chushin toshite' (Administrative Evaluation of Livelihood Support and Recommendation Based on Monitoring Results Based on the Self-Reliance Support Program).
Miyamoto, J. (2009) 'Seikatsu Hogo Seido ni okeru Shuro Shien no Yukosei to Seizonken no Hosho' (Effectiveness of Employment Support in the Livelihood Protection and Security of the Right to Live), *Kagawa Daigaku Keizai Seisaku Kenkyu* (*Journal of Economic Policy Studies*, Kagawa University) No. 5.
Miyamoto, T. (ed.) (2002) *Fukushi Kokka Saihen no Seiji* (The Politics of Welfare State Restructuring), Kyoto: Mineruba Shobo.
Niki, R. (2007) *Iryo Kaikaku* (Medical Care Reform), Tokyo: Keiso Shobo.
OECD (1981) *The Welfare State in Crisis*, Paris: OECD.
——(2001) *Employment Outlook*, Paris: OECD.
Osawa, M. (2007) *Gendai Nihon no Seikatsu Hosho Sisutemu* (The Livelihood Security System in Contemporary Japan), Tokyo: Iwanami Shoten.
Papadakis, E. and Taylor-Gooby, P. (1987) *The Private Provision of Public Welfare: State, Market and Community*, Brighton, Sussex: Wheatsheaf.
Shindo, M. (1996) *Fukushi Gyosei to Kanryosei* (Welfare Administration and Bureaucracy), Tokyo: Iwanami Shoten.
Society for the Study of Social Policy (SSSP) (ed.) (2006) *Shakai Seisaku niokeru Fukushi to Shuro* (Linking Welfare and Work), Kyoto: Horitsu-Bunka sha.
Special Committee on the Livelihood Protection System (2004) *Seikatsu Hogo no Arikata nikansuru Senmon Iinkai Hokokusho* (The Report of Special Committee on

the Livelihood Protection System). Online. Available at www.mhlw.go.jp/shingi/2004/12/s1215-8a.html (accessed 4 March 2011).

Takegawa, S. (1999) *Shakai Seisaku no Nakano Gendai* (Welfare State and Welfare Society), Tokyo: Tokyo Daigaku Shuppankai.

——(2005) 'Japan's Welfare Regime: Welfare Politics, Provider and Regulator', *Development and Society* 34, 2: 169–90.

——(2009a) *Shakai Seisaku no Shakaigaku* (The Sociology of Social Policy), Kyoto: Minerva Shobo.

——(2009b) 'International Circumstances as Factors in Building a Welfare State: Welfare Regimes in Europe, Japan and Korea', *International Journal of Japanese Sociology* 18: 79–96.

Uzuhashi, T. (1997) *Gendai Fukushi Kokka no Kokusai Hikaku* (International Comparison of Modern Welfare States), Tokyo: Nippon Hyoronsha.

——(2003) 'Koteki Fujo Seido wo Meguru Kokusaiteki Doko to Seisakuteki Gani' (International Trends of the Public Assistance System and Policy Implication)', *Hikaku no Nakano Fukushi Kokka* (Welfare States in Comparison), Kyoto: Minerva Shobo.

——(ed.) (2007) *Wakufea: Haijo kara hosetsu e?* (Workfare: From Exclusion to Inclusion?), Kyoto: Horitsu-Bunka sha.

7 Workfare in South Korea

Delivering unemployment benefits in the developmental welfare state

Huck-ju Kwon and Jooha Lee[1]

New directions of the developmental welfare state

East Asian welfare states may be characterized as developmental ones (Holliday 2000; Kwon 2005). This concept illustrates how they have become organized so that they utilize their social policies as instruments for economic development.

Countries outside East Asia have also adopted this approach to welfare. Sweden was an early pioneer, and the US and UK developed their own versions of it, with a neoliberal orientation, in the late 1980s. The developmentalist, sometimes called the productivist, approach generally refers to a strategy involving the two interrelated initiatives of linking income maintenance to work and making social investments in education, job training and other active labour market policies that have the objective of increasing productivity (Esping-Andersen 1996). Different institutional legacies and balances of domestic political forces, combined with changing socioeconomic circumstances, mean that the developmentalist strategy is likely to take different forms in different countries and at different times in the same country.

East Asian developmental welfare states tend to have the objective of protecting workers in strategic sectors in order to further economic development. The overriding concern of most of them has been to impose a minimal financial burden on the state, which has resulted in low levels of public spending on social welfare. The Korean state has therefore been less involved in providing social provision than its Western counterparts, but it has played a significant welfare role as a regulator (Kwon 1999; Shin 2000).

The Korean state shifted the responsibility for welfare on to companies and families, using its regulatory power to force the private sector to provide and finance certain types of social provision and care. Korean companies' commitment to lifetime employment and the automatic seniority system has also compensated for this lack of state welfare provision in addition to family- and company-provided welfare. The large business sector has been willing to provide its work force with company welfare and employment stability in order to secure a stable supply of skilled workers in the manufacturing and chemical industries (Chung 2006).

The general strategy's successes have included the impressive economic development of such countries as Korea and Taiwan during the past five decades. Its exclusive focus on economic objectives has, however, led to the neglect of the intrinsic goal of social policy, which is protecting the poor, the elderly and such other vulnerable people as workers in the informal sector, who are more vulnerable to unfavourable economic and social factors than those in the formal sector. Furthermore, for a long time, these counties provided unemployed people with no social protection.

The East Asian economic crisis of 1997–98 brutally exposed the weaknesses of this approach, however, and after it was over, such East Asian countries as Korea and Taiwan expanded their existing social policy programmes to cover those who had been left outside their welfare programmes. These reforms placed new emphasis on social protection for the unemployed and the poor (Shin 2000; Ramesh 2003; Holliday & Wilding 2003; Kwon 2005).

A debate has been taking place in the literature addressing East Asian social policy about the nature of the expansion of the region's welfare states. Kwon and Holliday (2007) argued that these states began expanding their welfare provision in order to meet the need for structural adjustment that arose from the economic crisis and that no change occurred in their economy-first rationales. Others, such as Kim (2008), have maintained that the extension of these welfare states has signified a new policy direction towards the establishment of social rights.

Both arguments certainly make good points. Kwon (2005) argued that Korea's welfare reforms resulting from the crisis involved both continuity and change. The changes included such new programmes as a minimum living standard guarantee (MLSG) – also referred to as the National Basic Livelihood Security Programme – and an extension of its Employment Insurance Programme (EIP), which had the intention of providing social protection to those whom Korea's developmental welfare state had previously neglected, thereby making it more inclusive. Korea, along with other East Asian countries, has also experienced continuity with regard to its state's welfare policies by maintaining a developmental orientation. The expansion of its provision of welfare during the economic crisis was actually part of a structural economic reform policy package, as it extended its unemployment benefits in order to facilitate the structural reform of its industries, which inevitably led to a sharp rise in unemployment. The EIP, which includes the extended unemployment benefits, has a strong workfare orientation, and the MLSG, which provides poor people with a national minimum income, also has workfare requirements.

The EIP, which the previous government had planned,[2] was implemented in 1995 under the terms of the Employment Insurance Act adopted in 1993. The government then viewed a flexible labour market as a prerequisite for enhancing economic competitiveness, and the EIP was a complementary element in the process of making the labour market flexible (Yi & Lee 2005: 154). According to the final report of the Employment Insurance Research Commission (1993), which had been established to draft the Employment Insurance

Bill, the EIP's aim was to facilitate Korea's industrial restructuring process of upgrading to high-tech industry and enhancing the economy's efficiency. As the state's role as a provider is minimal, the EIP is financed by premiums paid by the insured and their employers, with no financial contribution from the state except administration costs (Kwon 1999; Chung 2006).

This presence of both continuity and change leads to the conclusion that Korea's developmental welfare state has maintained its developmentalist orientation while simultaneously becoming more inclusive by providing social protection to the vulnerable. Introducing new policy programmes, however, does not guarantee their effective implementation for the achievement of their policy goals. This chapter therefore examines Korea's unemployment programmes' implementation at the local level. The next section first identifies the overall structural changes in Korea's approach to providing welfare that emerged in the ten years following the East Asian economic crisis of 1997–98. It then describes the range of social programmes and services that Korea has provided since then. The chapter proceeds to examine the difficulties that local officials have experienced in implementing the workfare programmes, including excerpts from interviews with some of them. The chapter subsequently addresses the difficulties that unemployed people face when claiming their benefits by reporting findings from a focus group interview (FGI) that we conducted with several of them. It then analyses these interviews and reaches conclusions with regard to whether Korea's developmental welfare state has successfully achieved its policy goal of inclusive social protection.

New features of Korea's developmental welfare state

The Korean welfare state that emerged ten years after the onset of the reforms prompted by the East Asian economic crisis included the five social insurance programmes of Industrial Accident Insurance (IAI), National Health Insurance (NHI), the National Pension Programme (NPP), the EIP and Long-Term Care Insurance (LTCI). It also included the two social assistance programmes of the MLSG and a basic old-age allowance, which the state provided for people aged 65 and older whose monthly incomes were less than 680,000, which is about US$600 at the current exchange rate, and special public pension programmes for civil servants, private school teachers and military personnel.

Introduced in 1961, IAI was Korea's first state welfare programme and illustrates the nature of its developmental welfare state. It originally covered workers in workplaces of 500 or more employees. The number of workplaces that it covers has increased gradually as Korea's industrialization has gathered momentum and, by mid-2010, all workplaces with more than one regular employee have to participate in it. It covered 44 per cent of all gainfully employed people in 2005. Those who fall outside the programme are farmers, self-employed people and casual employees.

The second of the Korean developmental welfare state's programmes is NHI. It became a compulsory programme in 1977, when it protected workers employed by large-scale industrial enterprises, public sector workers and private school teachers. Most employees in the industrial sector had access to it by 1987, but self-employed people, farmers and others without employers fell outside it. As Korea's democratization movement intensified in the late 1980s, social grievances against the NHI programme became a political issue, and all the candidates during the 1987 presidential election campaign promised its universalization.

In 1988–89, the democratically elected government extended NHI to the entire population, providing financial subvention for those people not paying premiums. The remaining problem was integrating the more than 300 fragmented health insurance funds operating under its umbrella throughout the country, as their financial conditions were so diverse that people had many different degrees of health care protection. The Kim Dae-jung government accomplished this in 2000, thereby achieving inclusion and equality in Korean health care.

LTCI is a new social insurance programme that the government implemented in 2008 in conjunction with NHI. It combines its payroll contributions with people's NHI premiums, so that everyone who pays NHI premiums pays an additional 3 per cent on them for LTCI. It provides long-term care services to people aged 60 and older who have difficulty with activities of daily living. Social workers interview the elderly applicants for these services to assess their needs. Once their applications have been approved, they can receive either in-home or institutionalized care. The care providers have contracts with the NHI programme, which also requires those receiving care to make co-payments.

The NPP is the Korean developmental welfare state's third main element. The government first considered introducing a national pension in the early 1970s in order to mobilize domestic savings for industrialization, but postponed its implementation because of the 1973 oil crisis, eventually reintroducing it in 1988. Because it is an insurance-structured programme, it began, similarly to NHI, with manufacturing sector employees and, by 1994, covered 26.7 per cent of the working population (Kwon 1999). Farmers, self-employed people and those employed under short-term contracts joined the programme in 1999. It underwent its most significant reform in 2007 when, in order to enhance its financial sustainability, it began the process of reducing its replacement rate for average earners from 60 per cent to 40 per cent over the next twenty years. This reform also triggered reforms of the public pension programmes for civil servants and school teachers.

The EIP was implemented in 1995 to provide unemployment benefits. As its name suggests, it both promotes employment and provides unemployment benefits, making it a typical workfare programme. It also provides job security grants and training grants to employers. Table 7.1 details this graphically. Job security grants subsidize employers who retain their employees instead of laying them off. The training grants provide eligible workers with training vouchers that they can redeem at training institutes of their choice to obtain training for new job skills. This programme was the last addition to Korea's

Table 7.1 The Employment Insurance Programme's structure

Area	Aim	Grants
Job security	Employment restructuring	Grants for retraining, re-employment and job change
	Promoting job creation	Grants for the employers of the elderly, long-term unemployment, women and childcare facilities
	Severance payments for construction workers	Contributions to the fund for severance payments for construction workers
Training and skill development	Supporting employers	Grants for training workers, training facilities and similar
	Supporting workers	Grants for further education, skill development and similar
	Supporting construction workers	Grants for further education, skill development and similar
Unemployment	Income support	Unemployment benefits
	Promoting job-seeking activities	Allowance for early job-finders; grants for moving to new jobs
Maternity	Maternity protection	Allowance for childbirth; allowance for maternity leave

Source: Mo (2005)

developmental welfare state before the East Asian economic crisis. This chapter will discuss it in more detail later.

As the Korean approach places so much emphasis on work, the government did not consider the provision of unemployment insurance to be an option in the 1980s. Its introduction in 1995 was a sign of the ongoing changes in the state's concept of welfare provision. It was nevertheless a lukewarm effort and failed to bring about any significant changes at the time; during the 1997 economic crisis, only 7.8 per cent of Korea's unemployed workers received benefits from it (Employment Insurance Corporation 2001). However, the government then extended the programme's coverage swiftly by loosening its eligibility requirements, and the proportion of unemployed workers receiving benefits rose to 33.1 per cent in 1999.

The MLSG is another important aspect of the new characteristics of Korea's developmental welfare state. Unlike Korea's other social welfare programmes, a movement originating in the country's civil society initiated its introduction (Ahn 2000). Its rationale is that all Koreans deserve at least a minimum standard of living as a matter of right, a radical departure from the previous assistance programme, whose scope and level of benefits had been notably limited. Funded entirely by central and local governments, it is a social assistance programme that provides benefits to poor people if their income is below the poverty line regardless of their age and family conditions, although it does require that its recipients aged between 18 and 64 participate in training, public work projects or community service if they are unemployed. Those who have family members who have responsibility for them are basically ineligible, but they can claim the benefit if the family members responsible are unable to provide support. Under the previous social assistance programme, everyone between the ages of 18 and 64 and all those with family members responsible for them were ineligible to receive benefits (Ministry of Health and Welfare 2000).

Figure 7.1 illustrates the overall trend of Korean government spending on social protection from 1999 to 2009. Overall spending increased in nominal terms as such existing social insurance programmes as the NPP and NHI matured. Expenditures on social insurance in particular increased steadily, mainly due to the NPP.

Therefore, the Korean state's approach to welfare provision now encompasses a wide range of social welfare programmes such as health insurance, pensions, unemployment benefits and a minimum standard of living. Its evolution from a bare social insurance structure to comprehensive social protection is a remarkable achievement. It is also clear that its programmes have steadily aimed to be more inclusive and to protect those who had been shut out.

Although Korean state welfare includes a range of social insurance programmes and social services, not all of them cover everyone. Table 7.2 compares the programmes' coverage by employment status among wage and salary earners in 2001 with that in 2007. The pension, health insurance and employment insurance programmes extended their coverage during that interval. It is important to note the presence of a clear difference between regular employees and temporary employees without secure long-term contracts. Although almost all regular employees participated in the NPP in 2007, only 33.9 per cent of

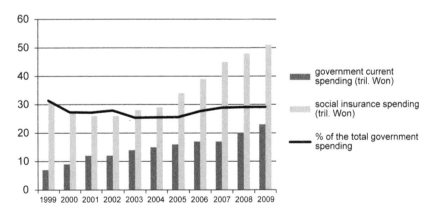

Figure 7.1 Government spending on social protection
Source: National Statistical Office

Table 7.2 Social insurance coverage (%) by employment status

		Wage and salary earners	Regular employees	Temporary employees
NPP	2001	51.8	92.7	19.3
	2007	62.6	98.8	33.9
NHI	2001	54.3	94.8	22.2
	2007	63.9	99.3	35.8
EIP	2001	46.9	80.0	20.7
	2007	55.6	83.8	33.3

Source: Kim, Y.S. (2001, 2007)
Note: Wage and salary earners include both regular employees and casual employees.

temporary workers did. A similar difference exists with regard to the other two programmes (Kim 2001, 2007).

Those who are not in paid employment can join the NHI programme as residence-based members, which enables almost everyone to be covered by health insurance. This, however, is only the case with regard to health insurance. Approximately 25 per cent of the working-age population is outside of the NPP, for example. Among its residence-based participants, 20.3 per cent pay contributions, and 27.6 per cent of all NPP participants make no contributions. This means that the NPP pays no pensions to a large segment of the population.

As the EIP is only for permanent wage and salary earners, self-employed people, farmers and temporary workers are simply outside it. Table 7.3 compares the demographics of those who participate in the EIP with those who do not. It shows that a significant majority of its participants are male, its largest age group is those aged between 30 and 39, and its largest educational

Table 7.3 Composition (%) of Employment Insurance Programme participants and non-participants

Demographic group		Among insiders	Among outsiders
Male		65.8	49.7
Female		34.2	50.3
Age (years)			
	29 and younger	24.5	19.0
	30–39	39.6	23.8
	40–49	21.8	34.2
	50–59	12.4	19.5
	60 and older	1.7	3.5
Education			
	Middle school or less	1.8	4.0
	High school	44.3	67.7
	Junior college	23.4	13.6
	University	27.4	12.5
	Postgraduate	3.3	2.2

Source: Kim, Y.S. (2010)

group is those with a high school education. Furthermore, workers in the construction, retailing and service sectors were less likely to participate in it than workers in the manufacturing sector (Kim 2010).

Local implementation of employment insurance

The Kim Dae-jung government quickly expanded the EIP's coverage at the onset of the 1997 economic crisis. Its unemployment benefit component had initially covered only workers in workplaces with more than thirty employees, and its employment stabilization and job skill development components workplaces with more than seventy employees. A series of reforms extended the coverage of all three components to all workplaces by October 1998. The number of recipients of unemployment benefits consequently rose from 49,117 in 1997 to 411,686 in 1998 (Korea Employment Information Service 2005).

The first eligibility requirement for unemployment benefits is that claimants pay contributions for at least a certain period of time before losing their jobs. They must also be actively seeking a job and demonstrate this by registering at an employment security centre and remaining ready and able to work. They lose their benefits if they refuse a job or training course to which their centre has directed them. Those who voluntarily leave their jobs without a justifiable reason such as economic restructuring, their firm's geographical relocation and difficulties in adapting to new technologies, or who lose their jobs due to negligence, do not qualify for the benefit. The government only relaxed the first of these eligibility conditions, the minimum contribution requirements, in the aftermath of the 1997 crisis.

The eligibility condition of actively seeking employment is closely related to the EIP's workfare elements. The OECD (2000) reported that the Korean unemployment benefit scheme contained such activation elements designed to encourage the re-employment of beneficiaries as job search requirements and employment promotion allowances. The programme also has other examples of job search requirements such as requiring claimants who apply for unemployment benefits to apply simultaneously for work, requiring unemployment beneficiaries to visit their employment security centres regularly to prove that they are job-hunting and providing sanctions for beneficiaries who have fraudulently circumvented the job search requirements (Ministry of Labour 2006). The implementation of the job search requirements, however, has not been as rigorous as that for which the Employment Insurance Act provides.

Local officials at the employment security centres have the responsibility of verifying the accuracy of job-seeking activities. In our first wave of interviews with such officers, several told us that they had been hampered by a shortage of office personnel. In a 2005 interview, for instance, one told us, 'In the present situation, we cannot classify claimants' desire for jobs at all, and even if they falsely report their job-search activities we grant the benefits regardless of whether such activities are true'.[3]

The programme's employment promotion allowances consist of an early re-employment allowance, a vocational training promotion allowance, a wide-area job-seeking allowance and a moving allowance. The programme pays early re-employment allowances to beneficiaries who find stable jobs or start their own businesses before exhausting the duration of their benefits. The vocational training promotion allowance is available to those who undergo training to which the head of their employment security centre has directed them. The programme may pay the wide-area job-seeking allowance to those who are looking for jobs that their employment security centre has offered them, but are more than 50 kilometres away from their residence. It pays the moving allowance to those who move to another place to start a new job or to undergo a training course as directed by the head of their employment security centre (Ministry of Labour 2006).

The percentage of the beneficiaries of the early re-employment allowance to total beneficiaries has steadily increased, but was still only 15 per cent in 2008. The ratios of those receiving the vocational training promotion, wide-area job-seeking and moving allowances to the total have also been negligible (Korea Employment Information Service 2005, 2008). These initiatives have therefore been of limited use in facilitating beneficiaries' re-entry into the labour market.

The eligibility condition addressing the nature of the job loss accounts for a large proportion of the ineligibility of those who fail to receive unemployment benefits. The criteria for determining the validity of the reasons for job loss are much tighter than those in many Organisation for Economic Co-operation and Development (OECD) countries, where in some cases even those who quit jobs without good cause are entitled to unemployment benefits after a certain amount of time (OECD 2000; Lee *et al.* 2006). It can be argued that the EIP's beneficiaries have represented too limited a proportion of Korea's unemployed workers for it to be considered a primary social protection against unemployment. A total of 41.1 per cent of all employment and 58.1 per cent of all paid workers were eligible for the EIP in June 2010 (Korea Employment Information Service 2010). This can be attributed to a number of factors in addition to the strict eligibility requirements.

In 2010, the EIP still applied to neither self-employed people nor unpaid family workers, who constitute a larger share of total employment in Korea than in other OECD countries. Self-employment in Korea was 29 per cent of all employment in 1999, the second highest in the OECD, and unpaid family workers constituted 9 per cent of the work force in that year, much higher than in all other OECD countries except Mexico, Greece and Turkey (OECD 2000).

Certain part-time workers, workers older than 65, civil servants and private school teachers are ineligible for coverage by the EIP (Article 8 of the Employment Insurance Act). Furthermore, many daily workers, part-time workers and workers in small businesses who should legally be covered by the EIP have not actually been insured, mainly because of limited administrative capacity and the non-payment of contributions, as the government extended EIP coverage to daily workers without hiring new staff. As a local employment security centre employee told us in a 2005 interview, 'Almost the same number of employment security centre officials are handling new entrants as well as existing beneficiaries. ... The quality of services cannot help decreasing as much as the number of beneficiaries increases'.

Sometimes, daily workers, part-time workers and employees of small businesses fail to be insured simply because their employers have neither registered them nor transferred their social contributions to the Employment Insurance Fund, creating gaps between de jure and de facto coverage. The Korean labour market has developed a deepening duality between regular employees and such casual employees as temporary and daily ones (Kim 2001, 2007, 2010). The OECD (2000) officially defines regular employees as those who work for more than one year and are paid the standard wage plus bonuses and overtime pay. Temporary workers are employed for a determined length of time, usually longer than a month and shorter than a year. Daily workers are those employed on a daily basis, but in practice, most daily workers tend to be employed at a particular establishment for longer than one day.

Korea has a relatively low rate of regular or permanent employment (OECD 2000), and the proportion of casual workers, who are often referred to as *outsiders*, in contrast to regular employee *insiders* who receive the protection of the social insurance programmes, has been increasing. The EIP covered only 35.4 per cent of all outsider workers as of March 2010, at which time it covered 82.3 per cent of insider workers (Kim 2010).

The government strengthened the job skill development programme under the EIP and other active labour market measures in order to alleviate the adverse impact of the 1997 crisis on Korea's labour market. For example, it provided vocational training to 360,000 people in 1998, eight times more than in 1997, and such private sector institutions as universities and other educational facilities participated in vocational training far more actively than ever before. By 2004, more than two million employees were participating in the EIP's job skill development programme and the training participation rate of insured workers was 27.1 per cent (Lee *et al.* 2006).

It is vital to consolidate and improve the role of the local employment security centres in order to make the implementation of Korea's active labour market policies effective (Fay 1996; OECD 2000). Such government documents as Ministry of Labour (2006) have also highlighted the importance of having effectively functioning employment security centres in order to promote the active labour market programmes but, although they have succeeded in providing basic job vacancy information and simple job matching, they have also had clear limitations in their delivery of intensive counselling and tailored career guidance.

Unlike in most other OECD countries, Korea's employment security centres operate under the direct authority of the Ministry of Labour and not as a separate, autonomous agency (OECD 2000: 148). This means that they do not have budgetary autonomy, their own source of financing or the authority to select their own officials, including their overall director. They are also subject to ministerial direction in policy matters. However, the central government has provided them with inadequate autonomy, staffing and budgetary support, resulting in their inability to provide adequate services (Lee *et al.* 2006; Lee 2009). The average number of allocated job-seekers for each employment security centre employee in 2005 was 400, which was four times larger than the standard recommended by the International Labour Organization (ILO) that the OECD used as a comparison standard (Ministry of Labour 2005). Employment security centre employees also have a heavy administrative workload and perform many other tasks in addition to job counselling. In a 2005 interview, one of them told us, 'The central government requires a great deal of general administrative work on top of job brokering'.

Another clear obstacle is insufficient financial resources, although building and developing infrastructure for the labour market such as the employment security centres is a prerequisite for the successful implementation of active labour market policies. According to the EIP's tenth anniversary report, its fund is supposed to finance Korea's labour market infrastructure (Kim 2006). Figure 7.2 shows that Korea had the lowest level of public expenditure on active labour market policies – including the employment security centres – as a percentage of gross domestic product (GDP) in the OECD. Even considering such related factors as the unemployment rate, the labour force participation rate and per capita GDP, Korean government spending on its active labour market measures is small by international standards (Keum 2005).

The EIP has included and emphasized such active labour market measures as its job skill development programme from the start, whereas traditional Western unemployment insurance or benefit systems have tended to concentrate initially on paying unemployment benefits. This implies that the Korean government intended the EIP to pursue active labour market policies

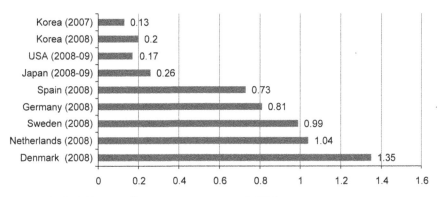

Figure 7.2 ALMP expenditure as a percentage of GDP
Source: OECD (2010)
Note: There is a statistical break in Korea between 2007 and 2008 due to an extensive revision of the reporting framework. The US fiscal year starts on 1 October and Japan's on 1 April

without direct government financing, as it is a compulsory social insurance system financed by employers and employees. Its job skill development programme is, however, the nation's key active labour market policy, so the government needs to take a certain amount of financial responsibility for it in its budget.

Claiming unemployment benefits at the local level

In order to capture the diversity of the experiences of unemployed people who attempt to claim unemployment benefits, we traced the different paths they take to do so. We conducted an FGI with six people who had different work experiences in August 2010. Table 7.4 presents the personal profiles of this FGI's participants.

The FGI clearly revealed that a big difference existed with regard to accessing unemployment benefits between participant F, a woman who had been an office worker, and the others. The difference involved their first step in the process of claiming the benefits, which involved meeting the eligibility requirements of having contributed to the EIP for a minimum of one year and the job loss being involuntary.

F said, 'I had to quit my job because the company carried out a restructuring programme. I heard from my friends that I'd need a letter from the company certifying that I was made unemployed involuntarily. I had no difficulty in getting the certificate from the company. I'm now in the last month of the six-month period of unemployment benefit payments. I think that the benefits have been very helpful to me in getting through to this month and I'm now searching for a new job'.

Some of them had been unable to get the certificate from their former employers, such as a female junior nurse referred to here as D, who said, 'Hospitals normally try to avoid involuntary unemployment. Managers tend to assign people to difficult jobs, such as those in emergency rooms, when they want them to quit. If a junior nurse quits a job because of such difficulties the hospitals don't give them a certificate of involuntary unemployment'.

Others had been unable to maintain a full year of EIP contributions. One was a male construction worker referred to here as B, who said, 'Because I worked in the construction sector it was very difficult to pay the contribution

Table 7.4 FGI participants' personal profiles

Person	Age	Previous employment	Unemployed benefits
A (male)	43	Construction worker	June 2010 to time of FGI
B (male)	59	Construction worker	January–August 2010
C (male)	34	Taxi driver	April–August 2010
D (female)	34	Junior nurse	September–December 1998
E (female)	29	Hairdresser	May–July 2010
F (female)	31	Office worker	February–August 2010

for a year. I only work when work is available. This is true of most construction workers. Luckily this time I managed to contribute for a year and I was able to claim the unemployment benefits'.

A male former taxi driver referred to here as C added, 'I know that the taxi companies don't give the certificates, but my manager gave me one. I'm now trying to find jobs where things are more established than in the taxi industry'.

Their difficulties are mainly the result of the EIP's requirements rather than the service that the employment security centres provide. Although the government mandated the eligibility requirement with regard to involuntary job loss to prevent people from abusing the programme, some employers apparently give certification even if people are voluntarily unemployed. We do not know why some employers have this attitude, but it is plausible that they do not want to appear to government officials to create unemployment. It could be the case that those employers have received grants from the EIP for retaining jobs.

Once unemployed people obtain a certificate, they need to visit their local employment security centre to claim their unemployment benefits. Officials at the centres check all their paperwork, including their certificates. The final eligibility requirement is to show that they are actively seeking jobs. The interviewees had different experiences in their local employment centres, and some of them were unhappy about the receptions they received.

An unemployed female hairdresser, referred to here as E, complained, 'The place was like a market. I found a long queue once I opened the door to the office. It was difficult to find where I should go. Someone told me that I should fill in the form on the computer but there was a long queue there as well'.

F explained, 'I think that there were too many people for the officials to handle all the documents. They looked tired'.

The officials at the local employment centres apparently do not treat people equally. An unemployed male construction worker, referred to here as A, did not have much education and was unhappy with his treatment at his local employment centre. He explained, 'I visited the local employment centre, since I received letters from the tax office saying that I'd contributed to the EIP for more than a year. When I tried to talk to an officer there he didn't listen to me carefully. He told me that I wasn't eligible without checking everything. I was so annoyed that I couldn't continue the conversation and just went home'. He later returned and successfully claimed his benefit.

Once unemployed people have started receiving their benefits, they need to show that they are actively searching for new jobs by regularly visiting their local employment centre and reporting their job-hunting activities either in writing or speaking face to face. The most common method is to bring the business cards of the companies they have visited. B reported that, in order to show his job-hunting activities, 'They told me that I should bring the business cards of the companies I visited or their telephone numbers. Sometimes they said it was okay but sometimes it wasn't enough. I don't know what to do. It seems to depend on how they feel'.

The FGI revealed that people went though different experiences in the process of moving from becoming unemployed to receiving unemployment benefits. Although the former office worker had no significant difficulties with this process, the others had encountered various obstacles. The most frequent problems that they experienced involved obtaining their certificates of involuntary unemployment from the companies for which they had worked. The exercise's clearest finding is that people did not have equal access to unemployment benefits.

Concluding remarks

The twenty-first century has been a time of growth for East Asian developmental welfare states. Whereas its overall structure has maintained its developmental orientation, the Korean state has introduced a range of programmes with the objective of protecting those who had been left outside. This chapter has examined how such continuity and change has been reflected at the local level, where policy objectives are achieved or fail to be achieved in practice, focusing on Korea's EIP. It has examined the case of unemployment benefits, which are in themselves evidence that Korea's welfare policies have undergone a significant change.

At the macro level, Korea now has a wide range of social policies, including IAI, NHI and the NPP, which have been the main pillars of its developmental welfare state and, more recently, the EIP, the MLSG, LTCI and such highly sophisticated programmes as the earned income tax credit. It therefore now meets the criteria of being an inclusively oriented welfare state, although it falls far short of an acceptable level of inclusion, as the EIP, for example, covers less than 60 per cent of the country's wage and salary earners. Although it covers most regular employees, it still covers only about 35 per cent of casual workers.

This chapter has sought to answer the question of whether Korea has implemented its new workfare programmes, particularly the EIP, effectively at the local level. It has found that local officials were unprepared to deal with the EIP's workfare elements on account of insufficient experience, personnel and financial resources. The change that the policy-makers at the top wanted to bring about failed to take place at the local level because of a lack of implementation capacity. We must note, however, that this was the case near the end of 2005, and improvements in implementation have occurred since then.

Our FGI with people claiming unemployment benefits revealed that some people have more difficulty claiming them than others, particularly those with poor education and those who work under temporary contracts. The implementation of the EIP clearly needs to be improved further in order to guarantee fairness while still helping and encouraging unemployed people to find new jobs.

Our analysis of Korea's developmental welfare state from the perspective of implementation presents a mixed overall picture. It has experienced steady progress with regard to the range of social protection it offers, but in terms of inclusion and equal access, it has fallen short of achieving its new policy goals with regard to protecting the unemployed. It has, however, made progress in this area. If the state continues to make efforts to address these shortfalls, it is highly likely to become more inclusive while maintaining its developmental credentials.

Notes

1 This paper draws largely on the authors' previous research such as Kwon (2010) and Lee (2009). This paper is part of the larger research project, Comparing Social Protection in East Asia: Coping Crisis and Reducing Poverty, supported by the Korea Research Foundation.
2 According to an internal document from the Ministry of Labour (1983), in the early 1980s, there was a consensus within the government on the future direction of the unemployment insurance system in Korea as follows. The government should not approach the matter of unemployment with a focus on cash benefits. Instead, the government should prevent unemployment itself in terms of stable economic growth and an effective labour market system. Therefore, the future Korean system should be named the Employment Insurance System rather than the Unemployment Insurance System.
3 Translations of all interview transcripts are by the authors.

Bibliography

Ahn, B.Y. (2000) 'Analysis of Enactment Procedure of National Basic Livelihood Security Act', *Korean Journal of Public Administration* 38: 1–50 (in Korean).

Chung, M.K. (2006) 'The Korean Developmental Welfare Regime: In Search of a New Regime Type in East Asia', *Shakai Seisaku Gakkai Shi (Journal of Social Policy and Labor Studies, Japan)* 16: 149–71.

Employment Insurance Corporation (2001) *Employment Insurance Review*, Seoul: Employment Insurance Corporation (in Korean).

Employment Insurance Research Commission (1993) *The Proposed Employment Insurance System for Korea*, Seoul: Korea Labour Institute (in Korean).

Esping-Andersen, G. (1996) *Welfare States in Transition: National Adpatations in Global Economies*, London: Sage.

Fay, R. (1996) 'Enhancing the Effectiveness of Active Labour Market Policies: Evidence from Programme Evaluation in OECD Countries', *Labour Market and Social Policy* – Occasional Papers no. 18, Paris: OECD.

Holliday, I. (2000) 'Productivist Welfare Capitalism: Social Policy in East Asia', *Political Studies* 48: 706–23.

Holliday, I. and Wilding, P. (eds) (2003) *Welfare Capitalism in East Asia: Social Policy in the Tiger Economies*, Basingstoke: Palgrave Macmillan.

Keum, J.H. (2005) 'Development Direction and Financial Prospect of the Employment Insurance', paper presented at Forum for the Development and Financial Stabilization of the Employment Insurance, 10th Anniversary, Seoul, May (in Korean).

Kim, D.H. (2006) 'Employment Insurance Finance', in Ministry of Labour (ed.) *1995–2005 Employment Insurance, 10th Anniversary*, Seoul: Ministry of Labour (in Korean).

Kim, W.K. (2010) 'An Analysis of the Probability of Participation in the Employment Insurance Program', Graduate School of Public Administration, Seoul National University, Seoul.

Kim, Y.M. (2008) 'Beyond East Asian Welfare Productivism in South Korea', *Policy & Politics* 36: 109–25.

Kim, Y.S. (2001) 'The Size and Conditions of Non-regular Employment', *Monthly Bulletin for Labour & Society*, vol. 59, Seoul: Korea Labour and Society Institute (in Korean).

——(2007) 'The Size and Conditions of Non-regular Employment', *Monthly Bulletin for Labour & Society*, vol. 123, Seoul: Korea Labour and Society Institute (in Korean).

——(2010) 'The Size and Conditions of Non-regular Employment', *Monthly Bulletin for Labour & Society*, vol. 153, Seoul: Korea Labour and Society Institute (in Korean).

Korea Employment Information Service (2005) *Yearly Statistics of Employment Insurance*. Online. Available at http://keis.or.kr/ (accessed 29 September 2010) (in Korean).

——(2008) *Yearly Statistics of Employment Insurance*. Online. Available at http://keis.or.kr/ (accessed 29 September 2010) (in Korean).

——(2010) *Monthly Statistics of Employment Insurance – June 2010*. Online. Available at http://keis.or.kr/ (accessed 29 September 2010) (in Korean).

Kwon, H.J. (1999) 'Inadequate Policy or Operational Failure? The Potential Crisis of the Korean National Pension Programme', *Social Policy & Administration* 33, 1: 20–38.

——(2005) 'Transforming the Developmental Welfare State in East Asia', *Development and Change* 36, 3: 477–97.

——(2010) 'The Developmental Welfare State and the Citizenship', Working paper. Seoul: The Korea Institute of Public Administration.

Kwon, S.M. and Holliday, I. (2007) 'The Korean Welfare State: A Paradox of Expansion in an Era of Globalization and Economic Crisis?', *International Journal of Social Welfare* 16, 3: 242–48.

Lee, J.H. (2009) 'Another Dimension of Welfare Reform: The Implementation of the Employment Insurance Programme in Korea', *International Journal of Social Welfare* 18, 3: 281–90.

Lee, K.Y. et al. (2006) 'EIS Implementation and Evaluation', in J.H. Keum (et al.) *Employment Insurance in Korea: The First Ten Years*, Seoul: Korea Labour Institute.

Ministry of Health and Welfare (2000) *Health and Welfare White Paper*, Seoul: Ministry of Health and Welfare (in Korean).

Ministry of Labour (1983) *Examination of Introducing the Employment Insurance System*, Seoul: Ministry of Labour (in Korean).

——(2005) 'Plan for Upgrading the Employment Assistance Service', paper presented at the Report Meeting for the Reform of the National Employment Assistance Service, Seoul, April (in Korean).

——(2006) *1995–2005 Employment Insurance, 10th Anniversary*, Seoul: Ministry of Labour (in Korean).

Mo, J.W. (2005) *Social Security*, Seoul: Hakjisa (in Korean).

OECD (2000) *Pushing Ahead with Reform in Korea: Labour Market and Social Safety-Net Policies*, Paris: OECD.

——(2010) *OECD Employment Outlook 2010: Moving beyond the Jobs Crisis*, Paris: OECD.

Ramesh, M. (2003) 'Globalization and Social Security Expansion in East Asia', in L. Weiss (ed.) *States in the Global Economy: Bringing Domestic Institutions Back In*, New York: Cambridge University Press.

Shin, D.M. (2000) 'Financial Crisis and Social Security: The Paradox of the Republic of Korea', *International Social Security Review* 53, 3: 83–107.

Yi, I.C. and Lee, B.H. (2005) 'Development Strategies and the Unemployment Polices in Korea', in H.J. Kwon (ed.) *Transforming the Developmental Welfare State in East Asia*, London: Palgrave/UNRISD.

8 Workfare in Singapore

Irene Y.H. Ng

Introduction

Workfare is understood very differently in Singapore compared with many other countries. Whereas workfare, as adopted by the editors of this book, refers to a 'public welfare approach' conditional on work, policy-makers in Singapore view workfare programmes very differently from welfare. Social policy in Singapore is anti-welfare (Peh 2006). Unlike in many other countries where workfare was started from welfare-to-work, Singapore's was started from non-welfare-to-work. Workfare recipients are not former welfare recipients, and had no formal social safety net in the past.

With the above qualifications, workfare can be reframed in this chapter on Singapore as government assistance programmes that push recipients to enter the labour market and improve their employability. We will start by giving the historical background to Singapore's social policy environment, thus giving the backdrop for the development of workfare in Singapore. The main workfare-related policies and programmes will then be described. We start with the Central Provident Fund (CPF), considered to be Singapore's main social security system. Although strictly not a workfare programme, it is a system that promotes work and through which workfare aid is also disbursed. Two direct workfare programmes are then discussed, namely ComCare Self-Reliance and Workfare Income Supplement (WIS). Besides these direct programmes, it is important also to have an overall understanding of the comprehensive efforts to increase skills and employability, and improve the availability of jobs. These continuing education and training (CET) programmes and macroeconomic policy efforts will be discussed before a critique of the impact of workfare efforts so far.

Why non-welfare-to-workfare

A non-welfare state

Social policy in Singapore is anti-welfare (Lian 2008). Even at the height of the global recession in February 2009, the Minister for Community Development,

Youth and Sports (MCYS), Vivian Balakrishnan, opened his Committee of Supply speech by reminding Singaporeans of their values of hard work and self-reliance. While outlining the expansion of programmes for those in financial difficulty during the downturn, he emphasized:

> ... we cannot afford and we should not design a permanent, unconditional and needs-based welfare system, despite the alluring simplicity of giving $400 here and $500 there with no questions asked. That is the road to ruin and it does not work. Nations that have gone down that route are worse off today. We need to make sure we keep on track and we maintain a system that encourages empowerment, not entitlement; dignity, not dependence; self-reliance, not state-reliance.
>
> MCYS (2009a)

The term 'self-reliance' is therefore evoked repeatedly to remind Singaporeans to work hard and not rely on the government. As defined by Minister Balakrishnan, 'self-reliance' means 'enabling a person to work, to provide for his family, to save for his rainy day and to do his best to build a better future. Self reliance does not mean selfish individualism. It recognises that we all have responsibilities to our families and to the community that sustains us' (MCYS 2010b).

With the emphasis on self-reliance, cash assistance in Singapore is given in small amounts, to ensure that financial aid does not become a disincentive to work. The only welfare provision given in cash without any conditions is probably Public Assistance (PA), a stringently means-tested programme for those who are not able to work and have little or no social and financial support. During the Committee of Supply debates in Parliament in 2007, Minister Balakrishnan announced increases in PA rates, but stressed that they would not be too generous so as not to take away the incentives of those who are working hard in low-paying jobs (MCYS 2007).

Singapore's main social security system is the CPF, to the extent that it provides old-age savings for salaried individuals (Lian 2008). It is a compulsory savings scheme where a proportion of the monthly earnings of all employed Singaporeans are put into the CPF. The contribution rate is currently 35 per cent for those aged 50 and below. Those more than 50 years old contribute lower rates (CPF Board 2010a). As a defined contribution system, CPF accounts are individual: whatever amount contributed belongs to the individual.

Besides savings for retirement needs, CPF has become an extensive system that also meets housing, education and health care needs. Part of the monthly contribution goes into the CPF member's Medisave account, which can only be used for stipulated health care costs. In addition, a portion of Medisave is used to purchase medical insurance through various plans in Medishield and other approved private insurance schemes. Hence, CPF can be used for medical expenses before one retires. CPF can also be withdrawn to pay for the purchase of housing and one's own or one's children's tertiary education. The latter acts as a loan that must be returned to the CPF account upon the completion of studies. Proceeds from the sale of homes must also be returned if financed by CPF savings.

Besides the above main uses, account holders can also use their CPF monies for approved investments. CPF interest rates are tax-free and generally higher than market rates. The government also shares one-off transfers through the CPF, such as lump sums to offset the goods and services tax, and for budget sharing in good years. Most of the transfers are given regressively, with low-income earners getting higher amounts. People who do not have CPF accounts, such as housewives, self-employed individuals and casual workers, are encouraged to deposit a small amount in CPF so that they can enjoy these transfers. As can be seen, the values of self-reliance and mutual obligation are again strongly reflected in the CPF system and its secondary uses. If you contribute to your own retirement and development, you can enjoy subsidies and benefits from the government.

The emphasis on human capital development as seen through the CPF is also articulated by Singapore's social policy, which is anchored on education, housing and health care as the three pillars of social security (Ministry of Finance 2007). Since independence in 1965, the Singapore government has built its education, housing and health care systems into institutions that are globally recognized as world class yet affordable. Today, Singapore has a highly educated work force, one of the longest lifespans and the highest home ownership rate in the world (Ng 2010a). Human resources are sometimes said to be the only resource in this small country, hence the government focuses its investments on building human capital so that individuals can help themselves. Besides CPF, PA and other financial assistance schemes targeted at specific vulnerable populations, such as families with young children, Singapore does not have any unemployment insurance, minimum wage or any form of guaranteed assistance to anyone with the ability to work or with a family member who can.

Effects of globalization

The introduction of workfare is therefore a rather drastic shift in the orientation of policy in Singapore. It had to change, as it dealt with the onslaught of globalization on low-wage workers. Not only was Singapore's income inequality widening (Ng 2010a), median and below earnings were stagnating or even declining (Yeoh 2007). From the media to policy-makers to the man on the street, it was increasingly recognized that there is now a group in Singapore who are able to work, but are still not able to make ends meet.

Globalization is taking its toll in several ways. As more countries have opened up to trade and investments, Singapore has become a more costly business location. Hence, to remain competitive in the global market, it has to restructure its economy and focus on high-tech and skills-intensive industries. The government has intervened aggressively by targeting specific industries

(Lim & Lee 2010). The effects of globalization and economic restructuring pull skilled and unskilled wages in opposite directions. For skilled professionals, the global competition to attract the best talent bids their wages up. For workers with low skills and poor education, lower cost destinations and cheaper foreign workers erode their wages. By some measures, Singapore is considered the most globalized economy in the world (Li 2010; Ng 2010a), making the ill-effects of globalization on bottom earners a more pressing problem here than in other countries. The *Singapore Competitiveness Report 2009* (Ketels *et al.* 2009: 15) suggests that the problem of inequality will 'likely become more pressing over time'.

Workfare in Singapore

Thus, with recognition of the challenges faced by eroding wages and the disappearing jobs of low-earning individuals, workfare became formalized in Singapore's social policy. The CPF, with its various functions of not only retirement savings, but also meeting housing and health care needs, had been the main tool of social security. However, if one does not contribute to the CPF, one does not receive the above benefits. To contribute to the CPF, one must be employed in a job that pays CPF or take the step to put money in. Hence, it is a system that is 'workfare' in the sense that, if one does not have formal work, one does not have CPF. And if one does not work enough, one will have insufficient CPF. This is the case for many low-earning individuals.

In 2005, the Ministerial Committee on Low Wage Workers (MCLWW) was set up 'to recommend measures to improve employability and income security for low wage workers and to help families break out of the poverty cycle' (MCLWW 2009). In January 2006, the Committee released its report, recommending a holistic package of strategies founded on four 'principles of workfare'. These principles included:

a) Continued economic growth and job creation as the best assurance that low-wage workers have for a better future;
b) Preservation of work ethic;
c) Equity and assistance for low-wage workers; and
d) Focus on children.

These principles clearly take a human capital development and labour market approach, with the emphasis again on self-reliance and mutual obligation. The values of self-reliance and mutual obligation were reiterated in MCYS's principles of its social safety net, which were presented at a family research network forum in 2009 as:

a) Self-reliance and mutual obligation;
b) Encouragement to work;

c) Families as first line of support; and
d) Many helping hands in supporting an individual.

Thus, with the workfare framework, 2006 marks the year in which workfare was introduced into Singapore, which this chapter presents in terms of four distinct initiatives: self-reliance programmes, WIS, skills upgrading and job creation.

Self-reliance programmes

Self-reliance programmes refer to the initiatives by MCYS to help work-able individuals find jobs, sustain earnings and tide themselves through financial difficulty. The first of such programmes began before the workfare framework was introduced in 2006. In 2003, MCYS initiated a Work Assistance Programme (WAP) (MCYS 2003). The programme was targeted to 'help low income Singaporeans tide over periods of retrenchment and get back to work quickly'. Whereas training and job search assistance had been a mainstay among government assistance, the new programme would give financial assistance with the requirement that participants actively seek a job. S$40million was set aside for WAP from October 2003 to the end of 2004.

WAP assisted unemployed individuals. A programme was also needed for families with earned income, but insufficient to meet household expenses. In 2005, the Self-Reliance Programme (SReP) was started. It helped families where the breadwinner's income was insufficient to meet household needs, or where no adult member was able to work temporarily, for example due to illness, caregiving needs or incarceration. The families receiving SReP were assisted through case management to deal with the situations that prevent employment or the meeting of household expenses. The case management functioned as a 'mutual obligation' where recipients were to work towards improving their situations. S$4.3 million was budgeted for SReP annually (MCYS 2004). WAP and SReP were provided by five Community Development Councils (CDCs) distributed throughout the country.

In 2006, after the workfare framework was adopted, WAP and SReP were consolidated into one scheme named Work Support (WS) (MCYS 2006), a programme slated to provide financial support and other assistance in order to help recipients find employment and achieve financial independence (MCYS 2010c). Available to households that earn less than S$1,500 per month, applicants must also satisfy a needs test, have little or no savings, have inadequate family and community support and demonstrate a willingness to take steps to become self-reliant. When on the programme, case officers work out an action plan with recipients, in which recipients sign an undertaking to take steps to improve their financial situation. The steps include activities related to job search, upgrading of skills, increasing hours of work or reducing expenses (MCYS 2010c). During this period, recipients receive monthly cash assistance, the amounts of which depend on household income and the number of work-capable adults and dependents in the household. Clients usually also receive assistance with utilities and conservancy charges. Case officers have the discretion to modify the amounts according to their assessment of client compliance and other presenting needs.

The consolidation of the two programmes into one helped to streamline the work of the CDCs. However, in terms of programme features, WS consists of two tracks that basically followed the same targets as the two earlier programmes. WS-Employment (WSE) assists families where there is no working member. Assistance of up to six months is provided to enable the person to work. For households with a working member yet struggling to make ends meet, a longer track of up to twenty-four months is provided. In addition, for households with children below the age of 18, case management is also provided. This means a closer monitoring by case officers of the progress of families on their action plan. Such issues are categorized into seven types, including employment, finance, health, children, shelter, food and social support (Ngiam & Ng 2011).

Adjustments continued to be made in response to changes and needs in the economy. ComCare Transitions (CCT) was introduced in 2008 to provide 'medium-term' help for those who are unable to work. These usually include individuals who face more challenges to work, such as a long-term illness (MCYS 2010a). During the 2008–9 recession, MCYS also made the eligibility and duration of WS more flexible in order to extend help to those who were retrenched (MCYS 2009b).

WS and CCT are supported by the ComCare Endowment Fund set up in 2005. The fund supports all kinds of social assistance programmes by the MCYS for low-income individuals (MCYS n.d.). Together, WS and CCT make up the ComCare Self-Reliance pillar of the fund. Figure 8.1 (see left vertical axis) shows that the number of cases seen by WS and CCT has been accelerating from fiscal years 2006 to 2009 (MCYS 2010d). The decrease in the number of WS cases since the introduction of CCT shows that some cases that used to be under WS were channelled to CCT. Figure 8.1 (right vertical axis) also gives the amount that has been disbursed into the ComCare Self-Reliance pillar made up of WS and CCT. Following the increase in the number of cases, the amount disbursed has been increasing (MCLWW 2009). Taking the ratio of the disbursed amount to the number of cases gives a per capita annual disbursement amount of S$2864 in 2006, S$3244 in 2007 and S$2843 in 2008. The disbursement amount for the whole financial year of 2009 is not yet available, but S$13million was reported to have been distributed for WS between April and December 2009 (Choo 2010). Projecting this amount into a full year gives a possible disbursement of S$17 million in 2009, which is 23 per cent more than the 2008 amount for WS and CCT combined.

The expansion of ComCare Self-Reliance was a result of not just increased reach to low-wage earners who used not to receive financial assistance, but also the financial crisis in 2008 and 2009. As Singapore has recovered from the recession and experienced positive economic growth, caseloads in 2010 have returned to pre-recession levels (Community Development Councils 2010).

Workfare in Singapore 137

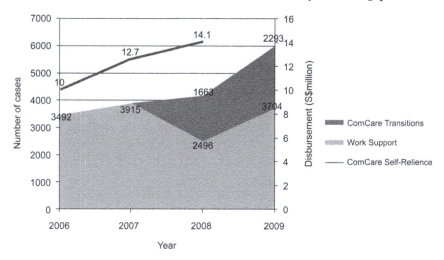

Figure 8.1 Number of cases and disbursement amounts in Work Support and ComCare Transitions
Sources: MCYS (2010d); Ministerial Committee on Low Wage Workers (2009)

Workfare Income Supplement

The Workfare Income Supplement (WIS) is probably the main and biggest initiative under the workfare framework. It was introduced in 2006 as a 'bonus', a one-off budget-sharing exercise. In 2007, it became a permanent scheme and was named WIS (CPF Board 2009). With this, WIS became the fourth pillar of Singapore's social safety net, which had comprised housing, education and medical (Ministry of Finance 2007).

It 'provides cash and CPF incentives to encourage older low wage workers to work and to prepare for long term retirement needs' (MCLWW 2009: 3). Specifically, it supplements the earnings of individuals who earn S$1,700 (revised from S$1,500 in 2010) or less per month, are 35 years and above and who stay in a property with an annual value of S$10,000 or less (CPF Board 2009; Ministry of Finance 2010). The supplement is paid as cash and into the individuals' CPF in the ratio of 1:2.5. This ensures social security not just for the present, but more importantly, for future old age security as well as for other needs accessible through CPF, including housing and medical care. Amounts given vary by age, earnings and employment status. The maximum pay-out is given to older workers whose earnings are in the mid-range of the earnings eligibility. In terms of employment status, those who are self- or informally employed and therefore do not have CPF can receive WIS by making contributions to their CPF Medisave account. However, the amount of WIS they get is only two-thirds of what employees get. The latter requirement of contribution to Medisave sends a clear signal of the importance placed by the government on setting aside funds for medical expenses.

138 *Irene Y.H. Ng*

Although viewed as the main workfare initiative in Singapore, WIS works more like the earned income tax credit (EITC) in the United States than welfare-to-work programmes in other countries. WIS is also distinctively different from other welfare-to-work programmes in several ways. First, the scheme aims to encourage work effort especially by older workers, and has no provision for younger workers. In contrast, workfare programmes in countries such as Australia (Macklin & Snowdon 2010), Hong Kong (Tang 2010) and Britain (White & Riley 2002) have specific programmes for young adults. Second, WIS is unique in being able to meet several objectives at once, where workers' immediate purchasing power, retirement needs and even medical needs are boosted in one sweep.

Figure 8.2 shows the annual disbursement of WIS (including workfare bonus) from 2006 to 2008. The numbers are clearly on the rise. However, there has also been criticism that, for informal workers who cannot benefit from WIS as they do not contribute to CPF, the reach of WIS has been limited. These informal workers are the very ones who might need earnings supplement most. Yet, having to put money into Medisave in order to receive WIS might decrease their purchasing power so much that it becomes not economically viable to do so (Yin 2007; Ministry of Manpower 2008; Goh 2010).

In response to the global recession, a one-off Workfare Special Payment for WIS recipients was announced in 2009. The cash top-up was to provide additional assistance to older low-wage workers to tide them over the recession, and was to be paid over three payments. Like WIS, older workers get more, with the maximum amount paid being S$1,200 or S$400 per payment (CPF Board 2010b). S$55 million worth of Special Payment was paid out in 2009, with a last instalment due in 2010 (Goh 2010).

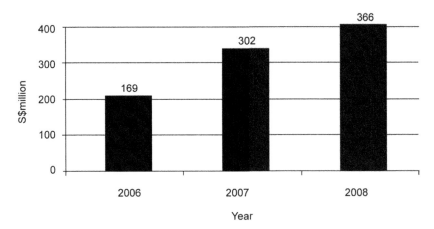

Figure 8.2 Disbursement amounts of WIS and Workfare Bonus, 2006–08

Skills upgrading

Skills training and upgrading programmes have been important in Singapore, and these were brought under the workfare framework to improve employability and financial independence. Including them as workfare also makes practical sense. For many, the CDCs are their first point of contact when needing employability assistance. They might then be referred to one of the ComCare programmes or to employment and training assistance, or both. For example, the action plan of a WS recipient might include a requirement to attend skills development.

Highly subsidized adult education and training has been in place since 1972, when the Skills Development Levy (SDL) Act required all employers to contribute a levy for all employees up to a cap. The levy contributes to the Skills Development Fund (SDF), which subsidizes employers up to 90 per cent for staff training (Singapore Workforce Development Agency 2010). In this way, employers are incentivized to upgrade the skills of their staff.

With the workfare framework, upgrading of the skills and wages of low-earning Singaporeans picked up pace. Two specific programmes were highlighted in the MCLWW Progress Report. The Workforce Development Agency (WDA) under the Ministry of Manpower (MOM) developed the Workfare Skills Qualification (WSQ) system. The WSQ maps out 'training and certification pathways for workers to enhance their skills and capabilities in specific sectors and occupations, and how companies and industries can upgrade their workers' skills standards' (MCLWW 2009: 15).

Whereas WSQ provides a mapped route to skills upgrading, the Employability Skills System (ESS) trains foundational work skills such as workplace literacy, numeracy, information and communication technologies. It seems that the workplace literacy and numeracy qualifications under the ESS are increasingly recognized by employers as alternatives to 'N' and 'O' levels (MCLWW 2009).

In 2008, the various training and upgrading programmes were brought under a Continuing Education and Training (CET) master plan to expand the reach of training programmes to more centres and workers. Then, in response to the economic recession, the Skills Upgrading and Resilience (SPUR) programme gave the CET master plan a further push as the government worked with employers to save jobs and build the capabilities of retrenched staff (MCLWW 2009).

Further, in 2010, as Singapore recovered from the recession, the government embarked on a development plan of 'inclusive growth', which means growth that shares the benefits with those who had lost out or faced difficulties keeping up in the past, including low-wage workers, families with children and the elderly (Ministry of Finance 2010). The main tool would be to increase productivity so as to improve wages. For initiatives aimed at low-wage workers, the wage gains through productivity would take place via the following:

a) Decreasing reliance on foreign workers through higher foreign worker levies imposed on employers;

b) Further strengthening the CET system; and
c) Enhancements to WIS that include, first, increasing WIS amounts and income eligibility (see the section on WIS), and second, a workfare training scheme (WTS) for all workers aged 35 years and older.

Whereas developing a 'first class' CET was aimed at attaining a comprehensive adult education infrastructure comparable to the education system for young students, the WIS enhancements were aimed specifically to improve the employability of older workers. Specifically, WTS gives workers cash grants – capped at S$400 per year – when they complete their training, and pays employers 90–95 per cent of absentee payroll and course fee outlays. It also structures a training programme for those with very low skills (Ministry of Finance 2010). By 2009, WSQ had trained 166,600 workers, and ESS 58,000 (MCLWW 2009).

Job creation

In a speech entitled 'Rethinking Welfare in the Great Recession' before the Senate Finance Committee on 21 September 2010, Gordon Berlin, the President of MDRC, observed the limited effectiveness of Temporary Assistance for Needy Families (TANF) as an anti-poverty strategy during the current 'great recession'. TANF was the policy that reformed welfare and pushed many welfare recipients to work. It had reduced welfare caseloads, increased women's employment rates and reduced childhood poverty. However, it has been unresponsive to the recession. Although the caseloads of other safety net programmes, such as food stamps and unemployment insurance, had risen to meet growing needs, the 'TANF caseload has increased only modestly' (Berlin 2010: 1). TANF was limited during a time of high unemployment as it is was premised on work being available.

Recalling one of the principles of Singapore's workfare framework, that continued economic growth and job creation are 'the best assurance that low wage workers have for a better future', the Singapore government has invested in developing industries that create jobs for low-income individuals. An example is the decision in 2005 to build two integrated resorts that include a casino in each as a major entertainment. Although morally controversial and unpopular, the pragmatic government took this step with the main aim of boosting the tourism industry. At the same time, the number of jobs at stake and the estimated spin-off of generating 35,000 jobs for low-income Singaporeans was emphasized (Ministry of Trade and Industry 2005)

In the same year, the Job Re-creation Programme (JRP) was started to tackle unemployment. The programme aims to:

a) redesign low-value, low-paying and non-attractive jobs;
b) source and identify new job opportunities for Singaporeans; and
c) train and help jobless Singaporeans adjust to the new jobs.

For this, a Job Redesign Incentive Scheme was put in place to subsidise the manpower, equipment and other costs of employers embarking on pilot projects to redesign jobs. Employers can receive up to S$100,000 support for each pilot project (Tripartite Forum on Job Re-creation 2005). From 2006 to 2008, JRP has helped more than 47,000 workers (MCLWW 2009).

Discussion

Workfare reached Singapore relatively late. Tang (2010) claims that Hong Kong was the first in Asia to implement welfare-to-work in the period 1997 to 1999 (Tang 2010: 100). Although workfare-style programmes such as the CPF and skills training had been operational in Singapore, the adoption of workfare as part of its social safety net in 2006 came eight years later, when the workfare framework and the WIS were established. Now, a few years on, and having undergone a major recession during this period, it is hard to tell what the impacts of workfare have been on the well-being of its recipients.

Aggregate statistics from government reports indicate that the programmes have benefited an increasing number of recipients as the programmes expanded. Every programme detailed in this chapter served an increasing number of clients every year. An increased number of beneficiaries is not an indicator of effectiveness, however. It only shows the expansion of workfare.

Research is required to truly discover the impact of the workfare programmes, the ideal being evaluations using randomized trials with control groups. Unfortunately, there are no published evaluations of the workfare programmes. It might also be too early for reports to be published, given that workfare has been in place for only a few years. In future, there might be publications from some of the evaluations being conducted now. For example, MCYS commissioned a research study to track recipients of WS for three years after programme completion (Musfirah 2010). Early indications from the study using programme information suggest that there has been no significant improvement in the economic situation of WS recipients before and after WS (Ng & Ho 2010). Although this finding seems to imply that WS has not helped, it is possible that the recipients' financial situation could have worsened without WS. Conclusions on effectiveness can only be made when results from the follow-up study become available in future.

At present, several macroeconomic trends suggest that the workfare programmes probably did have some effects. The first trend was the quick economic recovery that also saw caseloads in government assistance programmes declining with the recovery. The economy bounced back fairly quickly from the recession, although Singapore, being more vulnerable as a more open economy, was more badly hit than other Asian economies. Unlike TANF, which was not responsive to more assistance needed, the number of cases receiving assistance from the CDCs, including job placement and self-reliance programmes, swelled during the recession but has since abated. The quick economic recovery and

142 *Irene Y.H. Ng*

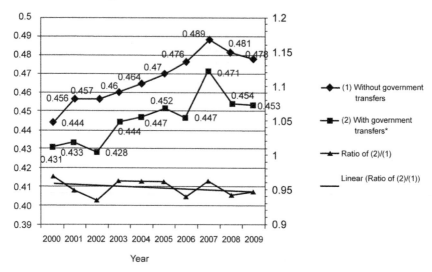

Figure 8.3 Gini coefficient among employed households, 2000–09
Source: Singapore Department of Statistics (2010)
Note:
* Government transfers include growth dividends; NS bonus; GST credits; senior citizen bonus; top-ups to CPF accounts; new Singapore shares; economic restructuring shares; workfare bonus and WIS; rebates on utilities, rental, service and conservancy charges; baby bonus; income tax and property tax rebates; and other schemes related to education and health care

counter-cyclical caseloads suggest responsive and well-targeted programmes for helping Singaporeans through financial difficulties.

A second macro trend is the movements in income inequality through time. Figure 8.3 is adapted from the Gini coefficient chart in the 2009 Income Trends Report by the Singapore Department of Statistics (2010). The chart shows data only from 2000, but Singapore's Gini coefficient has been on an upward trend since the 1980s (Ng 2010a). Chart 1 shows that, since the turn of the century, the upward trend has continued until the recession hit in 2008, after which the Gini coefficient moderated slightly. The effects of government taxes and benefits are seen in the line labelled (2), where government transfers have decreased the Gini coefficient by between 0.013 and 0.029 points (about 3–6 per cent) each year. Taking the ratio of the Gini coefficients without and with government transfers gives ratios fluctuating around a flat trend line at 0.955.

Interpreting the findings in this chart is complex. First, readers should be aware that the steep slopes and wide gaps between lines are partly optical because the scales of the axes are narrow. Compared with Gini estimates in other countries, Singapore's is relatively high. The lowest number of 0.4 in 2000 is high when compared internationally, and in 2007, it reached almost 0.5. On this basis, it is hard to judge the government's ability to narrow inequality. How significant is a lower Gini of between 3 per cent and 6 per cent? Further, looking at the flat trend line of the ratio of the Gini index without and with government transfers, the government does not seem to have made gains in narrowing the income gap by introducing workfare in 2006. The gap between the Gini coefficients before and after 2006 seems to have stayed more or less constant. In fact, the boom year of 2007 was also the year when the full gamut of workfare programmes were in place, yet 2007 looks like the year when government intervention was less able to lower the Gini coefficient.

These observations from the trends in the Gini coefficient point to the huge challenge that policy-makers face in mitigating the forces of economic development and restructuring that keep pulling the income distribution apart. The results in Figure 8.3 show that government efforts have been able to lower inequality by a more or less equal amount each year, but have not been able to reduce inequality from year to year. However, without government intervention, inequality would have been worse. Similarly, even as we maintain a healthy scepticism towards the number of low-wage workers that government reports claim to have helped, the plight of bottom earners would have been worse without the measures.

As has been demonstrated by the tweaks and enhancements in the various workfare programmes, workfare in Singapore will continue to evolve and expand. Policies in Singapore respond swiftly to changes in the economy. This chapter has presented some of the measures that the government has put in place quickly to aid Singaporeans through the recent recession. Some critics, however, question how sustainable Singapore's social safety net is in the long term. Lim and Lee (2010: 151), for example, criticized Singapore's economy as 'predicated on a particular form of state-mediated globalization which arguably empowers and enriches wealthy foreigners, and the state itself, more than it does average local citizens'. The discussion above on the trends in inequality also suggests that more might need to be done to turn around the widening income gap. Beyond workfare given through small incremental programmes, a more redistributive tax system might be needed, and those at the top might need to be compelled to contribute more to the jobs and remuneration of those at the bottom (Ng 2010b). Within the workfare infrastructure currently in place, this might mean strengthening the linkages with employers to provide genuine and meaningful pathways for the advancement of skills. The strengthening of linkages might take shape in stronger terms that compel employer participation.

The latest initiatives to raise productivity and generate inclusive growth are steps in the right direction. However, raising the productivity of low-skilled workers will be extremely challenging (Tan 2010), and it remains to be seen whether the measures in place are able to increase wages for all, or only those at the top; and whether economic growth in the next few years will be truly inclusive.

Another different framework to consider is the development of alternative forms of earnings besides employment-based earnings. For example, Choy has noted the 'untapped potential of domestically-oriented service industries'

(Choy 2010: 137). Examples might include small eateries (or hawker stalls as they are called in Singapore), hairstyling salons or delivery services. Such small businesses are increasingly overtaken by chains and franchises. Government subsidies can be given to promote such local and independent entrepreneurship. Similarly, in a *Straits Times* interview, urban development researcher Joel Kotkin suggested government subsidies for low-end jobs that do not pay well, so that occupations such as hawkers and plumbers are promoted and become viewed more favourably. Then, locals will be more willing to take these jobs and there can be less reliance on foreign workers (Basu 2010).

Beyond the issues of skills and stagnating wages, several studies have shown that many low-income families face multiple barriers to employment, such as physical and mental illness, caregiving obligations and behaviour and school issues of children (Danziger *et al.* 2002; Ng & Ho 2010). These barriers might originate from social and not economic factors. Such findings suggest that workfare programmes need to address non-economic issues as well in order to effectively help low-wage earners achieve self-reliance. However, social interventions seem to have been left to social services to pick up after government assistance programmes. A programme such as WS, for example, provides case management, but only in terms of client compliance with an action plan. Social issues that need to be worked out are often referred to family service centres (FSCs). Given that a substantial population of low-earning families need assistance to overcome barriers to employment, there might need to be more integrated and holistic help in the workfare programmes themselves (Ng & Ho 2010).

Research from other countries has shown some positive effects of Conditional Cash Transfer (CCT) programmes that conditions assistance not on work, but on other gains such as children's school completion, health improvement and attendance at self-improvement or training courses (Berlin 2010; Kammerman & Gatenio-Gabel 2010). As it becomes more challenging to improve skills and job opportunities, especially for those who face several barriers to employment and are harder to employ, workfare programmes might also have to move towards rewarding non-work activities.

Conclusion

Although a latecomer, Singapore's unique brand of workfare has been decisive and wide ranging. Its workfare framework includes not only work programmes that look similar to those in other countries, but also an earnings supplement that meets retirement and health needs and initiatives that overhaul adult continuing education and create jobs. Expansionary measures through workfare programmes have also been used to help retrenched and financially strapped Singaporeans during the recent global recession. However, the assistance in terms of cash amounts into recipients' pockets remains small, as the belief in self-reliance and mutual obligation is strong.

It is too early to assess how effective workfare has been in Singapore. Research is also lacking. However, aggregate data such as caseloads that are responsive to the economic environment and a widening income inequality slightly mitigated by government intervention suggest that workfare has had some beneficial effects. It seems to have kept inequality and stagnating wages from worsening. However, it has not reduced the problem. Workfare in Singapore will probably continue to expand and change. Some suggestions for alternative workfare approaches have been given in this chapter. These include: (a) mutual obligations imposed not just on low-wage earners, but also on employers to hire locally and improve their productivity; (b) a more redistributive tax system; (c) subsidies for small local businesses; (d) more holistic assistance to overcome barriers to employment beyond skills and education; and (e) rewards for meeting other development objectives besides work.

The adverse consequences on low-wage earners of globalization and economic restructuring will become more challenging to overcome. Especially for a small open economy where a strong work ethic are viewed as key to economic survival, workfare – and not welfare – will become a more important component of the social safety net. The infrastructure for a strong workfare regime is in place. The continuing challenge will be to balance sufficient and effective assistance without eroding the work ethic. The entrenched value of self-reliance will continue to be challenged.

Acknowledgements

I thank Linda Lim and Yap Mui Teng for help in reviewing this article.

Bibliography

Basu, R. (2010) 'Great Hawker or Great Scholar for a Great City?', *The Straits Times*, 13 October.

Berlin, G.L. (2010) 'Rethinking Welfare in the Great Recession: Issues in the Re-authorization of Temporary Assistance for Needy Families', Testimony before the Senate Finance Committee, 21 September. Online. Available at http://finance.senate.gov/imo/media/doc/092110gbtest.pdf (accessed 10 November 2010).

Central Provident Fund Board (2009) *FAQs on Workfare Income Supplement Scheme (WIS)*. Online. Available at http://mycpf.cpf.gov.sg/CPF/Templates/SubPage_Template.aspx?NRMODE=Published&NRORIGINALURL=%2fMembers%2fGen-Info%2fWIS%2fFAQs_WIS%2ehtm&NRNODEGUID=%7b0AFCD966-2976-44BA-ABB8-FF6084F17A72%7d& NRCACHEHINT = Guest#2 (accessed 29 January 2009).

——(2010a) *CPF Contribution*. Online. Available at http://mycpf.cpf.gov.sg/Members/Gen-Info/Con-Rates/ContriRa.htm (accessed 10 November 2010).

——(2010b) *WIS Special Payment Factsheet*. Online. Available at http://mycpf.cpf.gov.sg/NR/rdonlyres/42A04C4C-0C8E-4AE8-903D-C4C507C84738/0/WIS_Factsheet.pdf (accessed 10 November 2010).

Choo, E. (2010) 'ComCare sees Highest Number of Applicants in 2009, up 47% On-year', *Channel News Asia*, 27 January. Online. Available at www.channelnewsasia.com/stories/singaporelocalnews/view/1033436/1/.html (accessed 10 November 2010).

Choy, K.M. (2010) 'Singapore's Changing Economic Model', in T. Chong (ed.) *Management of Success: Singapore Revisited*, pp. 123–38, Singapore: Institute of South-east Asian Studies.

Community Development Councils (2010) *CDCs Observe Residents Seeking Employment Assistance have Reached Pre-Recession Levels*. Online. Available at www.cdc.org.sg/index.php?option=com_content&view=article&id=21&Itemid=31 (accessed 10 November 2010).

Danziger, S.K., Corcoran, M., Danziger, S., Heflin, C., Kalil, A., Levine, J., Rosen, D., Seefeldt, K., Siefert, K. and Tolman, R. (2002) *Barriers to the Employment of Welfare Recipients*, No. 02-508, Ann Arbor: Population Studies Center, University of Michigan. Online. Available at www.psc.isr.umich.edu/pubs/pdf/rr02-508.pdf (accessed 10 November 2010).

Goh, C.L. (2010) 'Ideas aplenty for Tweaks to Workfare Scheme', *The Straits Times*, 26 January.

Kammerman, S.B. and Gatenio-Gabel, S. (2010) 'Conditional Cash Transfers (CCT): A Child Policy Strategy in Asia', International Conference on Economic Stress, Human Capital and Families in Asia: Research and Policy Challenges, Plenary Session 1, 3–4 June, Singapore.

Ketels, C., Lall, A., and Neo, B.S. (2009) *Singapore Competitiveness Report 2009*, Singapore: Asia Competitiveness Institute, Lee Kuan Yew School of Public Policy, National University of Singapore. Online. Available at www.spp.nus.edu.sg/aci/docs/Singapore%20Competitiveness%20Report%202009.pdf (accessed 10 November 2010).

Li, D. (2010) 'Most Global Economy', *The Straits Times*, 29 January.

Lian, K.F. (2008) 'Is there a Social Policy in Singapore?' in Lian, K.F. and Tong, C.K. (eds) *Social Policy in Post Industrial Singapore*, pp.21–43, Leiden: Koninklijke Brill.

Lim, L.Y.C. and Lee, S.A. (2010) 'Globalizing State, Disappearing Nation: the Impact of Foreign Participation in the Singapore Economy', in T. Chong (ed.) *Management of Success: Singapore Revisited*, pp. 139–59. Singapore: Institute of South-east Asian Studies.

Macklin, J. and Snowdon, W. (2010) *Major Welfare Reforms to Support Vulnerable Australians* (media release). Australia: Ministry for Families, Housing, Community Services, and Indigenous Affairs. Online. Available at www.jennymacklin.fahcsia.gov.au/mediareleases/2010/pages/welfare_reforms_22jun10.aspx (accessed 10 November 2010).

Ministerial Committee on Low Wage Workers (2009) *Progress Report*. Singapore. Online. Available at www.moe.gov.sg/media/press/files/2009/06/progress-report-ministerial-committee-low-wage-workers.pdf (accessed 10 November 2010).

Ministry of Community Development Youth and Sports (MCYS) (2003) *Work Assistance Programme: Government Injects $40 mil to Help Low-Income Unemployed Singaporeans Transit Back to Work*. Online. Available at http://app1.mcys.gov.sg/PressRoom/WorkAssistanceProgrammeGovernmentInjects40.aspx (accessed 10 November 2010).

——(2004) *Self Reliance Programme*. Online. Available at http://app1.mcys.gov.sg/PressRoom/SelfRelianceProgramme.aspx (accessed 10 November 2010).

——(2006) *Committee of Supply (2006) Debate: ComCare and Low-Income Families*. Online. Available at http://app1.mcys.gov.sg/PressRoom/CommitteeofSupplyDebate2006ComcareandLow.aspx (accessed 10 November 2010).

——(2007) Speech by Dr Vivian Balakrishnan, Minister for Community Development, Youth and Sports and Second Minister for Information, Communications and

the Arts at the Committee of Supply Sitting 2007, 8 March 2007, 3.50 pm. Online. Available at http://app1.mcys.gov.sg/Portals/0/Summary/pressroom/12-2007-1.pdf (accessed 10 November 2010).
——(2009) 'Challenges Facing the Vulnerable and Policy Responses', 29 February. Paper presented at the 2nd Family Research Network Forum, Singapore.
——(2009a) Speech by Dr Vivian Balakrishnan, Minister, Ministry of Community Development, Youth and Sports at the FY 2009 Committee for Supply debate, 11 February 2009. Online. Available at http://app1.mcys.gov.sg/Portals/0/Summary/pressroom/Committee-for-Supply-Debate-2009-Opening-Speech-by-Minister-Principles-of-Social-Resilience.pdf (accessed 10 November 2010).
——(2009b) Speech by Dr Vivian Balakrishnan, Minister, Ministry of Community D, Youth and Sports at the FY 2009 Committee for Supply debate, 11 February 2009. Online. Available at www.mcys.gov.sg/MCDSFiles/Speeches/Articles/13-2009.pdf (accessed 10 November 2010).
——(2010a) *CCT: ComCare Transitions.* Online. Available at www.mcys.gov.sg/web/serv_E_CCT.html (accessed 3 February 2010).
——(2010b) Committee of Supply 2010 Debates: Min (CYS) Opening Speech. Online. Available at http://app1.mcys.gov.sg/PressRoom/COS2010DebatesMinCYSOpeningSpeech.aspx (accessed 10 November 2010).
——(2010c) *Help and Assistance: Work Support (WS) Scheme.* Online. Available at www.mcys.gov.sg/web/serv_E_WS.html (accessed 10 November 2010).
——(2010d) *Number of Social Assistance Cases.* Online. Available at http://app1.mcys.gov.sg/ResearchRoom/ResearchStatistics/NumberofSocialAssistanceCases.aspx (accessed 10 November 2010).
——(n.d.) *ComCare Annual Report FY2008.* Singapore. Online. Available at http://app1.mcys.gov.sg/Portals/0/Topic/Issues/ComCare%20Annual%20Report%20FY2008.pdf (accessed 10 November 2010).
Ministry of Finance (2007) *Budget Speech 2007.* Online. Available at www.mof.gov.sg/budget_2007/budget_speech/index.html (accessed 24 July 2010).
——(2010) *Budget Speech 2010.* Online. Available at www.mof.gov.sg/budget_2010/speech_toc/index.html (accessed 25 May 2010).
Ministry of Manpower (2008) Committee of Supply Speech (part 3) by Mr Gan Kim Yong, Minister of State for Manpower and Education, 5 March 2008, 12:00 am, Parliament. Online. Available at www.mom.gov.sg/newsroom/Pages/SpeechesDetail.aspx?listid=213 (accessed 10 November 2010).
Ministry of Trade and Industry (2005) Statement by Prime Minister Lee Hsien Loong on Integrated Resort on Monday, 18 April 2005 at Parliament House. Proposal to Develop Integrated Resorts. Online. Available at http://app.mti.gov.sg/data/pages/606/doc/Ministerial%20Statement%20-%20PM%2018apr05.pdf (accessed 10 November 2010).
Musfirah, H. (2010) 'Families Tracked to see if Help Given is Enough', *Today*, 4 June.
Ng, I.Y.H. (2010a) 'Globalized Intentions in Tension: The Case of Singapore (Globalisation and Indigenisation)'. *International Social Work* 53, 5: 671–85.
——(2010b) 'Can we Fix Inequality?' *SALT: Fostering the Non-Profit Community.* Online. Available at www.salt.org.sg/articles_list/detail/4c9aee09-99f4-4291-bfe6-0cc07c3410df (accessed 10 November 2010).
Ng, I.Y.H. and Ho, K.W. (2010) *Multi-stressed Low-Earning Families in Contemporary Policy Context: Lessons from Work Support Recipients in Singapore.* Unpublished manuscript.

Ngiam, T.L. and Ng, I.Y.H. (2011) 'Contemporary Welfare Policies and Social Wellbeing', in K. Mehta and A. Wee (eds) *Social Work in the Singapore Context*, 2nd edn, Singapore: Pearson.

Peh, S.H. (2006) 'Scandinavia-style Welfare not for S'pore', *The Straits Times*, 14 November.

Singapore Department of Statistics (2010) *Key Household Income Trends, 2009*. Occasional Paper on Income Statistics, August 2010.

Singapore Workforce Development Agency (2010) *Employer-based Funding*. Online. Available at http://app2.wda.gov.sg/web/Contents/Contents.aspx?ContId=436 (accessed 10 November 2010).

Tan, E.K.B. (2010) 'For the Prescription to Work ... Mindset Change and Inclusive Growth must be Abiding Commitments', *Today*, 6 February.

Tang, K. (2010) 'Welfare-to-work Reform in Hong Kong: Overview and Prospects', in J. Midgley and K. Tang (eds) *Social Policy and Poverty in East Asia: The Role of Social Security*, pp. 99–115, Oxford: Routledge.

The Skills Development Fund (SDF) (2003) Website. Online. Available at www.sdf.gov.sg/General/AboutContent.html (accessed 10 November 2010).

Tripartite Forum on Job Re-creation (2005) *Factsheet on Job Re-Creation Programme*. Online. Available at http://app-stg.wda.gov.sg/data/wda/factsheets/Jobs_Recreation_Programme_05032005.pdf (accessed 10 November 2010).

White, M. and Riley, R. (2002) *Findings from the Macro Evaluation of the New Deal for Young People*, No. 168. Department for Work and Pensions. Online. Available at http://campaigns.dwp.gov.uk/asd/asd5/rrep168.pdf (accessed 10 November 2010).

Yap, M.T. (2010) 'Social Assistance Programmes in Singapore', in J. Midgley and K. Tang (eds) *Social Policy and Poverty in East Asia: The Role of Social Security*, pp. 66–80, Oxford: Routledge.

Yeoh, K.L. (2007) 'Rethinking a New Social Compact for Singapore' *ETHOS* October, 3: 7–12. Online. Available at www.cscollege.gov.sg/cgl/pdf/ETHOS_IS03.pdf (accessed 10 November 2010).

Yin, J. (2007) *Low-Wage Workers Do Not Contribute to CPF*. Online. Available at www.thinkcentre.org/article.cfm?ArticleID=2870 (accessed 10 November 2010).

Part III
Conclusion

9 Workfare in East Asia
Development and characteristics
Chak Kwan Chan

Chapter 1 explained how the implementation of workfare measures in Western welfare states resulted from their declining manufacturing sectors, a large number of households in which no one had paid employment and politicians' perceptions of welfare dependence. As the work ethic and family relationships in East Asian cultures are different from those in Europe and America, this chapter examines the factors that have contributed to the introduction of workfare in East Asia and discusses whether workfare is a good approach for East Asian societies.

Changing economies and the Asian economic crisis

The development of workfare in East Asia needs to be examined in the context of economic restructuring and the impact of the 1997 Asian economic crisis. Since the 1980s, China and other developing Asian countries such as Malaysia, Indonesia, the Philippines and Viet Nam have attracted a lot of foreign direct investment (FDI) from global capitalists, directly threatening the livelihoods of manufacturing sector workers in the advanced economies.

More than 380,000 foreign enterprises, for example, established themselves in China between 1980 and 2001 (Zhu 2004). China became the world's second largest recipient of FDI in 2009, just after the United States (US) (*China Daily* 2010). Many businesses from other Asian countries have also moved their production lines to China. Hong Kong, for example, was China's biggest investor from 1978 to 2003, with investments of more than US$200 billion (Ho 2004), while the proportion of its own workforce in the manufacturing sector dropped from 36.5 per cent in 1981 to just 3.8 per cent in 2009 (Hong Kong Productivity Centre 1982; Information Services Department 2010). Hong Kong's service industries have meanwhile replaced manufacturing as its main economic pillar, employing 88 per cent of its total workforce in 2009 (Information Services Department 2010).

Such other Asian economies as those of Japan, Singapore and South Korea have experienced similar declines in their manufacturing sectors. The proportion of Singapore's workers employed in manufacturing dropped from 30 per cent in 1983 to 26 per cent in 1996 (Monetary Authority of Singapore 1997), the number of manufacturing workers in Japan decreased from 15.7 million in 1992 to 12.2 million in 2003 (Ito 2003), and the proportion of manufacturing workers in South Korea decreased 20 per cent, from 3.3 million to 2.7 million, from 1987 to 1997 (Stuivenwold & Timmer 2003).

An increasingly competitive global economy has therefore resulted in the decline of the advanced East Asian economies' traditionally strong manufacturing sectors, with their principal economic activity shifting to the service and finance sectors. These changes have brought about tremendous employment and training pressures on the workers they have displaced. The group they have affected most is middle-aged workers with low educational levels, as the changed economies no longer require their skills. The introduction of workfare in Singapore, for example, is to deal with the onslaught of globalization on its low-wage workers (Chapter 8).

The onset of the Asian economic crisis in 1997 exacerbated the pressure on East Asian governments to reform their welfare policies. The crisis was the result of structural weaknesses in East Asian economies such as macroeconomic policy errors, significant current account deficits, overinflated asset prices, overlending and corruption (House of Commons Library 1999). Its fallout included widespread industrial layoffs and rapidly increasing unemployment (Lee 1998).

Korea's unemployment rate increased from 2 per cent in 1996 to 6.8 per cent in 1998 (Kwon 2002), Macau's from 2.7 per cent in 1997 to 5.4 per cent in 1998 (Chan & Lei 2000), Hong Kong's from 2.2 per cent in 1997 to 6.1 per cent in 1999, Singapore's from 1.8 per cent to 3.7 per cent, and Taiwan's from 2.7 per cent to 3.1 per cent (Yu 2001). The Economic and Social Commission for Asia and the Pacific (ESCAP 2003) explained that the crisis clearly showed that East Asian countries had limited social safety nets and inadequate labour market policies for addressing the economic downturn, having previously relied on rapid economic growth to prevent unemployment and provide social protection. This resulted in the programmes that they devised in response to the crisis being 'hastily designed and their implementation rushed' (ESCAP 2003: 39).

Chang (Chapter 5) stressed that the most important factor that contributed to the implementation of workfare in Taiwan was the unprecedentedly high unemployment rate triggered by the Asian economic crisis. In Korea, the coverage of the Employment Insurance Programme was extended after the crisis. As a result, the number of unemployment benefit recipients jumped from 49,117 in 1997 to 411,686 in 1998 (Chapter 7). In Macau, a consensus arose during the crisis that the government needed to take action immediately to remedy the high unemployment rate (Chan & Lei 2000). The East Asian welfare model built on rapid economic growth and low employment was therefore unable to cope effectively with a rapidly increasing number of unemployed workers, so most governments took immediate action to create jobs or provide financial assistance on the condition that claimants attend training or accept assigned jobs.

Displaced workers as the main target

Chapter 1 described how single parents are one of the main groups that American and Western European workfare policies target. Although Japan and Hong Kong have concrete measures providing incentives for single parents to enter the labour market (Chapters 3 and 6), most of the workfare measures described in this book have mainly targeted displaced workers. This is because traditional two-parent families are still the dominant pattern in East Asia, and the number of single-parent families has remained relative small. For example, the proportion of single-parent households was 7.2 per cent in Japan and 7.4 per cent in Korea in 1995 compared with more than 20 per cent in many European countries (Jacobs 1998).

All the welfare systems described in this book except that in China have implemented workfare in response to the increasing number of displaced workers resulting from the decline of their manufacturing industries. Taiwan's government has had to address the problems caused by the decline of its manufacturing sector following China's implementation of its open door policy. It introduced several temporary measures to provide financial assistance for unemployed workers whose factories had closed or moved to the People's Republic of China (PRC). The 1994 Employment Promotion Measure for Workers Unemployed Due To Plant Closure or Shutdown, for example, offered financial assistance to affected workers who undertook vocational training or accepted assigned employment (Chapter 5).

The participants in Korea's public work projects were mainly 'low-skilled, less educated, and older workers' (Lee 2000: 17). Hong Kong launched its Initiatives for Wider Economic Participation in 2000 with the objective of creating jobs for low-skilled workers. The Hong Kong government also established an employment programme to help middle-aged jobseekers to learn new skills and implemented a work experience and training scheme that has offered financial assistance and training opportunities for unemployed people aged 14 to 24 (Chapter 3).

Macau's government launched several similar employment initiatives to help poorly educated middle-aged workers. Those attending job-training courses organized by the government and higher education institutions in 2002 could receive a generous allowance, and the 2004 Employment Assistance and Training Course attempted to help them to learn skills required by service industries and provided its participants with a training allowance, as with similar programmes (Chapter 4). All these governments, therefore, attempted to use training programmes to provide former manufacturing workers with new skills so that they could take advantage of new job opportunities in the expanding service industries.

The politics of workfare

The cases in this book are evidence that shifts in political power and social structures have shaped the contents and implementation of workfare. Hong

Kong and China have harsher workfare measures than the others, for example. Hong Kong requires those attempting to claim public unemployment assistance to meet welfare staff regularly and to provide concrete evidence of their job searches. They must also participate immediately in community work to receive their benefits. Some unemployed workers must do community work three full days a week for at least six months if they have received benefits for more than a year (Chan 2011). More importantly, its workfare programmes combine with its insufficient labour protection with regard to wages and working hours to create a class of working poor who cannot achieve self-reliance (Chan 2011).

In China, the Guangzhou municipal government terminates the benefits of public assistance beneficiaries who have rejected two job offers. Chapter 2 quotes a single mother whom the authorities ordered to accept jobs without offering her any support in caring for her children and elderly mother-in-law. Guangzhou also forces beneficiaries to accept unstable jobs with incomes lower than the benefit. Furthermore, those administering its workfare programmes failed to provide beneficiaries with such basic information as that they were eligible for vocational training and top-up allowances after accepting jobs. By not providing beneficiaries with effective channels through which to express their grievances and challenge officials' decisions, China's welfare bureaucrats have clearly put work first and have ignored beneficiaries' family care needs and health concerns (Chapter 2).

Both Hong Kong and Japan reduced single parents' benefits in an effort to induce them to enter the labour market. Japan, however, scrapped this policy following the downfall of the right-wing Koizumi government. Then, after the Democratic Party of Japan won the 2009 general election, it restored an extra livelihood support allowance for single parents and promised to abolish a previous reduction in their childcare benefits (Chapter 6). The Hong Kong government has unfortunately made no changes to its workfare measures since implementing them in 1999.

One explanation for this difference is that the political systems in Japan and Hong Kong have directly shaped the contents of their approaches to workfare. Japan is a democratic polity and its political parties have an incentive to change policies in response to public demand. Hong Kong, however, is a semi-democratic polity with a chief executive chosen mainly by its economic and social elite. Furthermore, the design of Hong Kong's Legislative Council gives its control to business and professional bodies. As Hong Kong's Chief Executive is elected mainly by pro-business and pro-China groups, the working class has little power to change the harsh welfare measures (Chan 2004).

Similarly, welfare claimants in China's one-party polity have little power to monitor government officials or to express their grievances about corrupt welfare administrators (Chan *et al.* 2008). The experiences of social assistance claimants in Hong Kong and China therefore illustrate that authoritarian polities and administrative-led governments can easily pass legislation that implements stigmatizing welfare policies with little concern for poor people's well-being.

In some countries, political parties have used workfare to enhance their legitimacy. The two main political parties in Taiwan, the Chinese Nationalist Party (CNP) and the Democratic Progressive Party (DPP), have both implemented workfare measures in order to win public support. The CNP President Teng-hui Lee, for example, approved the Unemployment Assistance Measure during the lead-up to the 1995 legislative elections, and DPP President Shui-bian Chen implemented the Plan for Expanding Employment through Public Service during the lead-up to the 2004 presidential election. Taiwan's elections have therefore clearly been the catalysts for the enactment of relevant economic and employment programmes (Chapter 5).

The main objectives of Macau's workfare programmes have been to reduce working class pressure with regard to importing migrant workers from mainland China, who composed more than 14 per cent of the total workforce in 1998 (Chan & Lei 2000). After the onset of the Asian economic crisis, the Macau government introduced a social literacy class to provide financial support for unemployed people. Then in 2002, it offered a generous allowance to unemployed workers who attended full-time training programmes that it and higher education institutions had organized (Chapter 4).

Having to cope with a high unemployment rate following the 1997 economic crisis and the 2002 outbreak of severe acute respiratory syndrome (SARS), the Hong Kong government launched a Youth Pre-employment Training Programme in 1999 and youth work experience and training schemes in 2002 in order to meet the training and financial needs of young people. It also implemented the Re-employment Training Programme for unemployed middle-aged workers to help them to learn how to do new jobs (Chapter 3).

Workfare is a conditional form of welfare support that requires unemployed people to accept jobs or attend training, almost always involving some punitive aspects, a degree of coercion or both. This raises the questions of why it is relatively popular in East Asia and how it can achieve the political objectives of reducing public pressure on governments and enhancing those governments' legitimacy.

Several factors could have reduced the stigmatizing effect of this type of programme. They have been specific and separate from traditional public assistance schemes, which tend to be associated with such negative conceptualizations as deprivation, helplessness and laziness. Being separate, workfare programmes can offer higher benefit rates that can reduce the degree of stigmatization to some extent.

Another factor is that East Asian governments introduced many of these workfare measures in response to the 1997 economic recession and the 2002 SARS outbreak. This prevented politicians from finding excuses for blaming individuals or families for their unemployment problems. The public also tends to hold a more positive view of unemployed people during economic crises, making it more politically acceptable to provide unemployed workers with special welfare measures at these times.

A third factor is that workfare programmes are also in harmony with traditional East Asian values with regard to the work ethic and individual duty, so these governments encountered little resistance in requiring beneficiaries to fulfil some duties in return for support. Furthermore, many East Asians, particularly Chinese people, consider study to be a positive activity that enhances people's knowledge and skills, which means that they are unlikely to resist requirements to attend training courses in order to receive benefits.

Workfare can, therefore, be an extremely stigmatizing approach in the less democratic East Asian countries in which governments can easily enact harsh measures. Welfare beneficiaries in such societies have limited opportunities to express their grievances and even fewer to change unreasonable requirements. Governments elsewhere in East Asia have manipulated workfare to enhance their legitimacy by providing special financial support and training programmes.

Has workfare become East Asia's dominant welfare approach?

Some have argued that East Asian welfare states are productivist and developmental ones that use social policy mainly for enhancing economic development (Chapter 1). Furthermore, Confucian ethics have strongly influenced their welfare cultures with their emphasis on personal responsibility and family obligations (Chapter 1). As this chapter noted earlier, however, the East Asian economies have had to confront the challenges of economic restructuring and global competition. In this context, it is reasonable to ask whether workfare has become its dominant welfare approach for providing unemployed workers with financial support while strengthening their work ethic.

It is important to stress that the variations in East Asian welfare programmes and political structures mean that the development of workfare has also varied in the seven economies upon which this book has focused. The nature of these workfare approaches can be broadly classified as institutionalized, temporary or decentralized and loose.

Institutionalized workfare

Hong Kong, Japan, South Korea and Singapore have well-organized welfare administration. Workfare has become their key welfare approach, with their governments having integrated it into their social security schemes.

Hong Kong people benefiting from the Comprehensive Social Assistance Scheme (CSSA) must participate in the Active Employment Assistance and Community Work programmes. They also have to meet their welfare officers regularly and do such non-paid community work as repainting public facilities, cutting weeds, spraying for mosquitoes, cleaning and counter services in public libraries. The Hong Kong government also implements short-term employment assistance projects such as the Special Job Attachment Programme, which offers extra financial support for some unemployed CSSA beneficiaries for training and job placements, and the New Dawn Project, which encourages single parents to enter the labour market by supporting them with childcare services (Chapter 3; Chan 2011).

The beneficiaries of Korea's National Basic Livelihood Security Programme are required to join Self-Support Services, which include employment skills training, job placement, business start-up training, community service and employment promotion services (Chapter 7; Jung 2005; United Nations High Commissioner for Human Rights 2010). Korea's Employment Insurance Programme requires its beneficiaries to search actively for jobs and suspends their benefits if they refuse jobs or training courses it offers them (Chapter 7).

Japan's Koizumi government introduced several workfare measures that targeted specific groups. In 2002, it required single mothers, for example, to seek employment support, attend vocational training and accept job placement. Later that year, it cut the level of their benefits and reduced their childcare allowance by half. It also passed an act that offered short-term accommodation and training for homeless people. It then established a programme that provided young people aged from 15 to 34 who were not in education or needed for household duties with vocational education and job placements. In addition, it launched a self-reliance support programme requiring selected groups receiving public assistance to attend vocational training or education and to accept subsidized jobs. In 2005, it established a programme to provide vocational training and employment opportunities for people with disabilities (Chapter 6). The combination of work and benefits has clearly become the Japanese government's key welfare approach, and it has designed various programmes targeting specific groups needing assistance.

In Singapore, workfare has become 'the fourth pillar' of its social security system (Poh 2007: 1); its guiding principle is that 'work should remain the more attractive alternative to social assistance' (Ministry of Health, Labour and Welfare 2010: 3). Accordingly, recipients of the Work Support programme have to work out an action plan with welfare officers with regard to job searches, upgrading skills, increasing hours of work and taking up assigned jobs (Chapter 8; Ministry of Health, Labour and Welfare 2010). From January to March 2010, the Community Development Councils, regional offices that are responsible for implementing the Work Support programme, helped 80 per cent of claimants to find jobs (Ministry of Health, Labour and Welfare, 2010). It should be noted that Singapore is the only case that has limited the time for receiving benefits. The maximum assistance period for the recipients of the Work Support programme is twenty-four months.

Also, compared with other cases illustrated in this book, Singapore's workfare measures have heavily targeted low-income and middle-aged workers instead of all categories of welfare beneficiaries. It introduced its Workfare Income Supplement (WIS) scheme in 2007 to 'supplement wages, encourage older low-wage workers to work regularly and build up their CPF [Central Provident Fund] savings' (Ministry of Manpower 2010: n.p.). It then implemented its Workfare Training Scheme in 2010 to provide financial incentives to encourage workers to attend training courses and to support employers in improving their employees' skills (Ministry of Manpower 2010). The WIS is similar to the earned income tax credit in the United States, which benefits mainly older workers rather than young ones (Chapter 8). Workfare in Singapore is therefore a long-term, institutionalized programme with the objective of keeping middle-aged, low-skilled workers in the labour market in order to prevent them from falling into the category of unemployed or low-income public assistance beneficiaries, as in Hong Kong. To some extent, Singapore's workfare is a prevention and reward strategy instead of Hong Kong's remedial and punitive approach.

By integrating workfare into their social security systems, Hong Kong, Japan, Korea and Singapore have accepted it as the key to manoeuvring unemployed people into the labour market so that they can maintain their traditional work ethic even in times of prosperity. Hong Kong's government, for example, has not relaxed its stringent workfare policies even when its economy recorded 6–8 per cent growth from 2004 to 2007 (Chapter 3), as workfare helps to reduce the number of claimants and thereby to preserve Hong Kong's minimal social security system (Chan 2011).

Temporary workfare

Taiwan's and Macau's workfare consists of temporary employment programmes, implemented in order to maintain social stability and to enhance the ruling parties' legitimacy in response to economic crises. Taiwan introduced more than twelve workfare programmes between 1989 and 2009 to address the needs of displaced workers and the victims of natural disasters. Its 1993 Employment Promotion Measure for Unemployed Workers Due to Plant Closures or Shutdowns, for example, provided a four-month benefit for workers affected by factory closures. However, its beneficiaries had to attend job training and/ or do community service work assigned by the authorities. This type of programme is a short-term strategy, used by the two ruling parties with new programme names to cope with Taiwan's worsening unemployment problem resulting from the relocation of production lines to the PRC (Chapter 5).

The Taiwanese government has also offered short-term assistance to the victims of natural disasters such as the 921 Earthquake Restoration Employment Services, Vocational Training and Temporary Work Allowance Measure in 2000, which required its beneficiaries to work at least three days a week (Chapter 5). Taiwan's government has clearly used such short-term workfare programmes to combat particular economic crises and to maintain the ruling parties' legitimacy.

Macau's government has similarly set up special programmes during economic downturns to reduce its working class's resistance to its labour importation scheme, which resulted in 14.6 per cent of Macau's workers actually being from China in 1998 while Macau's unemployment rates in 1999 and 2000 were more than 6 per cent (Chan & Lei 2000; Chapter 4). Understandably dissatisfied with the government's labour policy, local workers held several large demonstrations and the government had to deploy riot police to control them (Chapter 4). In order to address the workers' dissatisfaction, the Macau government relaxed the criteria for receiving unemployment relief in 2000 and also introduced social literacy classes involving the provision of benefits to those who attended elementary courses in such subjects as English and local culture and history (Chapter 4).

In 2004, the Macau government launched an employment assistance and training course, which was a special programme separate from the overall public assistance scheme, and a community-based assistance programme, which was a voluntary programme that offered additional benefits to social assistance claimants who voluntarily participated in it. Every Macau permanent resident has received MOP$5,000 from the government annually since 2008 under the Wealth Partaking Scheme, a shift in its welfare strategy from workfare to cash for all (Chapter 4).

South Korea and Hong Kong had also introduced short-term welfare measures to address the tremendous employment pressures resulting from the Asian economic crisis. The Korean government offered unemployed workers three-month temporary jobs with low salaries, which generated 400,000 jobs in 1999, and offered short-term income opportunities to desperate unemployed people (Lee 2000). Hong Kong implemented similar short-term training and job placement projects in 1999, 2004 and 2007 to reduce unemployment among young people (Chapter 3). Countries affected by economic crises had to design short-term programmes quickly to combat the problems caused by the resulting unemployment (ESCAP 2003). The short-term nature of these workfare projects reveals the inability of East Asian minimal social security systems to meet poor people's financial needs in times of economic downturn and some East Asian governments' political need to take quick actions in response to public grievances. They did not integrate these temporary projects fully into their existing social security schemes, however, because their objective was only to offer support to certain groups in times of crisis.

Decentralized and loose workfare

China's approach to workfare is decentralized and loose. A 1999 central government social assistance document stipulated that those receiving benefits from the minimum living standard scheme (MLSS) must perform non-profit community service (Chapter 2). The central government did not, however, specify how to put this principle into practice. More importantly, the MLSS is administered and primarily financed by local authorities, which set up their own rules for it according to their financial conditions and their senior officials' perceptions of workfare. The different local authorities therefore have different practices with regard to the scheme's work-first, vocational training and financial reward programmes (Chapter 2).

China's workfare is therefore clearly neither centralized nor organized. The contents and administration of the workfare programmes in the eight cities that Chapter 2 analysed vary significantly. Although all eight cities, for example, emphasised work-first by requiring beneficiaries to seek jobs actively or to accept jobs referred to them, only three offered them financial incentives to find paid employment (Chapter 2).

Furthermore, even at the local level, those who implement workfare do not do so systematically, as China's welfare officers tend to be either volunteers or bureaucrats without any relevant professional qualifications instead of welfare professionals or career counsellors (Chan 2008). Those in Guangzhou, for example, often fail to tell beneficiaries about the contents of workfare programmes or to offer them the training courses promised in the official documents (Chapter 2).

Three factors have apparently shaped the characteristics of China's workfare. One is that China's public assistance has always been so minimal that it has actually failed to meet even the beneficiaries' basic survival needs. As Chapter 2 reported, many beneficiaries have to get informal work in order to top up their benefits. Therefore, a harsh national workfare policy would obviously be unjustified and unnecessary. Another factor is that, as China is still building its welfare administration, its poor administrative structure and poorly trained welfare officials limit the effectiveness of its programmes. The final factor discussed here is that, as the local authorities administer and primarily finance China's existing social assistance scheme, those that have serious financial constraints have no intention of directing the resources required for implementing training programmes and offering financial incentives to unemployed workers. Given these constraints, only a small number of cities are introducing their own workfare programmes to address local concerns.

Evaluating the wisdom of workfare for East Asian societies

Chapter 1 explained how the Western welfare states' adoption of workfare has been a response to globalization and the increasing number of families without a member in paid employment due to family breakdowns. As this chapter reported earlier, however, East Asian countries have a significantly lower proportion of single parents than those in the West.

Furthermore, some East Asian governments base social security requirements on families rather than individuals, as the West does, and require family members to provide each other with mutual support. In these countries, it is extremely difficult for people living in the same household as their family members to make separate claims for social assistance, as officials consider only households' total incomes regardless of the various members' actual financial relationships (Chan 1998). Korea, for example, requires would be beneficiaries to seek support from close relatives before applying for public benefits (United Nation High Commissioner for Human Rights 2010).

As mutual help among family members outside nuclear families is a normal practice in many East Asian societies, these family-oriented social security systems have to some extent already reduced the number of single parents living on public benefits. This may partly explain why, of the seven polities this book has analysed, only Hong Kong and Japan have specific policies to induce single parents to enter the labour market, and the newly elected Japanese government in 2009 scrapped measures introduced by the previous government to reduce benefits for them. Family breakdowns are therefore apparently not a key concern for East Asian welfare states.

East Asian welfare states also do not have to combat a strong culture of dependence. Politicians in Western countries have used the problems of long-term unemployment, families with no employed members and single parents to justify the implementation of workfare (Chan 2011). Before the onset of the 1998 Asian economic crisis, most of the seven polities this book has analysed had relatively low unemployment rates and their social security claimants had been mainly elderly and disabled people (Chan 1998; United Nation High Commission for Human Rights 2010). This clearly indicates that East Asian cultures have a strong work ethic in which people stress self-reliance and mutual help within families. This book has shown that it is far from reasonable to implement workfare programmes by using extra public funds in societies in which most people have already perceived the government to be the last resort. Compared with Western welfare states, East Asian governments have clearly lacked a strong argument for imposing stringent workfare programmes.

As this book has also shown, many East Asian countries introduced workfare during times of economic recession and rapidly increasing numbers of unemployed workers, particularly with ad hoc, quickly assembled, short-term employment and training programmes intended to solve the urgent financial needs of unemployed workers who had no protection from effective unemployment insurance schemes. Such polities as South Korea and Macau later relaxed their unemployment insurance criteria and amended their public assistance schemes to allow able-bodied, young unemployed people to receive public benefits. However, they linked this relaxation of benefit rules to employment and training requirements. Workfare in some East Asian countries has therefore been a mechanism to prevent welfare dependence rather than to combat an existing dependence problem.

Hong Kong and Japan are the only two polities that this book has examined that have comprehensive policies for inducing specific categories of beneficiaries to enter the labour market. Both of them had enjoyed a long period of sustained economic growth since the 1960s due to their strong manufacturing sectors, but after China and other new Asian economies began industrializing, they had to cope with investors moving their capital and production lines to places with lower production costs. Even before the Asian economic crisis, Hong Kong and Japan had been experiencing economic restructuring and an increasing number of displaced workers. To them, workfare became a mechanism to help reduce the stress that unemployed workers' welfare needs put on their residual social security systems by encouraging the displaced workers to upgrade their skills and by pressing them to take low-paid jobs.

Workfare's effectiveness in helping displaced workers to find new jobs in expanding service and finance sectors *depends on the quality of the programmes devised, the qualifications of welfare staff, the extent of labour protection legislation and the willingness of the government to create jobs in times of economic downturn.* Some governments set up workfare programmes mainly to punish beneficiaries instead of providing them with sufficient time and support to earn better qualifications. Two of the seven Chinese cities that Chapter 2 analysed offered unemployed beneficiaries no job training programmes. Macau required unemployed workers to attend short-term literacy and culture classes instead of longer training programmes with higher vocational qualifications. These classes were ineffective in preparing the unemployed workers for new jobs (Chapter 4). Hong Kong required unemployed beneficiaries to do such work as repainting public facilities, cutting weeds and cleaning beaches, the effectiveness of which in helping displaced workers to acquire new skills in a changing economy is obviously questionable.

In many of the polities this book has analysed, moreover, most welfare advisers or officers have had insufficient training to offer beneficiaries adequate support. In China, most welfare workers have no professional qualifications. In many cases, they have ordered beneficiaries to accept jobs for which they are unqualified or overqualified or have ignored single parents' duty to care for others (Chapter 2). Hong Kong's public assistance officers do not have any career or counselling qualifications but only receive a short-term training course (Chan 1998). Chan and Bowpitt (2005) reported that Hong Kong welfare officers ill-treated beneficiaries in addition to providing them with insufficient support. The Korean government fails to provide sufficient resources for the Employment Security Centres, which can provide only such simple services as advertising job vacancies and job matching and has limited ability to deliver intensive counselling and career guidance (Chapter 7).

Furthermore, labour protection in East Asia tends to be notably limited. When introducing workfare in 1999, the Hong Kong government enacted no legislation to protect workers with regard to wages and working hours; it is not until May 2011 that a minimum wage policy will be introduced. The absence of wage protection means that many formerly unemployed beneficiaries still need to receive public benefits after accepting employment. Their benefit status has, therefore, only changed from the category of unemployed to low income according to Hong Kong's Comprehensive Social Security Allowance (CSSA) scheme's case classification (Chan 2011). China's minimum wage was reported to be lower than that in thirty-two African countries, which fails to provide workers with a decent living standard (*The Epoch Times* 25 February 2010). Wages in Macau were so low that the government was forced to implement a wage subsidy scheme (Chapter 4). Similarly, there is no national minimum wage in Singapore so that some working-poor families have to receive public benefits to top up their income (Chapter 8). Thus, it is evident that self-reliance is actually a myth in some Asian economies that strictly implement harsh workfare measures but fail to establish a fair and protective labour market.

Some East Asian governments have therefore not attempted to protect workers with labour legislation, have failed to offer displaced workers effective training programmes and have not employed qualified professionals to provide career guidance and psychological support to unemployed workers. These weaknesses have clearly revealed the true face of workfare in those countries, which is a cheap employment promotion strategy that governments use to justify their minimal and stigmatizing social assistance schemes, and through which they suppress demands for welfare and coerce unemployment beneficiaries into the labour market or their family mutual help networks.

Workfare also helps to keep wages low by maintaining a large pool of labour in the market. The median monthly income in Hong Kong, for example, only increased from HK$9,500 to HK$10,000 from 1996 to 2006, and the monthly income of low-skilled workers even fell, from HK$6,000 in 1997 to HK$5,000 in 2006 (Chapter 3). Such low wages prevent those who work for them from being self-sufficient and force them to continue to receive public assistance in order to survive. Unsurprisingly, approximately 80 per cent of the CSSA scheme's low-wage beneficiaries receive benefits for more than three years (Chapter 3). Chan (2011: 29) described Hong Kong's combination of a highly exploitative labour market and a coercive and stigmatizing social security system as a twenty-first century 'open workhouse'. Exploiting the values of self-reliance and personal responsibility in the form of employment, community work and training, workfare has offered some governments a new moral justification for oppressing poor people in the competitive global economy.

Job creation, rather than compulsory community work, therefore seems to be a better response to the economic restructuring and loss of jobs resulting from globalization, as it addresses poor people's financial and employment needs better while maintaining the work ethic and the values of self-reliance and mutual family support. It was evident that the implementation of workfare did not increase the employment rates of single parents, homeless people, unemployed young people and other beneficiaries of Japan's public assistance schemes (Chapter 6). This was because a shortage of jobs, rather than welfare dependence, is the main cause of unemployment in the age of globalization (Chapter 6). With a minimal social assistance scheme, the Singapore government, for example, has limited choice but takes an active role in creating jobs through public projects or by subsidizing employers to upgrade their workers' skills (Chapter 8). In 2005, a project to build two integrated resorts created 3,500 jobs for low-income Singaporeans (Chapter 8). In short, the effectiveness of workfare in sending more social assistance recipients to the labour market is actually constrained by poor economic conditions. With fewer job opportunities for low-skilled and displaced workers in advanced economies, job creation may therefore occasionally be necessary because it can immediately address the financial needs of unemployed workers without eroding traditional Asian family and work values.

Conclusion

The introduction of workfare following the onset of the Asian economic crisis provided unemployed people with financial assistance, thereby helping East Asian welfare states to maintain the work ethic during an economic downturn. Its development has varied among the seven polities this book has analysed because of their political and economic differences. Broadly speaking, some have institutionalized workfare, treating it as a key element of their social security system, some have used it as the basis of special programmes for addressing economic crises or for enhancing the legitimacy of the ruling parties, and China has based its decentralized welfare scheme on responding to regional needs.

Such basic workfare assumptions as the value of self-reliance and personal responsibility are compatible with the welfare ethos of East Asian societies, which emphasize the work ethic and mutual help among family members. The key concern here is that governments have manipulated it to suppress the demand for welfare without providing the necessary conditions for unemployed people to find new jobs and achieve self-reliance such as protecting workers' incomes, equipping jobseekers with adequate skills and providing unemployed people with personalized plans to improve their status. They have instead forced welfare beneficiaries to participate in community service work unlikely to enhance their employability. In particular, the combination of strong administrative-led governments and coercive workfare strategies has made social assistance in such polities involve highly stigmatizing schemes that help to suppress wages and maintain minimal welfare systems.

Effective workfare programmes are therefore likely to be expensive policies rather than cheap solutions. If governments truly have the objectives of enhancing displaced workers' employability and helping them to find new jobs that fit into the changing global economy, they have to invest more resources in providing them with well-organized vocational courses and offering them effective social and psychological support to overcome employment barriers. Governments can only justify controlling such citizens' behaviour if they provide sufficient support for their efforts to rejoin the labour force. Workfare and its associated stringent measures otherwise become a punishment of the poor and the unemployed, and the state becomes purely an agent of rich people working in the interests of capital instead of the general public.

Bibliography

Chan, C.K. (1998) 'Welfare Policies and the Construction of Welfare Relations in a Residual Welfare State. The Case of Hong Kong', *Social Policy and Administration* 32, 3: 278–91.
——(2004) 'Caring for the Poor versus degrading the Poor: The Case of Hong Kong Newspaper Charity', *International Journal of Social Welfare* 13, 2: 266–75.
——(2008) 'The Concept of Well-being and its Implications to Chinese Social Policy', *Chinese Public Policy Review* 2: 104–15 (in Chinese).

—— (2011) 'Hong Kong: Workfare in the World's Freest Economy', *International Journal of Social Welfare* 20, 1: 22–32.
Chan, C.K. and Bowpitt, G. (2005) *Human Dignity and Welfare Systems*, Bristol: The Policy Press.
Chan, C.K., Ngok, K.L. and Phillips, D. (2008) *Social Policy in China: Development and Well-Being*, Bristol: The Policy Press.
Chan, S.S. and Lei, C.K. (2000) *Unemployment and Labour Market Adjustment: The Case of Macau*, Macau: University of Macau.
China Daily (2010) '29% FDI Surge shows Confidence', 18 August. Online. Available at www.chinadaily.com.cn/bizchina/2010-08/18/content_11167903.htm (accessed 12 November 2010).
ESCAP (2003) 'A Note on Unemployment in the Wake of the Asian Economic Crisis and Some Responses', *Bulletin on Asia-Pacific Perspectives 2002/03*: 38–46. Available at www.unescap.org/drpad/publication/bulletin%202002/ch3.pdf (accessed 20 October 2010).
Ho, W.H. (2004). *Economic Development of China and Its Impact on Hong Kong*, Hong Kong: Hong Kong Policy Research Institute. Online. Available at www.hkpri.org.hk/passagesPDF/othersSpeech/2004/Economic%20Development%20of%20China%20and%20its%20Impact%20to%20Hong%20Kong.pdf (accessed 5 June 2010).
Holliday, I. (2000) 'Productivist Welfare Capitalism: Social Policy in East Asia', *Political Studies* 48, 4: 706–23.
Hong Kong Productivity Centre (1982) *General Review of the Manufacturing Industry*, Hong Kong: The Hong Kong Productivity Centre. Available at http://sunzi.lib.hku.hk/hkjo/view/41/4100007.pdf (accessed 20 October 2010).
House of Commons Library (1999) *The Asian Economic Crisis*, London: Economic Policy and Statistics Section, House of Commons Library.
Information Services Department (2010) *Hong Kong: The Facts*, Hong Kong: Information Services Department. Online. Available at www.gov.hk/en/about/abouthk/factsheets/docs/trade&industry.pdf (accessed 10 November 2010).
Ito, M. (2003) *Hollowing-out of the Japanese Manufacturing Industry and Regional Employment Development*, Tokyo: The Japan Institute for Labour Policy and Training.
Jacobs, D. (1998) *Social Welfare Systems in East Asia: A Comparative Analysis Including Private Welfare*, London: London School of Economics.
Jung, I.Y. (2005) 'Social Assistance Reform in Post-economic Crisis Korea: The Policy-making Process of the National Basic Livelihood Security Act', paper presented at the East Asian Social Policy Workshop: Transformation in East Asian Social Policy, University of Bath, 13–15 January.
Kwon, H.J. (2002) 'Advocacy Coalitions and the Politics of Welfare in Korea after the Economic Crisis', *Policy & Politics* 31, 1: 69–83.
Lee, E. (1998) *The Asian Financial Crisis: The Challenge for Social Policy*, Geneva: International Labour Office.
Lee, J. (2000) 'Income Assistance and Employment Creation through Public Works in Korea', paper presented at the International Conference on Economic Crisis and Labour Market Reform: The Case of Korea, Seoul, 7 May. Online. Available at http://unpan1.un.org/intradoc/groups/public/documents/APCITY/UNPAN020150.pdf (accessed 25 October 2010).
Ministry of Health, Labour and Welfare (2010) *The 8th ASEAN & Japan High Level Officials Meeting on Caring Societies – Country Report: Singapore*, Tokyo: Office of International Cooperation, International Affairs Division, Minister's Secretariat for

the Ministry of Health, Labour and Welfare. Online. Available at www.mhlw.go.jp/bunya/kokusaigyomu/asean/2010/dl/cr08-singapore.pdf (accessed 26 November 2010).

Ministry of Manpower (2010) *Workfare*, Singapore: Ministry of Manpower. Online. Available at www.mom.gov.sg/employment-practices/employment-rights-conditions/workfare/Pages/workfare-income-supplement.aspx (accessed 25 October 2010).

Monetary Authority of Singapore (1997) *Quality of Employment Growth in Singapore: 1983–96*, Singapore: Monetary Authority of Singapore. Online. Available at www.mas.gov.sg/publications/staff_papers/MAS_Occasional_Papers_No_2_Oct_1997.html (accessed: 2 November 2010).

Poh, J. (2007) 'Workfare: The Fourth Pillar of Social Security in Singapore', *Ethos Issue* 3 October. Online. Available at www.cscollege.gov.sg/cgl/pub_ethos_5j1.htm (accessed 20 October 2010).

Stuivenwold, E. and Timmer, M. (2003) *Manufacturing Performance in Indonesia, South Korea and Taiwan before and after the Crisis*. Online. Available at www.e-biblioteka.lt/resursai/ES/memorandumai/gd63.pdf (accessed 2 November 2010).

The Epoch Times (2010) 'China's Minimum Wage One of the Lowest in the World', 25 February. Online. Available at www.theepochtimes.com/n2/content/view/30453/ (accessed 13 December 2010).

United Nations High Commissioner for Human Rights (2010) *Responses to the Office of the United Nation High Commissioner for Human Rights*, Geneva: United Nations High Commissioner for Human Rights. Online. Available at www2.ohchr.org/english/issues/poverty/expert/docs/responses/Korea.pdf (accessed 1 November 2010).

Yu, T.S. (2001) 'An Overview of the Financial Crisis in East Asia', in T.S. Yu and D. Xu (eds) *From Crisis to Recovery: East Asia Rising Again?* pp. 1–28, Singapore: World Scientific Publishing.

Zhu, Y. (2004) 'Workers, Unions and the State: Migrant Workers in China's Labour-intensive Foreign Enterprises', *Development and Change* 35, 5: 1011–36.

Index

1997–98 Asian financial crisis 151, 152, 155; Hong Kong 41, 155, 159; South Korea 116, 122, 124, 159
2008 global economic crisis: Hong Kong 41, 45, 46; Japan 108; Singapore 136; Taiwan 78, 81, 83, 96, 152

administrative-led government 164; China 22, 24, 25, 154, 160; Hong Kong 42, 154; Macau 60
authoritarian government: China 154; East Asia 10; Hong Kong 154; Taiwan 79; workfare 10, 154

capitalism 96; productivist/developmental welfare 8, 9–10, 37, 79, 82, 115, 139, 143, 145, 156 (Hong Kong 41, 56; Macau 61, 66); welfare systems 5, 8–9; Western countries 5
Chan, Chak Kwan 3–13, 151–66; *see also* workfare, East Asia; workfare, Western countries
Chan, Wing Kit: China 17–40
Chang, Chin-Fen: Taiwan 78–99
China 17–40, 151, 154; administrative-led government 22, 24, 25, 154, 160; employment 24, 31, 33–34, 160; Human Development Index 78; market-oriented reforms 17, 18, 21, 22, 24; poverty 19, 21, 22, 24, 25, 31, 32, 34, 154; rural population 17, 19, 34; self-reliance 24, 25; Shanghai 20–21, 26, 27, 33, 35; state-owned enterprises (SOEs) 17, 18, 20, 21, 28, 31; tax 23, 32; unemployment 18–19, 23, 24, 34 (*daiye* 18, 19, 20; urban unemployment 19, 22, 24, 25; *xiagang* 18, 19, 20–21, 22, 23, 24, 26, 30); work ethic 24, 33, 37; *see also* China, welfare; China, workfare
China, welfare 160, 162; anti-unemployment policies 19–22, 24, 34; disabilities, people with 17; disadvantaged groups 17, 22, 24, 34; minimum living standard scheme (MLSS) 17, 19, 21–22, 23–25, 34–37, 159 (problems 22–23, 31–33, 34); public assistance 17, 19, 23, 24, 154, 160; re-employment services centre 19, 20–21, 23; social insurance 17, 21, 23, 24; social security system 17, 21–22, 23, 24, 160; unemployment insurance 19–20, 24; welfare dependency 18, 23, 33–34, 37; *see also* China; China, workfare
China, workfare 17, 22–28, 153–54, 159–60, 162; assessment 29–31, 37, 160, 162; community service 24, 25, 26, 28, 159; decentralized, loose workfare 159–60, 164; emergence of 23–26; Guangzhou case 18, 26, 28–31, 37, 154, 160; local government 24, 25, 26–28, 34, 37, 159–60 (financial incentives 25, 27, 28, 29, 31, 37, 159, 160; training 25, 26, 27, 28, 30, 31, 37, 159; work-first 25, 26, 28, 29–31, 37, 159, 160); politics 154; principles 24; reasons for implementing 34, 37; single parents 30–31, 154, 162; *see also* China; China, welfare
Choi, Alex H.: Macau 60–77;
citizen 4, 9, 10
community service 164; China 24, 25, 26, 28, 159; compulsory 163; Hong Kong 52, 154; South Korea 120
Confucian welfare system 8, 9, 45, 156

Index

democracy: Hong Kong 154; Japan 154; social democracy 3; Taiwan 78; workfare 10, 156
demography: ageing population 5, 6, 7, 8, 44, 50; Hong Kong 43–44 (life expectancy 41, 43–44)
developed countries 32, 33, 107; Japan 102, 104, 107; Taiwan 78, 82
developing countries 5, 19, 151
disabilities, people with 161; China 17; Hong Kong 47, 50; Japan 106, 107, 108, 109, 110, 111, 157; United Kingdom 7
disadvantaged groups 4, 41, 43, 54, 55, 95, 97; China 17, 22, 24, 34; Hong Kong 42, 43, 54, 55; Taiwan 95, 97

Economic and Social Commission for Asia and the Pacific (ESCAP) 152
economic restructuring 122, 134, 145, 151, 161, 163; *see also* manufacturing sector
economy 151–52; China, foreign direct investment (FDI) 151; East Asia 9–10, 151–52, 156; Taiwan 78, 80–82, 87, 88; *see also* 1997–98 Asian financial crisis; 2008 global economic crisis; economic restructuring; Hong Kong, economy
education 4, 156; China 28, 30; Hong Kong 41, 42, 44; Japan, vocational education 104, 111, 157; job-training 4, 55, 152, 153, 156, 163 (Japan 104; Macau 67, 68, 69, 75, 153, 155, 159; South Korea 118–19, 120, 122, 123, 124); labour market inclusion 4, 5–6, 121–22, 164; Macau, literacy classes 66, 67, 68, 69, 75, 155, 159, 162; Singapore, skills upgrading 135, 139–40, 141, 157–58, 163; South Korea 121–22, 127, 128
employability: disadvantaged groups 4, 55; job-training 4, 55; Singapore 131, 134, 139, 140; workfare 4, 164
employment: casual employment 6, 23, 29, 30, 32, 34, 117, 124, 128, 133; China 24, 31, 33–34, 160; flexible employment 34, 70, 160; Hong Kong 42–43, 44, 45, 56–57; Japan, employment/welfare relation 100, 105, 112, 163; job creation 45–46, 56, 135, 140–41, 152, 153, 163; as means of combating poverty 8, 43; part-time employment 6, 34, 51, 53, 89, 123, 124; permanent employment 107, 108, 110, 124; self-employment 23, 48, 117, 118, 121, 123, 133; South Korea 123–24; Taiwan 84–85; temporary employment 6, 45–46, 86, 159; unregistered employment 24, 31, 33–34; *see also* employability; unemployment
Europe 3, 5, 6, 94, 151; activation 3; ageing population 6; Economic Policy Committee 6, 7; family disintegration 7; unemployment 5, 6; Western Europe 3

family: disintegration in Western countries 5, 6, 7–8, 160; East Asia 10, 151, 153, 156, 160–61, 163, 164; extended family 9; family-oriented social security systems 9, 22, 32, 33, 67, 75, 84, 120, 160–61; Hong Kong 9, 42, 43, 45; Japan 9, 102; *see also* single parents

globalization 5; Singapore 133–34, 143, 145; Taiwan 80–82, 88, 96; workfare 100, 151, 163

health insurance 21, 102; South Korea 117–18, 120, 121, 128; Taiwan 79, 82, 96
Hong Kong 41–59, 154; administrative-led government 42, 154; Comprehensive Social Assistance Scheme (CSSA) 48–49, 50–54, 55, 56, 156, 162, 163; demography 41, 43–44; disabilities, people with 47, 50; disadvantaged groups 42, 43, 54, 55; education 41, 42, 44; the elderly 44–45, 47, 49, 50, 53, 56; employment 42–43, 44, 45, 56–57; family 9, 42, 43, 45; Human Development Index 41, 78; job creation 45–46, 56, 153; NGOs 46, 47, 48, 51, 52, 54, 55, 56; poverty 46, 56, 154; public assistance 162, 163; self-reliance 42, 43, 50, 52, 53, 54, 55, 56, 154; social enterprises 54–55; social policy 41–42, 43, 156, 158; unemployed's assistance 43, 47–50, 51, 154 (young people 43, 48–49, 50, 53, 153, 159); unemployment 41, 43, 45–46, 49, 51, 55, 56, 78, 152; welfare 9, 42–43, 154, 156, 162; workhouse 163; *see also* Hong Kong, economy; Hong Kong, workfare

Hong Kong, economy 41, 42, 43, 44, 45, 55, 151–52, 158, 161; 1997–98 Asian financial crisis 41, 155, 159; 2008 global economic crisis 41, 45, 46; income disparity 43, 46–47, 163; Initiatives for Wider Economic Participation 45–46, 153; labour market 42, 43–47, 50, 56, 161, 162, 163; manufacturing sector 44, 45, 161; productivist welfare capitalism 41, 56; tax 42, 57; *see also* Hong Kong; Hong Kong, workfare

Hong Kong, workfare 50–54, 55, 56, 57, 141, 153–54, 156–57, 158, 161, 162, 163; Active Employment Assistance (AEA) 51, 156; community work 51, 52, 154, 156, 162, 163; disregarded earnings provision 53–54; institutionalized workfare 156–57, 158; New Dawn Project 52, 156–57; politics 154; Re-employment Training Programme 47, 155; single parents 49, 52–53, 55, 153, 154, 157, 161; Support for Self-reliance scheme (SFS) 50, 51–52; temporary workfare 159; Youth Pre-employment Training Programme (YPTP) 48, 155; Youth Work Experience and Training Scheme (YMETS) 48, 155; *see also* Hong Kong; Hong Kong, economy

Human Development Index 78; China 78; Hong Kong 41, 78; Singapore 78; South Korea 78; Taiwan 78

Hung, Eva P.W.: Macau 60–77

International Labour Organization (ILO) 6, 41, 125
investment 5, 151

Japan 9, 100–114, 151–52, 154, 161; 2008 financial crisis 108; Democratic Party of Japan (DPJ) 109–10, 154; employment/welfare relation 100, 105, 112, 163; family 9, 102; Fukuda, Yasuo 107, 108; Koizumi, Junichiro 101; Liberal Democratic Party (LDP) 108, 109; manufacturing sector 152, 161; neoliberalism 101–2, 108, 110, 112; privatization 101, 102; tax 101, 109; unemployment 112, 163 (young people 104); vocational education 104, 111, 157; welfare 9, 100, 101–2, 105, 111, 112, 156; *see also* Japan, workfare

Japan, workfare 102–12, 154, 161, 163; assessment 110–12, 163; Democratic Party of Japan (DPJ) 109–10; disabilities, people with 106, 107, 108, 109, 110, 111, 157; five-year plan: from welfare to employment 106–8, 109, 111; homeless people 103–4, 106, 110, 157; institutionalized workfare 156, 157, 158; Koizumi government 102–6, 108, 109, 111, 157; large-boned policy 102, 104, 108; local government 105; neoliberalism 102, 108, 112; politics 154; public assistance 101, 104–5, 106–7, 109, 110, 111, 157; reasons for implementing workfare 110, 111; refundable tax credits 109; self-reliance support 102–10; single parents 102–3, 105, 106, 107, 109, 111, 153, 154, 157, 161; young people 104, 106, 109, 110–11, 157; *see also* Japan

Kwon, Huck-Ju: South Korea 115–30

labour market: China, workforce 19; Europe 5–6; globalization 5; Hong Kong 42, 43–47, 56, 161, 162, 163 (polarized labour force 43, 46; workforce 44–45, 50); job creation 45–46, 56, 135, 140–41, 152, 153, 163; labour market inclusion 4, 5–6, 121–22, 164; labour protection 162–63; low-wage workers 45, 70–71, 133, 134, 136, 138, 139, 143, 144, 145, 152, 157, 163; middle-aged workers 43, 152, 153, 155, 157; pushing welfare beneficiaries into 4, 6, 8, 43, 69, 74, 131, 155, 162, 163; Singapore 131, 134; workfare 4; *see also* education; employability; employment; unemployment

Lee, Jooha: South Korea 115–30
Leung, Joe C.B.: Hong Kong 41–59

Macau 60–77, 162; casino economy 60–61, 62–63, 66, 67, 72, 74; dependency culture 62, 68, 69; Ho, Edmund 60, 66, 68, 71, 72, 73; manufacturing sector 68, 75; migrant worker system 61, 63–64, 65, 66, 67, 70–72, 73, 74, 75, 155, 158–59; poverty 60, 61, 73, 74; tax 62–63, 72, 74; unemployment 60, 61, 62, 66, 67,

68, 70, 71, 75, 152, 158; *see also* Macau, welfare; Macau, workfare
Macau, welfare 61, 62–66, 73, 74, 75; cash for all 60, 62, 71–74, 159; job training 67, 68, 69, 75, 153, 155; legitimacy and the colonial regime 61, 62–66; productivist welfare capitalism 61, 66; social insurance 65, 75; social security system 62–66, 74, 75 (emergence of 62–65, 66; expansions 65–66; Portuguese social security system 64–65; Social Security Fund (SSF) 65, 66, 67, 68, 75); Standing Committee for the Coordination of Social Affairs (SCCSA) 64, 65, 75; unemployment assistance 65, 66, 75 (unemployment relief (UR) 66, 67, 75); Wealth Partaking Scheme 60, 73, 75, 159; *see also* Macau; Macau, workfare
Macau, workfare 60, 66–71, 74, 153, 158, 161; Active Life Service Scheme (ALSS) 69–71, 75; assessment 69, 70–71; emergence of 61–62, 68, 74; Employment Assistance and Training Course (EATC) 68, 69, 153, 155, 159; literacy classes 66, 67, 68, 69, 75, 155, 159, 162; politics of 71, 74, 158; reasons for implementing workfare 68, 74, 153, 155; temporary workfare 158–59; Workfare–Community Based Employment Assistance Programme (WCEA) 69–71, 75; *see also* Macau; Macau, welfare
manufacturing sector 153; decline 44, 45, 68, 81, 85, 151–52, 153; Hong Kong 44, 45, 161; Japan 152, 161; Macau 68, 75; Singapore 151; South Korea 115, 118, 122, 152; Taiwan 81, 85, 95, 153; *see also* economic restructuring

neoliberalism 91, 100–102, 115; Japan 101–2, 108, 110, 112; privatization 100; social policy 101–2, 108; workfare 100
Ng, Irene Y.H.: Singapore 131–48
Ngok, Kinglun: China 17–40
non-governmental organizations (NGOs) 96; Hong Kong 46, 47, 48, 51, 52, 54, 55, 56

Organisation for Economic Co-operation and Development (OECD) 41, 107, 123, 124; Western countries 5, 6

Peng, Zhaiwen: China 17–40
pension: Macau 62, 64, 65; South Korea, National Pension Programme (NPP) 117, 118, 120–21, 128; Taiwan 79, 82, 87; Western countries 7
politics: Macau 65, 66, 67, 71, 74; Taiwan 82–83, 88, 96, 155; *se also* democracy; workfare, politics of
poverty: child poverty 7, 8; China 19, 21, 22, 24, 25, 31, 32, 34, 154; employment as means of combating 8, 43; Hong Kong 46, 56, 154; Macau 60, 61, 73, 74; South Korea 116, 119–20
public assistance 8, 161; China 17, 19, 23, 24, 154, 160; Hong Kong 162, 163; Japan 101, 104–5, 106–7, 109, 110, 111, 157; Singapore 132, 158; Taiwan 82 (1980 Public Assistance Act 79, 84, 87); United Kingdom 7

rural area: China 17, 19, 34; farmer 17, 23, 79, 82, 94, 117, 118, 121

self-reliance 161, 162, 163, 164; China 24, 25; definition 132; Hong Kong 42, 43, 50, 52, 53, 54, 55, 56, 154; Japan 102–10; Singapore 131, 132, 134, 135–37, 141, 144, 145
severe acute respiratory syndrome (SARS) 45, 68, 155
Singapore 131–48, 151–52, 162; 2008 global economic crisis 136; cash assistance 135, 137, 138, 140, 144; Central Provident Fund (CPF) 131, 132–33, 134, 137, 141, 157; globalization 133–34, 143, 145; human capital development 133, 134; Human Development Index 78; income inequality 133–34, 142–43, 145; manufacturing sector 151; non-welfare state 131–33; public assistance 132, 158; self-reliance 131, 132, 134, 135–37, 141, 144, 145; social policy 131–32, 133, 134, 156, 157, 158; unemployment 78, 133, 140, 152; work ethic 134, 145; *see also* Singapore, workfare
Singapore, workfare 134–45, 157–58, 163; alternative workfare approaches 143–44, 145; assessment 141–45;

Community Development Councils (CDCs) 135, 136, 139, 141, 157; definition 131; emergence of 134–35; employability 131, 134, 139, 140; institutionalized workfare 156, 157–58; job creation 135, 140–41, 163 (Job Re-creation Programme (JRP) 140–41); labour market 131, 134; limited time for receiving benefits 157; low-wage workers 133, 134, 136, 138, 139, 143, 144, 145, 152, 157; principles of 134, 140; productivity 139, 143, 145; reasons for implementing workfare 152, 158; self-reliance programmes 131, 135–37, 141 (ComCare Self-Reliance 131, 136; ComCare Transitions (CCT) 136; Work Assistance Programme (WAP) 135; Work Support (WS) 135, 136, 141, 144, 157; skills upgrading 135, 139–40, 141, 157–58, 163 (Continuing Education and Training (CET) programmes 131, 139, 140; Workfare Skills Qualification (WSQ) system 139, 140; Workfare Training Scheme (WTS) 140, 157–58); Temporary Assistance for Needy Families (TANF) 140, 141; Workfare Income Supplement (WIS) 131, 135, 137–38, 140, 141, 157, 158; *see also* Singapore

single parents 153; China 30–31, 154, 162; East Asia 160–61; Hong Kong 49, 52–53, 55, 153, 154, 157, 161; Japan 102–3, 105, 106, 107, 109, 111, 153, 154, 157, 161; South Korea 153; Western countries 7–8, 153, 160; *see also* family

social inclusion 4; South Korea 116, 117, 118, 120, 128–29

social insurance: China17, 21, 23, 24; Hong Kong 52; Macau 65, 75; South Korea 117–19, 120–21, 124, 126; Taiwan 79–80, 82; *see also* social security system

social policy 3, 152; East Asia 10, 115; Hong Kong 41–42, 43, 156, 158; as instrument for economic development 115; neoliberalism 101–2, 108; privatization 100; Singapore 131–32, 133, 134, 156, 157, 158; South Korea 116, 117; *see also* social security system

social security system 7; *activation* 33; China 17, 21–22, 23, 24, 160; East Asia 159, 161; Europe 6; family-oriented social security systems 9, 22, 32, 33, 67, 75, 84, 120, 160–61; income-support programmes 32; Singapore, Central Provident Fund (CPF) 131, 132–33, 134, 137, 141, 157; Taiwan 79, 84; Western countries 7, 10, 32; workfare 156, 158, 159; *see also* Macau, welfare; social policy

South Korea 115–30, 151–52, 153, 161, 162; 1997–98 Asian financial crisis 116, 122, 124, 159; claiming unemployment benefits 126–28; community service 120; education 121–22, 127, 128; employment 123–24; Human Development Index 78; Kim Dae-jung 118, 122; manufacturing sector 115, 118, 122, 152; poverty 116, 119–20; unemployment 78, 116, 129, 152; *see also* South Korea, welfare; South Korea, workfare

South Korea, welfare 156; activation 122, 125–26; developmental welfare 115–16, 117–22, 128–29; Employment Insurance Programme (EIP) 116–17, 118–19, 121–28, 129, 152, 157 (authority 124–25; eligibility requirement 122, 123–24; employees 125; financial resources 125); Industrial Accident Insurance (IAI) 117, 128; local level 117, 122–28; Long-Term Care Insurance (LTCI) 117, 118, 128; minimum living standard guarantee (MLSG) 116, 117, 119–20, 128, 157; National Health Insurance (NHI) 117–18, 120, 121, 128; National Pension Programme (NPP) 117, 118, 120–21, 128; single parents 153; social inclusion 116, 117, 118, 120, 128–29; social insurance 117–19, 120–21, 124, 126; social policy 116, 117, 156, 158, 160; training 118–19, 120, 122, 123, 124; *see also* South Korea; South Korea, workfare

South Korea, workfare 116, 117, 118; assessment 126–29; institutionalized workfare 156, 157, 158; temporary workfare 159; *see also* South Korea; South Korea, welfare

stigmatization 111, 154, 155, 156, 163, 164

Taiwan 78–99, 152; 2008 financial crisis 78, 81, 83, 96, 152; authoritarian rule

79; Council of Labour Affairs (CLA) 79, 84, 85, 86, 87, 88, 90, 91, 96; democracy 78; Democratic Progressive Party (DPP) 79, 82–83, 88, 89, 96, 155; developed country 78, 82; economy 78, 80–82, 87, 88; employment 84–85; globalization 80–82, 88, 96; Human Development Index 78; manufacturing sector 81, 85, 95, 153; Nationalist Party (NP) 79, 82, 83, 89, 96, 155; politics 82–83, 88, 96, 155; tax 82, 96; unemployment 78, 80, 81–82, 83, 88, 89, 91, 92–93, 94, 95, 96, 152 (young people 89–90); *see also* Taiwan, welfare; Taiwan, workfare

Taiwan, welfare 78–80, 81, 82, 116; conservative/productivist developmental 79, 82; disadvantaged groups 95, 97; health insurance 79, 82, 96; labour insurance 79, 82, 84, 88, 96; pension 79, 82, 87; social insurance 79–80, 82; social security system 79, 84; unemployment assistance 79, 80, 84–87, 88–90, 92–93, 158; unemployment insurance policy 79, 94, 96; *see also* Taiwan; Taiwan, workfare

Taiwan, workfare 79, 81, 83–95, 155, 158; 1980 Public Assistance Act 79, 84, 87; assessment 90–97 (effectiveness 91, 94–95; political and economic factors 90–91, 96); emergency measures 80, 82, 83, 87–90, 158 (1999 earthquake, restoration programmes 87–88, 94–95, 158; 2001 global recessions, employment promotion programmes 88–89; 2008 financial crisis, employment promotion programmes 89–90; 2009 Typhoon Morakot, restoration programmes 90); politics of 91, 96, 155, 158; reasons for implementing workfare 80, 83, 86, 89, 152, 153; regular measures 80, 83–87 (based on employment status 84–87; based on residential status 83–84; Employment Promotion Measure (EPM) 85–86, 87, 153; Measure of Employment Promotion (MEP) 87; Unemployment Assistance Measure (UAM) 86–87, 155); temporary workfare 158; *see also* Taiwan; Taiwan, welfare

Takegawa, Shogo: Japan 100–114
tax 5, 8, 42, 142; China 23, 32; East Asia 10; Hong Kong 42, 57; Japan 101, 109; Macau 62–63, 72, 74; Taiwan 82, 96; tax revenue 5, 8, 62–63, 72

unemployment 7, 152, 155, 161; China 18–19, 23, 24, 34 (*daiye* 18, 19, 20; urban unemployment 19, 22, 24, 25; *xiagang* 18, 19, 20–21, 22, 23, 24, 26, 30); displaced workers as the main workfare target 153, 161–62, 163; economic crisis 45; Europe 5, 6; Hong Kong 41, 43, 45–46, 49, 51, 55, 56, 78; Japan 112, 163; jobless 7, 19, 20, 24, 67, 75, 95; layoffs 18, 85, 152; Macau 60, 61, 62, 66, 67, 68, 70, 71, 75, 152, 158; Singapore 78, 133, 140, 152; South Korea 78, 116, 129; Taiwan 78, 80, 81–82, 83, 88, 89, 91, 92–93, 94, 95, 96, 152; worklessness 7; young people 41, 45, 89–90, 104; *see also* employability; employment

unemployment assistance 155; China 19–20, 24; Hong Kong 43, 47–50, 51 (young people 43, 48–49, 50, 53, 153, 159); Macau 65, 66, 75 (unemployment relief (UR) 66, 67, 75); South Korea 116–17, 118–19, 121–28, 129; Taiwan 79, 80, 84–87, 88–90, 92–93, 158 (unemployment insurance policy 79, 94, 96); South Korea, Employment Insurance Programme (EIP) 116–17, 118–19, 121–28, 129; *see also* Japan, workfare; unemployment

United Kingdom 100; developmental welfare state 115; disabilities, people with 7; family disintegration 7; neoliberalism 100, 101, 115; New Labour government 7, 8; privatization 101; public assistance 7; unemployment, young people 104; welfare dependency 8; workfare 4, 5, 7, 8; worklessness 7

United States 138; 9/11/2001 88; developmental welfare state 115; family disintegration 7; neoliberalism 100, 101, 115; welfare dependency 7–8; welfare policy 3; workfare 4, 7–8, 84, 100

welfare: East Asia 115, 116, 152, 156; Hong Kong 9, 42–43, 154, 156, 162;

Index   173

Japan 9, 100, 101–2, 105, 111, 112, 156; productivist/developmental welfare 8, 9–10, 37, 41, 56, 61, 66, 79, 82, 115–17, 139, 143, 145, 156; reform 8, 152; Singapore, non-welfare state 131–33; stigmatization 154, 163; stringent measures 8, 10, 65; Sweden 115; welfare workers 124–25, 162, 163; welfare to work 61; Western countries 8, 102; *see also* China, welfare; Macau, welfare; Taiwan, welfare; South Korea, welfare

welfare dependency 161; activation 33; definition 23, 33; East Asia 161; Macau 62, 68, 69; Western countries 7–8, 10, 151

work ethic: China 24, 33, 37; East Asia 104, 151, 156, 158, 161, 163, 164; Singapore 134, 145

workfare: activation 3, 33, 37, 122, 125–26; citizens' rights and duties 4; coercion 4, 155, 164; common elements 4; definition 3–4, 8, 100, 131, 155; employability 4, 131; labour market 4, 101, 131; neoliberal social policy 100–101, 110; punishment 29, 155, 158, 164; pushing welfare beneficiaries into labor market 4, 6, 8, 43, 69, 74, 131, 155, 162, 163; stringent measures 158, 161, 164; *see also* workfare, East Asia; workfare, Western countries

workfare, assessment 160–64; China 29–31, 37, 160, 162; Japan 110–12, 163; Macau 69, 70–71; Singapore 141–45; South Korea 126–29; Taiwan 90–97; *see also* workfare, East Asia

workfare, East Asia 4, 8–11, 151–66; 1997–98 Asian financial crisis 151, 152, 155; changing economies and the Asian economic crisis 151–52; Confucian welfare system 8, 9, 45, 156; decentralized, loose workfare 159–60, 164; definitions 8–9, 163; displaced workers as the main target 153, 161–62, 163; globalization 100, 151, 163; institutionalized workfare 156–58, 164; middle-aged workers 43, 152, 153, 155, 157; productivist/developmental welfare 8, 9–10, 37, 41, 56, 61, 66, 79, 82, 115–17, 139, 143, 145, 156; social policy 152; stigmatization 111, 155, 156, 164; temporary workfare 158?–9, 164; unemployment 152, 155; *see also* workfare *under specific names of countries*; workfare; workfare, assessment; workfare, politics of; workfare, reasons for implementing

workfare, politics of 153–56, 158; China 154; Hong Kong 154; Japan 154; Macau 71, 74, 158; Taiwan 91, 96, 155, 158; *see also* workfare, East Asia

workfare, reasons for implementing 10, 110, 152, 153, 155, 161, 162; China 34, 37; Japan 110, 111; Macau 68, 74, 153, 155; Singapore 152, 158; Taiwan 80, 83, 86, 89, 152, 153; *see also* workfare, East Asia

workfare, Western countries 3–8, 10, 94, 100, 151, 160; ageing population 5, 6–7, 8; definition 4–5, 8, 100; family disintegration 5, 6, 7–8, 160; reasons for implementing workfare 4–8, 101, 110, 151, 160 (economic changes 5–6, 151, 160; social changes 6–8, 151, 160); single parents 7–8, 153, 160; United Kingdom 4, 5, 7, 8; United States 4, 7–8, 100; welfare dependency 7–8, 10, 151; workfare's deterrent effects 6; *see also* workfare

young people: Japan, workfare 104, 106, 109, 110–11, 157; Hong Kong (unemployed's assistance 43, 48–49, 50, 53, 153, 159; Youth Pre-employment Training Programme (YPTP) 48, 155; Youth Work Experience and Training Scheme (YMETS) 48, 155); unemployment 41, 45, 89–90, 104